Media Nations

Media Nations

Communicating Belonging and Exclusion in the Modern World

Sabina Mihelj

First published 2011 by
PALGRAVE MACMILLAN

Palgrave Macmillan in the UK is an imprint of Macmillan Publishers
Limited, registered in England, company number 785998, of
Houndmills, Basingstoke, Hampshire RG21 6XS.

Palgrave Macmillan in the US is a division of St Martin's Press LLC,
175 Fifth Avenue, New York, NY 10010.

Palgrave Macmillan is the global academic imprint of the above
companies and has companies and representatives throughout the
world.

Palgrave® and Macmillan® are registered trademarks in the United
States, the United Kingdom, Europe and other countries

ISBN 978–0–230–23185–6 hardback
ISBN 978–0–230–23186–3 paperback

This book is printed on paper suitable for recycling and made from
fully managed and sustained forest sources. Logging, pulping and
manufacturing processes are expected to conform to the environmental regulations of the country of origin.

A catalogue record for this book is available from the British Library.

A catalog record for this book is available from the Library of Congress.

10   9   8   7   6   5   4   3   2   1
20 19 18 17 16 15 14 13 12 11

Printed in China

Contents

List of Figures and Tables

Figures

Tables

Acknowledgments

Tracing the origins of one's intellectual interest in particular topics can easily turn into a navel-gazing exercise, and I do not intend to indulge in that here. Still, I would like to acknowledge the contributions of those individuals who, as teachers and mentors, first aroused my interest in the media and nationalism: Neva Zajc, journalist and editor at the Radio Koper-Capodistria in Koper, Slovenia, sociologist Silva Mežnarić, formerly Research Counsellor at the Institute for Migration and Ethnicity Research in Zagreb, Croatia, and sociologist Jože Vogrinc, Associate Professor at the Department of Sociology, University of Ljubljana. Without them, I would have probably never ended up writing a book on media nations.

In the process of researching and writing this book I have relied on many different people and institutions. Above all, I am indebted to colleagues and friends who have helped turn the Department of Social Sciences at Loughborough University into a true intellectual home. The full list of names is far too long to be included here, but I should at the very least mention Graham Murdock, who was the first to encourage me to write a general book about nationalism and the media, and Mike Pickering, who has provided support, inspiration and advice throughout the writing process. In addition, I would like to thank other colleagues and friends – both from Loughborough and beyond – who have kindly read and commented on earlier versions of the manuscript or its parts: Vaclav Štětka, Jovan Byford, Daniel Chernilo, Iris Wigger, Mojca Pajnik and Emily Keightley. My ideas have also been shaped by discussions with other members of the Cultural and Media Analysis Group at Loughborough, as well as by exchanges at various seminars, workshops and conferences where I have presented some of the ideas advanced in the book. All the remaining mistakes are of course solely mine.

Material support for the realization of this project came from several institutions, including the British Academy, the Ministry of Science of the Republic of Slovenia, the Norwegian Research Council, and Loughborough University. I am grateful to Veronika Bajt, Miloš Pankov and Vlado Kotnik who, in their various capacities as research assistants or co-investigators, helped collect and transcribe some of the material covered in the book, as well as to Mengmeng Zhang and Yuwei Wang for their help with tracing one of the images used.

Let me also acknowledge that Chapters 5 and 7 are in part based on prior publications. Parts of Chapter 5 have appeared in 'Television News, Narrative Conventions and National Imagination', *Discourse and Communication* 3(1): 57–78, co-written with Veronika Bajt and Miloš Pankov (Sage, 2009), while the last section of Chapter 7 draws on 'Television News and the Dynamics of National Remembering', in Castelló, Enric, Alexander Dhoest and Hugh O'Donnell (eds) *The Nation on Screen: Discourses of the National in Global Television* (Cambridge: Cambridge Scholars, 2009).

Thanks are also due to Linda Auld and Paul Sing at Palgrave for their efficient management of the editorial and publication process, and to Paul Stringer for his meticulous copy-editing.

Finally, I would like to thank my friends and family, and above all my partner, Jovan Byford, for always being there for me.

Introduction: Why Media Nations?

In contemporary fragmented media landscapes, moving further and further away from the 'one-for-all' mode of address established during the period of public broadcasting monopoly, the existence of national media cultures and national audiences seems elusive. The post-1989 enthusiasm for globalization has prompted many to deny the importance and endurance of nationalism, and to promulgate idyllic visions of a postnational, cosmopolitan society. Nation-states and national attachments, we have been told, are merely anachronistic remnants of the past, bound to dissipate with the onset of a global modernity. If we are to truly understand the nature of the increasingly globalized media industries, transnational cultural flows and diasporic media, we should dispense with our old vocabularies, steeped in methodological nationalism, and instead learn to think beyond the nation.

Yet, as explained at greater length later on in the book, positing a necessary link between the progress of globalization and the decline of national loyalties and national media is a mistake. For some, the vision of a global future is a threatening prospect, and one that has to be countered with renewed loyalty to the nation. For others, globalization simply means a new set of opportunities for nation-building and national promotion, this time on a worldwide scale. Outside of the narrow circle of cosmopolitan elites and diasporic communities, whose allegiances span across several countries, being a member of a nation – and normally one single nation – is still seen as an indispensable attribute of humanity. In often hardly noticeable ways, national belonging continues to inform people's perceptions of the world, collective memories and expressions of belonging. It is also repeatedly used to legitimate, as well as to challenge, the functioning of representative institutions, and to further collective action.

The hasty dismissal of nation-states and nationhood as irrelevant to contemporary concerns also sits uneasily with the persistent reproduction of prejudice against immigrants and minorities in the media, and

1

with outbursts of nationalist fervour prompted by terrorist attacks. Can we really understand and explain these phenomena without recourse to a theory of nationalism and mass communication? Curiously, this is precisely what the bulk of research and scholarly debate seems to be assuming. While the mediated construction of ethnic and racial prejudice continues to generate considerable scholarly debate, the role of the media in manufacturing national identity and inclusion has slipped down the academic agenda. For almost two decades, no single book has attempted to advance a general argument about the relationship between nationalism and mass communication. *Media Nations* aims to fill this gap.

The lack of reflection on the continued influence of nationhood in contemporary mass communication is not the only reason for the rather stale character of recent research on the topic. Three further blind spots add to this predicament. First, the study of the media and nationalism has become unhelpfully split into two sub-fields that only rarely speak to each other: on the one hand, the analysis of nationalism as a discourse or imagination embedded in different media texts and genres; on the other hand, the examination of institutional structures, policies and socio-economic contexts that give rise to nationalist discourse. Second, the debate is all too often locked into false dichotomies: globalization vs. nationalism, cosmopolitanism vs. parochialism, 'good' civic nationalism vs. 'bad' ethnic nationalism. And third, despite the growing body of case studies from around the world, general theories of nationalism and mass communication remain lamentably ethnocentric, and fail to address the multiple trajectories of modernity and nation-formation around the globe. *Media Nations* offers a corrective to these trends.

In order to make the concepts of nationalism, nation-state and national identity relevant to the understanding of modern forms of mass communication, we need to begin with a critical revision of established concepts and approaches. Benedict Anderson's *Imagined Communities* – first published in 1983 and the single most often quoted reference in existing examinations of nationalism and mass communication – provides an appropriate starting point. As Chapter 1 demonstrates, the popularity of Anderson's work is all too often based on a rather partial reading, which has tended to privilege the role of national imagination over the particular socio-economic context of its genesis and diffusion. The understanding of nations as 'imagined communities' has inspired many to analyse the multifarious forms of national imagination over a broad range of media genres and forms. The other fundamental part of Anderson's argument, which ties national imagination to print capitalism as a particular mode of production and distribution of the printed word, has often remained neglected. We therefore know relatively little about how nationalism as a particular form of discourse or cultural imagination is tied to the institutional structures of modern media, and to their broader economic, political and social realities.

To provide the necessary basis for addressing these issues, Chapter 1 develops an alternative approach to nationalism and mass communication, which combines the understanding of nationalism as a form of discourse with an emphasis on its link with power and politics. On the one hand, nationalism is an internally contested vision and division of the world, which sees the social world as fundamentally divided and structured along national lines. On the other hand, nationalism is also a principle of legitimation, which holds that in order to achieve legitimacy, an institution needs to act as a representative of the nation, or be otherwise devoted primarily to serving the nation and its interests. This principle of legitimation is potentially applicable to virtually any institution, including the different media institutions, and facilitates the embedding of the subjective nationalist visions and divisions into objective relations and categories that affect our everyday lives. This understanding of nationalism and mass communication can help us bridge the gap between text-based, cultural analysis of nationalism in the media, and the more sociological concerns with the impact of media institutions and their political and economic background.

Chapter 2 addresses one of the key conceptual dichotomies that pervade recent thinking about media nations, namely the one that pits nationalism against globalization. At first sight, it may seem awkward to discuss globalization so early on in the book. After all, we are accustomed to seeing globalization as a recent phenomenon, which historically comes only after the formation of nation-states and national cultures and in many ways spells their imminent demise. As suggested earlier, it is precisely this way of seeing that often serves as a pretext for neglecting the issues of nationalism and nationhood altogether. And this is exactly why this potential objection to the study of media nations needs to be put to rest early on. The development of a global international order and the intensification of trans-border exchanges certainly had profound consequences for the nature of state sovereignty and collective belonging. Yet we should be wary of exaggerating the novelty and extent of these processes, and of downplaying the persistence of various forms of segregation and exclusion in mass communication.

As Chapter 2 shows, nation-states and national identities continue to function as the main building blocks of worldwide systems, and are in fact responsible for making the global interactions possible despite the diversity of cultural assumptions and attitudes. Their very presence imposes a globally intelligible *grammar of nationhood* onto virtually every form of transnational governance, trade and communicative exchange; regardless of which country we turn to, we are likely to encounter national parliaments, national broadcasting systems, national symbols and national sports teams, which make even the remotest country appear somehow familiar and 'knowable'. This universal grammar of nationhood operates in each of the three major areas of globalization – economy, politics and culture – and is visible both at the level of policy regulation and media economy as well as the level of particular media genres and texts and their cross-cultural appropriation.

Having dealt with the unhelpful dichotomy between nationhood and global communication, we can then move on, in Chapters 3 and 4, to theories of multiple modernities, which provide a more suitable and persuasive framework for thinking about nationalism and the media. Classic theories of modernization have been rightly criticized for their Eurocentricity and the tendency to see social change as unilinear and irreversible. They leave little room for the specificities of modernization in the rest of the world, and brush over divergent developments within the West itself. Recent approaches to modernization, discussed in Chapter 3, tell a very different story: they acknowledge that the encounters between the global forces of modernization and local cultures and institutions gave rise to several competing visions of what it means to be modern. While some equate modernity with economic liberalization, others believe modern societies are unsustainable without the presence of a strong state capable of imposing limits on the market. The importance of communal identities, be they religious, national or ethno-racial, is disputed as well. For instance, while some visions of modernity champion a strict division between religious institutions and the state, others maintain religion can and should continue to serve as the key interpretive and moral framework in the modern world. These different, often competing visions of modernity finds resonances in recent comparative work on media and communication models. Drawing on this body of work, the second part of Chapter 3 identifies three key modern visions of mass communication – liberal, communist and fascist – and explains how they relate to the rival visions of modernity and to the three key principles of modern social organization – state bureaucracy, market exchange and community.

Chapter 4 takes a step further, demonstrating how these multiple routes to modernity and the associated models of mass communication inflect national imagination in particular ways, and give rise to different lines of inclusion and exclusion. If nation-formation is taking place in a society characterized by a liberal approach to economy and minimal state intervention, and within the context of a predominantly liberal media system that depends on advertising revenue rather than state subsidies, the prevailing markers of national belonging will most likely be tied to the consumption and possession of material goods. In contrast, if nation-formation occurs within the context of planned economy, and within a communist media system that is closely regulated by the communist party-state, national imagination is likely to centre on the community of comrades and the vision of a classless society. In discussing the formation of these diverse 'grammars of nationhood', and their links with different visions of modernity and models of mass communication, Chapter 4 draws on competing explanations of the historical growth of nationalism. It also shows how these explanations can be fruitfully combined into an analytical framework that is capable of accounting for the diversity of nation-building processes around the world.

The second half of Chapter 4 moves beyond historical forms of nation-formation and mediated communication, and examines recent changes in media systems and national imagination, spurred by democratization, economic liberalization and technological changes. Is the triadic framework of media models, modernization and national grammars still capable of accounting for the diversity of media systems and mediated forms of national imagination in the contemporary world? Or are the media nations that surround us today becoming increasingly alike, as befits the growing convergence towards one single model of modernity, characterized by market economy and liberal democracy? As shown in the chapter, the key analytical distinctions that underpin the triadic model continue to provide a helpful vocabulary for describing contemporary forms of media nations, their similarities and differences. We may well be increasingly accustomed to imagine and construct our commonalities and differences through our consumer choices and preferences, yet the way we do that still varies in accordance with the relative influence of the three key principles of modern social organization mentioned earlier: state bureaucracy, market exchange and community.

Chapter 5 asks whether and how the mediated grammar of nationhood varies in times of peace and in times of war, and discusses how these differences relate to the socio-political context, elite behaviour and attitudes, and the media – politics relationship. The chapter starts by drawing a distinction between two fundamental types of experience of nationhood present in the modern world – the constraining nationalist reality of the battleground, or 'hot' nationalism, and the trivial presence of nationhood away from the front, or 'banal' nationalism. It then goes on to demonstrate that these two experiences of nationhood are not as far removed from each other as we would like to think. When faced with the onset of war or a natural catastrophe, every media nation, regardless of the particular kind of national grammar it is sustained by, tends to undergo similar changes. The media – politics relationship tightens, professional routines of reporting are temporarily abandoned, journalists adopt a patriotic stance, treat their audience as a homogeneous, united nation, and marginalize dissenting voices. In other words, the mediated imagery centred on the figure of the informed, rational, deliberate citizen gives way to the one organized around the figures of the nation-warrior and the nation-victim. To demonstrate this, the chapter looks at two cases of conflict reporting, taken from two markedly different socio-political and media contexts: the TV news coverage of the early phase of the Yugoslav Wars in 1991 and the *New York Times'* response to the 9/11 attacks in 2001.

Chapter 6 adds yet another dimension to the discussion of different types of media nations, namely the intertwining of nationalist, familial and gendered discourse in the modern media. Whether explicitly based on ideas of ethnic lineage or not, the nation is often thought of as an extended family, and nationalist discourses around the globe are structured around notions of kinship relationships and gender roles. The contemporary obsession with veiled Muslim women, anxieties over falling birth rates in Western nations, as well as periodic outbursts of moral panic surrounding the sexualization of girls' and women's bodies, all form part of the same symbolic universe, within which private practices become not only a matter of public concern, but a key marker of difference between 'us' and 'them'. The chapter starts with a brief overview of general approaches to gender in nationalism theory, and then builds on arguments developed in preceding chapters to examine how the gendered orders of nationhood vary depending on the prevailing vision of modernity and the corresponding configurations of media, politics, economy and culture in different national contexts. The chapter concludes by examining how the mediation of gendered forms of nationhood shifts in the context of war.

If nations are indeed, as Anderson suggested, imagined as 'sociological organisms' moving steadily through time, how do the media construct this aspect of national imagination? This question is addressed in Chapter 7, which starts by outlining the general links between the historical standardization of clock time and calendar time and the development of modern mass communication and nation-states. Although the link between the modern media and the standardization of time-keeping is often discussed in connection with globalization and postmodernity, the chapter shows that the worldwide adoption of the uniform ways of time-reckoning left plenty of room for national variation. Using selected examples, it explains how the universal system of timekeeping became implicated in the mediated construction of a national sense of the passage of time, and then looks into how the divergent patterns of national calendars relate to the different grammars of nationhood and routes to modernity examined in Chapters 3 and 4. The last section of the chapter turns to the mediation of national perceptions of time in the context of war, and examines how journalistic uses of the past relate to the patterns of wartime national imagination discussed in Chapter 5.

The final chapter takes stock of the key arguments developed over the course of the book, and asks whether the persistence of nations and nationalism, both in the media and more broadly, should be a cause for concern. In both everyday talk and academic discourse, nationalism and national communication are routinely associated with narrow-mindedness and intolerance, and scholars and politicians alike seem to be permanently on the lookout for forms of communication and solidarity that are capable of overcoming these drawbacks, be they in the form of 'civic' nationhood and communication, or of cosmopolitan types of belonging and mediation. Yet we should not forget that nationalism also provides the basis for social inclusion and solidarity, and that both its historical rise and contemporary transmutations are closely intertwined with processes of democratization as well as struggles against discrimination and oppression. Unfortunately, it is impossible to divorce the ugly face of nationalism from its other, inclusive side; every form of nationalism carries with it this fundamental duality. As argued in the chapter even the 'good' forms of nationalism and belonging are not as harmless as we are often led to believe, and therefore cannot be adopted as universally preferred forms of collective identification and solidarity. A similar argument is developed in relation to the competing approaches to managing cultural diversity, both in societies at large and specifically within the media sector, as well as with regard to cosmopolitanism and the communicative spaces that transcend the nation.

This book brings together two rather distinct and wide-ranging fields of scholarly inquiry – nationalism studies on the one hand and media and communication studies on the other. In addition, it also draws inspiration from the tradition of comparative-historical analysis in the social sciences. Given the vast scope of literature and research relevant to these fields, many issues had to be left unexplored or addressed only very briefly. The range of empirical evidence examined has its limitations as well. While the narrative case studies presented in the chapter offer valuable insights into the multiple processes and causal mechanisms at work in media nations, the scope for broader generalizations is rather narrow.

Still, it should be noted that developing such generalizations was not really the aim. Instead, the character of *Media Nations* is largely exploratory. As long as it will help bring nationalism, nation-state and national identity back onto the agenda of media and communication research, and stimulate further comparative and historical research in this area, then this book will have achieved its aim.

1

Mediating Nationhood: Connecting Culture and Power

The link between culture and power lies at the core of any form of nationalism in the modern world. Over the course of the past few centuries, nationalist movements around the world transformed culture into a fundamental basis of social organization and power relationships. Those laying claim to power could no longer rely solely on divine will or heredity, but were increasingly expected to share the culture of those they wished to govern. This tight connection between culture and power came most clearly to the fore in those nationalist movements that endeavoured to make the boundaries of the state coincide with the boundaries of culture: secessionist movements demanding a separate state for their own nation, or unification movements pushing for the integration of culturally similar yet independent political units into a common state. For Ernest Gellner, such 'fusion of culture and polity' constitutes the essence of nationalism (1983: 14).

The assumption that culture forms the basis of any legitimate claim to power is shared also by those nationalist movements that stop short of demanding a fully sovereign nation-state. Examples can be found in the recent developments in Scotland and Catalonia: in both cases, claims for national self-determination and independent statehood have gradually receded, and nationalist leaders settled for regional parliaments and territorial autonomy (Greer 2007). Finally, the link between culture and power also underpins the myriad mundane practices and habits of thought that keep nationalism alive on an everyday basis; the routine references to 'our' state' or 'our' politicians, for example, or the habitual distinctions between 'domestic' and 'foreign' news (Billig 1995). In oblique and hardly noticeable ways, these everyday practices serve to consolidate a vision of the world that is segmented along cultural lines, and within which the power to represent is premised first and foremost on the ability to represent a particular culture, however defined.

No nationalism theory can afford to ignore the relationship between culture and power. Very often, however, nationalism scholars resort to a rather one-sided view of this relationship, and define nationalism either as a political principle or movement (e.g. Gellner 1983) or as a particular state of mind, form of discourse or cultural representation (e.g. Özkırımlı 2005). These two types of definitions correspond with two different approaches to culture: one that treats culture as a mere by-product of power relationships and pays little attention to the internal structure and logic of cultural representations as such, and another that examines culture in its own right, but often fails to explain how it relates to the wider economic and political context.

Much of the existing literature on nationalism and the media shares the same drawbacks. On the one hand, we find several studies that are concerned primarily with the processes of political instrumentalization and negotiation through which media institutions, for example newspapers, radio and television stations, or cinema industries, came to be used and perceived as instruments of nation-building or national promotion in the international arena (e.g. Jarvie 1992; Price 1995; Maxwell 1995). On the other hand, we come across a wide array of writings that explore the ways in which various mediated cultural forms, for instance editorials, reports, news bulletins, soap operas, and films, have contributed to the reproduction of nationalist discourse, representations, myths or symbols (e.g. Bishop and Jaworski 2003; Chan 2005; Frosh and Wolfsfeld 2007). Synthetic accounts that embrace both aspects at once and examine how they relate to each other are rather rare (but see e.g. Collins 1990). Standing somewhat aside from this is the growing body of work by media anthropologists, which investigates the mediation of nationhood through the texture of everyday life-worlds (e.g. Gillespie 1995; Mankekar 1999; Abu-Lughod 2005; Madianou 2005; Postill 2006). This literature has important implications for the arguments we develop in subsequent chapters, but is typically limited to a single national context and avoids developing a synthetic account of the media and nationalism as we do in this book.

This chapter starts by discussing the reasons responsible for this state of affairs in the study of nationalism and the media. It does so by means of examining the legacy of Benedict Anderson's theory of nations as 'imagined communities', probably the single most quoted idea in nationalism literature over the past two decades. After identifying the key weaknesses of this legacy, an alternative definition of nationalism is proposed, one that combines the understanding of nationalism as a form of discourse and imagination with an emphasis on its link with power. The third section of the chapter outlines how this definition of nationalism can be applied to the study of nationalism and the media.

The Legacy of *Imagined Communities*

As with all theories of social phenomena, the competing approaches to nations and nationalism are inevitably inflected by the social and political contexts in which they are advanced. This is particularly obvious when we look at the nineteenth- and early twentieth-century debates about nationalism and nations and their ties with parallel nation-building projects. Ernest Renan's ([1892] 2001) definition of the nation as 'a daily plebiscite', for instance, was developed in response to the disputes over Alsace-Lorraine, a territory France lost to the new German state after the Franco-Prussian war of 1870–71. Unlike his German contemporary Heinrich von Treitschke, who believed that the people of Alsace-Lorraine should be restored to their true German selves even if that went against their will, Renan believed in the primacy of the popular will over and above the ties of language, blood and soil (Harvey 2001). Given the Francophile sympathies of the population living in the disputed territories, this voluntarist definition of nationhood of course challenged the legitimacy of German annexation.

Stalin's ([1913] 1994: 20) notoriously restrictive definition of the nation as a 'historically evolved, stable community of language, territory, economic life, and psychological makeup manifested in common culture', which requires that all these characteristics are present for a group to qualify as a nation, was also heavily influenced by the internal struggles for power Stalin was involved in at the time. His definition was quite explicitly devised as an attack on the rival understanding of the nation formulated by Austrian Marxists Otto Bauer and Karl Renner, according to which a nation was not necessarily attached to a defined territory, but defined by common culture. The Austro-Marxist definition was tailored to suit the complexities of the national question in the Austro-Hungarian Empire, whose numerous nationalities were so intertwined as to make regional-territorial autonomy impossible. At the same time, this definition presented a threat to the unity of the Russian Social Democratic Party, since it provided leverage for the establishment of rival social democratic parties within the Russian empire (Davis 1978: 73–75).

Although the links between politics and scholarship may no longer be so evident, contemporary scholarly debates about nationalism continue to share affinities with wider political and ideological contexts. Theories emphasizing the mythical, invented character of nations and nationalism are at least potentially compatible with political and intellectual agendas seeking to escape the logic of nationalism and usher in postnational forms of imagination and belonging. In contrast, theories that emphasize the embeddedness of modern nations in pre-modern cultural ties can be used to boost support for nationalist political agendas, or call for better protection of minority cultures. There is of course no doubt that public uses of scholarly arguments often involve simplifications and even misinterpretations. Yet, for better or for worse, it is precisely such simplistic, misleading interpretations that often play a key role in deciding which types of analysis or explanation will come into fashion at a particular moment in time. Especially when it comes to scholarly works that become part of the canon of required readings, it is useful to keep in mind that their popularity is in part owed to reasons that extend well beyond the limits of scholarly deliberations, and are sometimes at odds with the authors' own arguments and intentions.

It is against this background that we need to assess the impact and legacy of Benedict Anderson's *Imagined Communities* (1991: 6), which taught us to think of nations as 'imagined political communities [...] imagined as both inherently limited and sovereign'. Arguably, much of the book's worldwide appeal has to do with the iconoclastic potential of its title, and its compatibility with anti-nationalist sentiments gathering momentum towards the end of the Cold War. Fuelled partly by global-ization debates and cosmopolitan visions, and partly by the need to chal-lenge the resurgence of nationalism in post-1989 Europe, these sentiments provided one of the key driving forces responsible for the impressive array of translations of Anderson's book into local languages around the world. The fact that much of the book is rather sympathetic towards nationalism, and quite explicitly aimed at rehabilitating nations and nationalisms as potentially positive forces in human history (cf. Anderson 1991: 141), did not seem to matter.

The case of the Serbo-Croatian translation, published at a point when nationalist passions were pushing the multinational Yugoslav federation ever closer to a violent disintegration, is particularly instructive in this respect. The short foreword to the book, written by the sociologist Silva Mežnarić (1990), makes it clear that the book was intended to function as an intellectual weapon in the struggle against the rising tide of competing nationalisms in the country. Anderson's reflections on the origins and spread of nationalism, argues Mežnarić, require a constant interrogation of the process of nationalization and one's own involvement in it. As such, they are also bound to open up the possibility of rejecting the nationalist appeal, and choosing the option of not belonging.

Yugoslav intellectuals were not alone in trying to use Anderson's book to inspire critical reflections about nationalist myths and claims. Takashi and Saya Shirashi, who brought *Imagined Communities* to Japan in 1987, did so with the explicit aim to counter Japanese exceptionalism and the concomitant belief that any comparisons between Japan and other countries are either impossible or irrelevant (Anderson 2006: 211). The Greek translation, which appeared in 1996, had a very similar objective, namely challenging the dominant narrative of Greek national history, as well as countering Greek claims over the name of Macedonia (ibid.: 219).

Much of the recent scholarly writing on nationalism continues to share this anti-nationalist impetus, and often uses the idea of nations as imagined communities as a springboard for developing alternative, post-national or cosmopolitan forms of collective imagination and belonging. If it was imagination that gave rise to nations, argues Ümut Özkırımlı (2005: 205), then the roots of a postnational order also lie in imagination. Although Özkırımlı is not oblivious of the persistence of nationalism and its embeddedness in institutions and everyday practices, he nevertheless insists on the necessity of a 'thought experiment' that would free us from the 'inexonerable logic of nationalism'. In a similar vein, Spencer and Wollman (2002: 255) are refusing to accept the notion that nationalism is here to stay, and are interested instead in understanding nationalism with the ultimate aim of moving beyond national categories and priorities, and envisaging 'a future where more universalistic loyalties could replace national identifications'.

However, the iconoclastic potential of *Imagined Communities* was not the only reason for its popularity. Had it been so, the classic modernist theories of nations and nationalism, which dominated the field of nationalism from roughly the end of World War II to the 1980s, could have provided equally powerful intellectual weapons. For Ernest Gellner, one of the foremost proponents of the modernist approach, the nature of nationalism was 'amnesiastic' and 'profoundly distorting', and the nation was no more than 'a vision of reality through a prism of illusion' (1983: 57–58). Eric Hobsbawm (1990: 177–78) shared these views: for him, nations and nationalism were just 'symptoms' and 'illusions' that 'appear more influential and omnipresent than they actually are'. Both authors believed nations and nationalisms were mere reflections of far more fundamental realities: Gellner emphasized the role of modernization and in particular industrialization, while Hobsbawm saw the prime movers in decolonization, revolution and the intervention of outside powers.

In contrast to Hobsbawm and Gellner, Anderson took national imagination and more broadly the cultural aspects of nationalism seriously, and regarded them as worthy of equally detailed treatment as the wider political and economic determinants. It is this appreciation of the constitutive role of culture and imagination that provided the second key reason for the popularity of Anderson's theory. It inspired a wide array of works examining the exact content and forms of national imagining over a variety of contemporary and historical contexts, and consequently made debates about nationalism much more attractive to academic disciplines professionally concerned with the internal logic and history of cultural forms: cultural and literary studies, art history, drama and theatre studies, as well as media and communication studies. The understanding of nations as cultural constructs led to a rethinking of established ideas about 'national cinema' and 'national literature', and gave rise to an outpouring of publications looking into how various nations of the world have been imagined and re-imagined through different cultural forms and genres, including music and dance, radio, literature, cinema, as well as drama and theatre (e.g. Hayes 2000; Hjort and MacKenzie 2000; Askew 2002; Ryan 2002; Wilmer 2002).

It is worth noting that the appearance of Anderson's book also coincided with the rise of discourse analysis and constructivist approaches to social reality, and with the concomitant decline of Marxist theory and class analysis over a range of social sciences and humanities. Within the field of media and communication studies, this trend initially found its expression in the growth of interest in the media as cultural forms and in the establishment of cultural studies as an autonomous field of inquiry. Although welcome and much needed, this development only rarely inspired truly multifaceted examinations of the media, and instead often worked to the detriment of economic and political analysis of media institutions. More recently, this tendency was coupled with an idealist version of discourse analysis, which neglects the extent to which discursive choices are limited by the social context in which they are made. Even critical discourse analysis, whose proponents often acknowledge that discourse is embedded in social structures and institutions, has tended 'to treat discourse as a thing that in itself can include or exclude, reproduce social inequalities or effect social change' (Richardson 2006: 26).

It should come as no surprise that these developments provided fertile grounds not only for an enthusiastic reception of Anderson's

theory, but also for its rather partial reading and application, which privileged the role of national imagination over the particular socio-
economic context of its genesis and diffusion. The other fundamental
part of Anderson's argument, which ties national imagination to print
capitalism as a particular mode of production and distribution of the
printed word, was often left unexplored. In sum, the popularity of
Imagined Communities can therefore in part be seen as a symptom of
rather unfortunate trends in recent research, which had the combined
effect of replacing the one-sided, overly determinist and materialist
analysis of nationalism with an equally narrow, predominantly text-
based analysis that divorces nationalist discourse from its moorings in
social, political and economic realities. As a consequence, we know
relatively little about how nationalism as a particular form of discourse
or cultural imagination is tied to the institutional structures of modern
media and to the broader economic, political and social realities.

One of the aims of this book is to challenge this trend, and overcome
the fragmentation of research into separate strands of text-based and
sociologically informed analysis of nationalism and mass communication. No matter how problematic its relationship to reality may be, we
need to acknowledge that nationalism also structures the world it tries to
describe (Calhoun 2007: 147) and becomes entrenched in institutional-
ized categories and practices that affect our everyday lives (Billig 1995;
Brubaker et al. 2006). Despite the porous nature of cultural boundaries,
international migration and the ability of individuals to maintain multiple attachments to places and collectivities near and far, modern nation-
states do manage to create and maintain complex webs of cultural traits,
social formations and systems of symbolic exchange, and can therefore
be treated as relatively stable and thick 'culture areas' (Postill 2006:
15–17).

The fact that nations are products of imagination and construction
does not prevent them from structuring the world we live in, becoming
embedded in a variety of routines and expressions, and acquiring deep
emotional legitimacy. As such, they inevitably also impose restrictions
on any subsequent attempts at national imagination, and in particular on
any individual attempts at identity construction. We may well feel that
nationality does not really matter, or may even refuse to identify with a
nation, yet we will have little choice when faced with a questionnaire
requiring one to tick the appropriate box under 'nationality'. Self-identification, however complex, will also matter precious little when one is
being discriminated against or physically attacked. A substantial proportion of the Jewish population in inter-war Europe was fully assimilated
into the respective national cultures, to the extent that many Jews

preferred to identify themselves as German, French or Hungarian rather than Jewish. Yet, in the light of the anti-Semitic legislation implemented by Nazi Germany and its allies, this kind of self-identification carried little weight.

Or, to combine ideas from Anderson and Marx: people do indeed imagine nations, but not in circumstances of their own choosing. Unmasking the principles of the symbolic or discursive construction and reproduction of nationhood is therefore not enough. We also need to understand the diverse social, political and economic mechanisms that condition these processes, and tie them to, on the one hand, the macro-level relations of power, operating through state policies and apparent in the ownership structures of privately owned institutions, as well as, on the other hand, the mundane forms of social interaction, everyday practices and routines involved in the negotiation and reproduction of power relations at the micro-level. To that end, we first need to unpack the relationship between nationalist discourse and power. Unless we do that, the task of critiquing the excesses of nationalism will continue to appear easier than it actually is.

A clarification is in order at this point. It will have become apparent by now that I am consistently using the term national *imagination* rather than national *imaginary*. The two terms are often used as synonyms, but for reasons I can address only very briefly I have decided to omit the latter entirely from my discussion. First, in its ordinary sense, the term 'imaginary' is often taken to mean the opposite of 'real', and this is clearly not how nationalism has been conceived either by Anderson or in this book. Second, the term imaginary, as used in existing literature on nationalism and the media, frequently comes burdened with the baggage of (usually Lacanian) psychoanalytical theory. As such, it is ill-suited for the study of nationalism, primarily because it is based on the rather dubious assumption that concepts originally developed to account for identification and subject-formation at individual level will be applicable to large-scale political and social processes (cf. Walsh 1996). This assumption is rather difficult to sustain, not least because it accepts and takes for granted precisely one of the key tenets of nationalist discourse that deserve critical interrogation – namely, the idea that nations have been constituted as unified subjects and behave as 'collective individuals'. This approach certainly cannot provide an adequate starting point for describing and explaining the actual functioning of nationalist discourse, whose power – as we will see later on – largely derives from its internal malleability and plurality. The concepts of discourse, imagination, power and legitimacy offer a much better starting point for tackling these issues.

Defining Nationalism: Discourse, Legitimacy and Power

There is of course nothing intrinsically wrong with defining nationalism as a discourse, and nations as imagined communities. In a way, such definitions allow us to capture what is common to *all* nationalisms and nations, without falling prey to the endless disputes over whether nationalism is essentially a political movement, a political doctrine or a sentiment, or over whether a nation is defined by a common political will or shared cultural traits (Calhoun 1997: 20–22). However, without expanding the definition of nationalism to include the tie between nationalist discourse and power, we are on thin ice. As Jonathan Hearn (2006: 247) rightly points out, nationalism should be conceived not only as a matter of discourse, culture or ideology, but also as 'an ascendant type in a long and evolving line of forms of social organization, of concatenations of power and culture'. It is true that nationalism is much more than a political doctrine, and that we should see it as 'a particular way of seeing and interpreting the world, a frame of reference that helps us make sense of and structure the reality that surrounds us' (Özkırımlı 2005: 163). Nevertheless, nationalism *also* has to do with politics and with power more generally – not in the narrow sense suggested by Ernest Gellner (1983), who defined nationalism as a political doctrine that requires cultural and political units to coincide, but as a much more broadly applicable *principle of legitimation*, used to shore up support for different forms of power, be they economic, political or cultural, at both macro- and micro-levels.

To conceptualize the relationship between nationalism as discourse and nationalism as a principle of legitimation, it is worth recalling Pierre Bourdieu's (1989) theory of social space and social power. Although this theory does not focus directly on nationalism, it is concerned precisely with the relationship between discourse and its broader social context – or between, as Bourdieu would say, the subjective representations of the world held by various social agents, and the objective structures and relations of power which they help engender and in which they are, at the same time, embedded. This relational approach helps us understand that representations are not constructed in a social vacuum, but vary with the position within social space, and are constrained by objective social structures and relations. Constraint does not imply total and absolute determination: although the world cannot be represented in just any way one would like, it is also not entirely determined by objective structures and relations. At any time, the social world can be constructed or represented in several different ways, following different systems of classification and naming, which in turn give rise to different principles of identity- and group-formation. This multiplicity opens up opportunities for symbolic struggles over the perception of the social world, which are at the same time also struggles over the relative influence of different sets of objective structures and relations of power.

Such struggles occur also within the realm of nationalism itself, between different nationalist visions of the world. Each of these visions defines 'the nation' in slightly different ways, drawing on different symbolic resources and applying either a voluntarist or an organicist understanding of the nation, or a mixture of both (Zimmer 2003). In this sense, the nation always functions as a polyvalent symbol, whose multiple meanings are 'competed over by different groups manoeuvring to capture the symbol's definition and its legitimating effects' (Verdery 1996: 228). The contrasting definitions of Britishness offered by the far-right British National Party and the UK's Liberal Democratic Party provide an excellent case in point. On the one hand, the British National Party defines Britishness primarily by reference to race: one of the party's major political objectives, as defined in its constitution, consists of 'stemming and reversing the tide of non-white immigration and to restoring [...] the overwhelmingly white make-up of the British population that existed in Britain prior to 1948' (British National Party 2004: 3). The Liberal Democrats, on the other hand, adopt an almost diametrically opposed vision of Britain: as their constitution proclaims, the members of the party 'reject all prejudice and discrimination based upon race, colour, religion, age, disability, sex or sexual orientation, and oppose all forms of entrenched privilege and inequality' (Liberal Democratic Party 2006). This is not to say that all members of the two parties will conform to the same definition of Britishness at all times. Instead, they may well adopt different and even mutually incompatible definitions, depending on the particular context and aims. We will return to these and other examples of internal contestation later in the book. For the moment, it should suffice to underline the coexistence of competing imaginings of the same nation. Without acknowledging this, we can easily fall prey to treating national imagination as homogeneous and even harmonious, and miss its inherently contested nature.

As follows from the above, nationalism can be seen as an internally contested vision and division of the world, which makes us see the social world as fundamentally divided and structured along national lines. The presence of contestation does not mean that the possibilities for imagining a particular nation are unlimited, or that all the different imaginings will be equally influential or widespread. To understand this, we need to remind ourselves that the competing nationalist visions of the world are also involved in the construction of, and are embedded in, the material institutional structures and power relations that are themselves organized along national distinctions. To be able to function in this way, nationalism clearly needs to entail more than just a particular vision and division of the world. In addition, it must also function as a principle of legitimation – a principle that facilitates its own institutionalization and hence endows national fictions with the power to structure the reality and its representations. As a principle of legitimation, nationalism holds that in order to achieve legitimacy, an institution needs to act as a representative of the nation, or be otherwise devoted to serving the nation and its interests. This principle of legitimation is potentially applicable to virtually any institution, not only to the institutions of political representation such as governments or political parties, but also to various social, economic and cultural institutions, including schools, the family and of course the media.

In this sense, nationalism can be applied even to institutions that are otherwise governed by principles of legitimation that have little to do with nationalism, such as, for example, religious or monarchic institutions – in as much as these institutions also aim to devote their activities to a particular nation. For instance, several religious institutions in nineteenth- and twentieth-century Europe have reacted to the rising influence of nationalism not by rejecting it, but by presenting themselves as institutions of vital importance for national defence and survival. The support of some of the Protestant churches and movements for German nationalism in the first half of the twentieth century (Baranowski 1995), and the close involvement of different religious institutions in the proliferation of nationalism in the former Yugoslavia in the 1990s (Perica 2002) are only some examples among many.

Institutions therefore clearly play a key role in translating representations of the world and the classificatory systems they entail into objective structures and relations. As such, they are also central to the exercise of power conferred by different representations and classifications. In order to become taken for granted elements of reality, and achieve power to form and transform that reality, the groups engendered by different visions of the social world need to become enshrined in particular institutions that act as their representatives. Or, as Bourdieu argued: 'the power of constitution, a power to make a new group, through mobilization, or to make it exist by proxy, by speaking on its behalf as an authorized spokesperson, can be obtained only as the outcome of a long process of institutionalization, at the end of which a representative is instituted, who receives from the group the power to make the group' (1989: 23). Once perceived as real, a group such as a nation, and more specifically the institutions and individuals that are recognized as its legitimate representatives, also wield particular forms of power, that is, the ability to affect the world in some way or another, whether by means of physical force or symbols. This understanding of the ties between representations, institutions and power constitutes the core of the approach to nationalism and mass communication adopted in this book.

A caveat is required at this point. Introducing the issue of legitimacy into a debate about nationalism – a debate, that is, about a discourse that has been enmeshed in a lot of violence and served to justify political regimes, policies and actions that hardly anyone would want to regard as legitimate – may of course seem problematic. Legitimacy is a vexing concept, not least because it is value-laden, and because human values are not universal. A regime that looks abhorrent to one observer may well seem entirely legitimate to another – at the very least, it will appear legitimate to the regime's rulers. Yet we do not need to enter such muddy waters in order to be able to discuss nationalism in relation to legitimacy. As Christopher Ansell (2001: 8706) points out, part of the trouble with the notion of legitimacy is that it implies a fairly static, measurable quality possessed by a regime or institution. Such a static notion cannot account for the manifold practices and processes through which legitimacy is produced, maintained, or weakened – that is, practices and processes of legitimation. These include processes of explaining and justifying a particular institutional order (Berger and Luckmann 1967), along with the self-referential, self-justifying activity of rulers and institutions themselves (Barker 2001). Most importantly, such processes do not necessarily succeed in generating consent by the subordinate, and may in fact not even be aimed at generating it.

It is such processes that we have in mind when saying that nationalism is a principle of legitimation. Nationalism assumes that to be legitimate, an institution needs to act as a representative of the nation, yet it does not at the same time require that representativeness be established by means of democratic voting. Or, as Jack Snyder (2000: 36) cogently puts it: nationalism is 'a doctrine of rule in the name of the people but not necessarily by the people'. This peculiar feature makes nationalism imminently compatible not only with democratic rule, but also with the forms of authority characteristic of the Middle Ages and the early modern period, when those who exercised power, as Habermas ([1962] 1989: 8) puts it, represented their power 'before' the people, and not 'for the people'.

To recapitulate: nationalism, as understood in this book, is both a particular type of discourse and a specific principle of legitimation. On the one hand, nationalism is an internally contested vision and division of the world, which sees the social world as fundamentally divided and structured along national lines. On the other hand, nationalism is also a principle of legitimation, which holds that in order to achieve legitimacy, an institution needs to act as a representative of the nation, or be otherwise devoted primarily to serving the nation and its interests. This principle of legitimation is potentially applicable to virtually any institution, including the different media institutions, and facilitates the embedding of the subjective nationalist visions and divisions into objective relations and categories that affect our everyday lives. After this initial ground-clearing exercise, it is now time to consider what the definition of nationalism developed in this section means for our understanding of the relationship between nationalism and mass communication.

The Media and Nationalism: Imagined Communities and Facilities of Mass Communication

Defining nationalism in the manner outlined on previous pages clearly requires us to reconnect the text-based analysis of national imagination to the analysis of the material and institutional structures and settings within which they are produced, circulated and consumed – in short, the various *facilities of mass communication*. These include three kinds of things involved in either recording or transmitting information: (a) common codes, such as languages and alphabets; (b) information and communication technologies, for instance paper, magnetic tapes, DVDs, the printing press, microphones, cameras, radio and television sets, mobile phones, personal computers and the like; and (c) institutions that govern or run the production, use or distribution of information by relying on these codes and technologies. The latter comprise both the relevant legislative and executive bodies responsible for such things as choosing and implementing different laws governing the public use of languages, alphabets or grammars, as well as the various privately or publicly funded institutions such as publishing companies, television and radio stations, computer software and hardware suppliers, advertising agencies, record labels, film production companies and distributors and so on.

In itself, the recognition of the importance of material and institutional aspects of mass communication in the formation and spreading of national imagination is of course far from new. It can be traced over a range of different theoretical approaches to nationalism, and constitutes a recurrent element of scholarly literature on nationalism ever since the mid-twentieth century (Schlesinger 2000). One of the earliest and most prominent examples can be found in Karl W. Deutsch's (1953) *Nationalism and Social Communication*, which takes into account not only the institutions and technologies of the periodical press, radio and television, but also the standardized systems of symbols such as languages and alphabets, the material facilities for the storage of information such as libraries and public monuments, and even collective memories and habits. For Deutsch, the existence of such facilities of communication in fact provides the single most important basis for the formation of 'a people', which he defines as '[a] larger group of persons linked by such complementary habits and facilities of communication' (ibid.: 70). All that distinguishes such a group from a full-fledged nation is power, more specifically 'a measure of effective control over the behaviour of its members' exercised either through informal social arrangements or through formal social', political or economic institutions (ibid.: 78).

Three decades later, Ernest Gellner, Benedict Anderson and Elizabeth Eisenstein developed similar arguments to Deutsch, though each with a somewhat different twist, and without explicitly drawing on Deutsch's work. For Gellner (1983: 127), the new medium and style of mass communication, namely the 'abstract, centralized, standardized, one-to-many communication', coupled with the concomitant standardization of languages, 'itself automatically engendered the core idea of nationalism, quite irrespective of what in particular is being put into the specific messages transmitted'. The key therefore lay not in the specific content of messages transmitted, but in the sheer existence of shared, centralized and standardized channels of communication, which distinguished those who could understand the messages from those who could not. Anderson's (1991: 32–36, 42–43) explanation was, at its core, no different. One of the key factors contributing to the rise of nationalism in Europe and European colonies also lay in the modern means of communication, namely print technology, and more specifically in its 'half-fortuitous, but explosive, interaction' with the capitalist system of production and human linguistic diversity. The introduction of print gave spoken vernacular languages a new fixity, transforming the continuum of local vernaculars into clearly distinct languages. Aided by the capitalist drive for ever-expanding markets of readers, these languages in turn gave rise to unified fields of communication and exchange below Latin, and were also increasingly adopted for purposes of administration and hence execution of power. Last but not least, the new media of mass communication, including, in particular, newspapers and novels, also promoted the creation of imagined communities of readers, who, although never meeting in person, felt they all belonged to the same national community.

Several other key theorists of nationalism, as well as historians and communication theorists concerned with the social and cultural impact of print and communication technologies (e.g. Innis [1951] 2007; Eisenstein 1979) could be added to this list, all sharing the same basic conviction about the tight link between the particular facilities of modern mass communication – most often the printing press, but also radio and television – and the spreading of national consciousness. However, none of them actually succeed in explaining why a group sharing certain facilities of communication should think of itself as a nation, or why common facilities of communication should necessarily induce cohesion and agreement. It is of course true that, as Anderson (1991: 32–36) argues, print capitalism establishes a particular relationship between the newspaper and the market of its readers, which gives rise to the nearly simultaneous consumption of the newspaper by thousands or even millions of readers, who all potentially share an awareness of each other as members of the same community, without ever meeting in person. However, we have little grounds for suggesting that this 'extraordinary mass ceremony' will inevitably result in the formation of a *national* imagined community. In short, Anderson (ibid.: 26) may well be correct that '[t]he idea of a sociological organism moving calendrically through homogeneous, empty time is a precise analogue of the idea of the nation', yet this same idea also corresponds to several other imagined communities, including particular village or city inhabitants, religious congregations, and even professional groups.

Examples abound, regardless of which facilities of communication we consider and which historical period or part of the world we turn to. For instance, one of the predecessors of modern newspapers in Europe, *Anzeiger* (Advertiser), published in Dresden in 1730, did not address itself to a national audience, but 'to all those within and without the city who would buy or sell, lease or rent, lend or borrow' (quoted in Smith 1979: 8). Although this publication fits the category of print capitalism, and is published in a vernacular language (German) rather than Latin, it does not aim to appeal to a whole nation. Another case in point is provided by the multiple forms of collective imagination fostered by the various newspapers published in China in the late nineteenth and early twentieth century. Shanghai alone was home both to Chinese newspapers like *Shebao* and *Minguo ribao*, to newspapers tied to native-place communities such as *Ningbo baihua bao* (Ningbo Vernacular) and *Guang-Zhao zhoubao* (Guangzhou and Zhaoqing Weekly), as well as to the Japanese paper *Shanhai*, which regularly brought news not only from Shanghai and Japan, but also from Korea (Goodman 2004: 2). Similarly complex webs of relations between imagined communities, languages and communicative facilities can be found in nineteenth- and twentieth-century Europe. While playing a crucial role in the building of European nations, various technologies, including telecommunication networks, railroads, highways, energy systems and various consumer products, were also used for the purposes of collective integration at a transnational level (Misa and Schot 2005).

An analogous intertwining of integration and disintegration, linking and de-linking, can also be found below the national level. As Susan Douglas' (2004) study of US radio reminds us, broadcasting had indeed played a crucial role in helping people around the world to imagine themselves as a nation, yet the very same medium also helped perpetuate the multiple ethnic, racial, generational, class, regional and gender divisions within nations, as well as allowed individuals to tune into imagined communities fuelled by subcultural rejection and subversion of mainstream national tastes and preferences. Much the same applies also to the functioning of language as a basic facility of communication. From the centre, the introduction of a common language may well be seen as 'unification', yet when observed from the periphery, the same process can be interpreted as 'cultural invasion' and 'linguistic assimilation' of non-dominant groups and languages, such as for instance Welsh, a Celtic language spoken in Wales in the United Kingdom, or Occitan, a Romance language historically spoken in Southern France as well as in parts of Italy and Spain (Burke 2004: 167). To take an example from beyond Europe, when the Directorate General of Information and Broadcasting in India attempted to change the English name of All India Radio into Hindi 'Akashvani' (Sky Voice), newspapers in Tamil Nadu reported protests against the 'imposition of Hindi' (Kumar 2006: 261–62). The attempt at promoting Hindi as a national language was therefore perceived not as a welcome instance of integration into the nationwide media sphere, but as an unwelcome invasion of a foreign language.

It is true that different communication technologies may be prone to different forms of social and cultural appropriation, and hence also display elective affinities with different kinds of collective imagination. Radio, for example, proved to be a versatile technology, and its relative accessibility made it amenable to a wide variety of uses inspired by bottom-up experimentation and appropriation, and thus to a range of small-scale or local forms of collective imagination. It is not a coincidence, for example, that radio was and still is one of the preferred facilities of mass communication among various minorities. Newspapers and print media in general often performed a similar function, yet their impact remained limited to literate segments of the population, and to those able to afford them. As such, they were also inclined to foster elite forms of collective imagination and identification. On the other hand, film and television, although appealing to audiences across gender, age and class divides, were also rather costly enterprises, and therefore, compared to radio, more vulnerable to both state appropriation and corporate interests. As a consequence, they were much more often used as means of promoting particular forms of collective imagination on a large scale – national or even transnational. None of this, however, makes any of these technologies as such particularly conducive *only* to national imagination.

In short, to assume that any facility of communication is uniquely predisposed to serve as a purveyor of national imagination or as an instrument of integration is misleading. As the above-mentioned examples suggest, facilities of mass communication are able to accommodate a range of different kinds of imagined communities, and can simultaneously cut both ways: serve as instruments of integration, while also being used as tools of exclusion and fragmentation, and often simultaneously so. An increase in the intensity of communication therefore does not necessarily bring about agreement and cohesion, but can instead end up enhancing differences and fostering internal conflicts. Furthermore, even when cohesion is achieved, it does not automatically assume a national form (for similar arguments, see e.g. Connor 1994: 28–66; Schlesinger 1991: 158). Shared facilities of communication may therefore represent an indispensable, but certainly not sufficient, means of achieving and maintaining cohesion within a certain group, and of spreading national imagination.

This has important implications for the understanding of some of the recent developments in the sphere of mass communication, including the rise of satellite television and transnational broadcasting, the proliferation of diasporic media and the establishment of the various Internet-based transnational channels of communication. Much of the recent literature tends to suggest that these phenomena present a serious challenge to the national order of mass communication, and encourage entirely unprecedented links between the media, nations and states. Yet if the ties between older means of mass communication and national imagination were not as tight as it is often assumed, we need to qualify such claims and develop a more nuanced understanding of relations between mediation and identification in different historical periods. This route is pursued in Chapter 2.

2

Media Nations in a Globalized World

Modern communication technologies are often singled out as a key ingredient in globalization processes, providing the basis for the expansion, strengthening and speeding-up of global connections and networks. With the intensification of global interdependence among states, runs the argument, the line between domestic and foreign news events is becoming blurred. Major political events such as the fall of the Berlin Wall in 1989, the 9/11 attacks, or the recent US presidential election are reported globally, and often take precedence over domestic news (cf. Wark 1994). Popular music, film and television fiction have long detached themselves from national environments and constitute key ingredients of cultural diets consumed worldwide. Similarly, international sporting contests including the Olympic Games and the football World Cup regularly attract millions of viewers worldwide and play a key role in the development of global culture and society (Roche 2000). News retailers such as Reuters, Associated Press and Agence France Presse distribute news stories, video footage and images to clients around the globe, making not only the content of news but also the accompanying visual imagery very much alike, wherever we are.

The territorial organization of communication flows has changed as well. The growth of satellite television and the Internet gave rise to an unprecedented intensification of cross-border information flows, which brought into doubt the capacities of states to maintain sovereign power over their communicative spaces (Price 2002). The proliferation of diasporic media further loosened the hold of established monopolies over spaces of communication and culture and fostered the formation of multiple attachments and hybrid identities (Georgiou 2006). The production and distribution of media products and communications services is also increasingly organized on a transnational scale. Rupert

Murdoch's News Corporation, one of the world's largest media conglomerates, owns some of the key daily newspapers in the UK, USA and Australasia, as well as some of the most successful broadcasting networks, film studios, music catalogues, satellite and cable TV channels, and numerous websites. In 2008, Nokia, the biggest manufacturer of mobile phones as well as a major player in the development of telecommunications networks, had its production units spread around the world, and was selling its products in over 150 countries (Nokia 2009). In the same year, Bertelsmann, a media corporation particularly influential in Europe, operated in over 50 countries (Bertelsmann 2009).

The evidence of media's involvement in globalization processes is clearly compelling, and has tempted several observers to announce the imminent demise of national media organizations and cultures. Writing in the mid-1990s, Mike Featherstone and Scott Lash have suggested that the global is starting 'to replace the nation-state as the decisive framework for social life', and that global actors, including the media, 'are standing alongside and beginning to replace their national counterparts' (1995: 1–2). Many authors have called for an abandonment of nation-state-centred analysis, and instead urged us to embrace 'methodological cosmopolitanism' (Beck 2000), replace the nation-state as the basic unit of analysis with that of the 'global system' (Robinson 1998), and focus on the examination of 'networked connections' and 'the space of flows' (Castells 2009). Yet, at the same time, we also know that the modern media continue to be involved in the reproduction of nationalism, in spite of the ongoing intensification of global media flows. Even in long-established nation-states, nationalism continues to be reproduced by means of banal reminders of nationhood weaved into political speeches and everyday media discourses (Billig 1995). The newest communication technologies such as satellite broadcasting and the Internet, which are often heralded as the harbingers of globalization, are not immune to nationalism either. All the evidence suggests that they serve as key platforms for the performance of national identities and circulation of national myths (Eriksen 2007).

How can we understand this double-edged nature of modern information and communication technologies, that is, their simultaneous involvement in both globalization and nationalism? Should we understand the outbursts of nationalist sentiments on the Internet or the xenophobic portrayals of immigrants and Muslims in British tabloids as mere atavisms, anachronistic remnants of the bygone era when the world was dominated by nation-states (Kaldor 2004)? Or should we, by contrast, see these outbursts as evidence of the continued vitality of nations and nationalism, and as proof of the ultimate failure of transnational communication and the cosmopolitan project (Smith 1995)? In other words, should we embrace the optimistic talk about the compression of time and space, the global village and cosmopolitan consciousness? Or should we discount it as mere wishful thinking that is obscuring the persistence of national patterns of belonging?

The answer to all of these questions is no. Although they are starting from very different assumptions about the nature of globalization, all of them assume that globalization and nationalism are fundamentally opposed and incompatible, and the nation-state in particular is often singled out as a key obstacle to globalization, which acts as 'a fetter on meaningful social transformations', 'a containment structure against change' and 'deactivator of progressive initiatives' (Luke 1995: 97). Yet this assumption is misleading. Now, as in the past, nation-state formation and globalization have been and continue to be closely intertwined rather than antithetical. Historically, 'nation-state presupposed a broader global expansion', and the rise of transnational economic and cultural exchanges went hand-in-hand with the rise of nation-states (Mann 1997: 477). To put it differently, the perception of globalization as a threat to nation-states and national culture is far too simplistic to account for the nature of interaction between the global and the national in the contemporary world (Rantanen 2002; Hopper 2007).

This is not to say that nothing has changed. The development of a global international order and the intensification of trans-border exchanges certainly had profound consequences for the nature of state sovereignty and challenged established forms of national imagination and belonging. Yet, at the same time, nation-states continue to function as the main building blocks of worldwide systems, and in fact flourish globally precisely thanks to the establishment of such global systems. Indeed, nation-states are responsible for making the global interactions possible despite the diversity of cultural assumptions and attitudes: their very presence imposes a globally intelligible *grammar of nationhood* onto virtually every form of transnational governance, trade and communicative exchange. Regardless of which country we turn to, we are likely to encounter national parliaments, national broadcasting systems, national symbols and national sports teams, which make even the remotest country appear somehow familiar and 'knowable'.

This common grammar of nationhood provides a standardized system of categorizing and organizing difference on a global scale, and is at the root of what Anderson (1998) called the 'modular' or 'serial' nature of nationalism. Global standardization and homogenization therefore does not imply an obliteration of difference. To the contrary, as this chapter will demonstrate, globalization requires – and in fact thrives on – differences, but constructs and organizes them in uniform ways. The basis of this uniformity is provided precisely by the world-wide adoption of a common grammar of nationhood; far from being an obstacle to globalization, nationhood constitutes one of its fundamental premises.

The imbrications of nationhood and globalization and their causes are explored further in the next section, which also investigates the notion of globalization itself and compares it to alternative ways of theorizing social change. The chapter then moves on to consider how the serial grammar of nationhood operates in each of the three major areas of globalization – economy, politics and culture – paying particular attention to the role of the media. The discussion draws on a range of historical and contemporary cases, including the creation of international broadcasting organizations, the media coverage of global events, recent shifts in the regulation of the telecommunications sector, the emergence of an international regime for governing the Internet, the impact of satellite television on cultural identity formation, and the proliferation and adaptation of reality television formats.

Globalization, Nation-states and Nationhood

Globalization is a word of fairly recent origins. Although 'globe-talk' (Holton 1998) is a ubiquitous feature of contemporary discourse, and can be found in political speeches, journalistic commentaries, business circles and academic writing, it gained wider currency only in the second half of the twentieth century. Prior to that, many processes and trends that are now commonly discussed under the banner of 'globalization' were theorized under the headings of 'modernization', 'industrialization', or 'capitalism' (Gilman 2007: 259ff). Pertti Alasuutari (2000) usefully points to the striking similarities between processes commonly discussed by contemporary globalization theorists and issues addressed in Marx and Engels' *Communist Manifesto* (1848). Both are concerned with the rise of global markets and industries, the global consumption of goods and the increasing interdependence of nations, as well as the global nature of intellectual exchanges and the rise of world culture, yet discuss them in somewhat different terms. This is not to say that nothing has changed since the nineteenth century: from the mid-twentieth century onwards, the global economy became dominated by transnational corporations, and new information and communication technologies have increased the speed and intensity of cross-border communication well beyond what was common in the past. Nevertheless, globalization is very often simply a new label 'under which one can [...] recycle many old problems and themes' (Gilman 2007: 261).

To put it differently, globalization theory should be regarded as one of the many possible ways of theorizing social change, albeit currently the most popular and widely accepted one. Several competing accounts are currently vying for recognition in the scholarly community: some argue that contemporary societies are centred on notions of risk (Beck 1999), some claim that they are best understood as information societies (Bell 1976; Castells 2009), while others prefer the term surveillance society (Lyon 2001). Many also insist on the continued relevance of theories of dependency, cultural imperialism and modernity. Each of these theories has its weaknesses and strengths, and their persuasiveness varies depending on the particular aspect of modern change we are interested in.

While globalization theory may be helpful in charting the intensification, proliferation and speeding-up of transnational networks and flows across a range of political, economic as well as cultural spheres, it often exaggerates the novelty and extent of these processes, and downplays the persistence of various forms of segregation and exclusion. Due to that, some authors insist that many of the phenomena discussed under the banner of globalization, especially global inequalities and exploitative relationships between rich and poor societies, are better seen as features of a particular stage in the development of capitalism (Sparks 2007; Lash and Lury 2007). Others favour the theory of modernization, interpreting globalization primarily as the incorporation of societies globally into capitalist modernity – a process that, until the last decades of the twentieth century, remained incomplete due to the persistence of two alternative forms of modernity: socialism and colonialism (Giddens 1991; Dirlik 2003).

We will return to these alternative ways of thinking about social change – and in particular to theories of modernization – in Chapter 3. For the purposes of this chapter, we will focus solely on the relationship between globalization and nationhood, and in particular on their interconnections and mutual interdependence. I will argue that many processes that are currently seen as features of globalization can be understood as aspects of the global rise of the modern nation-state as a key unit of political power and action, and of the parallel global spread of nationalism as the dominant discourse of political legitimacy and cultural identity. Whether we look at economy, politics or culture, nation-states and nationhood have often been instrumental in creating the global order, and constitute its key building blocks to this day. As the subsequent pages will demonstrate, globalization often proceeded by means of a global spread of particular national forms and institutions – nation-states, national parliaments, national markets, national flags, national broadcasting systems and so on – and, more broadly, by means of the global spread of nationalism as a particular political principle. Or, as Robertson argues: 'the commitment to the idea of the national society is a crucial ingredient of the contemporary form of globalization' (1992: 112).

At the cultural level, the key prerequisites for the global spread of nations lie in the nature of national imagination. The imagined communities of nations are always conceived as limited – that is, as communities with 'finite, if elastic, boundaries, beyond which lie other nations' (Anderson 1991: 7). Imagining the nation thus always entails imagining a world of nations, and brings along an awareness of how things are done elsewhere, among other nations (Foster 2002: 11). This awareness is particularly strong among peripheral nations, which often try to emulate or appropriate models developed by the world's most powerful nations, or are, alternatively, keen on rejecting them and developing alternative models of nation-building. Ironically, even post-colonial states, established after decolonization in the 1940s and 1950s, were all quite consciously replicating the model of the modern state established in the West, marginalizing alternative models of state and forms of rule (cf. Chatterjee 1986). Similar 'mimetic' behaviour can be found in Central and Eastern European states after the end of Cold War. Whether willingly or not, they all borrowed from and adapted models of political and economic institutions typical of Western European states.

As a consequence, all nations today 'are imagined as equivalent co-habitants of this continuous global domain through the use of similar categories to describe their internal features' (Cheah 2003: 10). This is not to say that Western models of nationhood are the only ones available, or that it is possible to speak of a single 'Western' model as such. As Chapters 3 and 4 will demonstrate, societies around the world adopted rather different visions of modernity, and these went hand in hand with different types of nation-making. However, regardless of these differences, all modern states and media systems ultimately conform to the established grammar of nationhood – they organize national media events, set up national broadcasting systems, found national associations of journalists and so on – in order to become recognizable on the world stage, and thereby become compatible with global systems of media exchange.

Globalization, Nationalism and Economy

Different authors writing about global transformations tend to emphasize different aspects of contemporary processes of change. Immanuel
Wallerstein (1984) gives pride of place to economic developments and
understands globalization primarily in terms of the global spread of
capitalist economy and the associated unequal division of labour. While
these developments have long historical roots, it is worth pointing out
that well into the twentieth century, economic globalization had
occurred primarily by means of international economic exchanges
performed by economic institutions tied to individual nation-states. In
contrast, the second half of the twentieth century has seen the spreading
of multinational corporations and a heavy flow of foreign direct investment, as well as the establishment of transnational regulatory institutions – the World Bank, the International Monetary Fund and the World
Trade Organization (Holton 1998: 52–58). Despite these shifts,
however, much of the global economy is still segmented along national
lines, and relies on the established inter-state order. The transnational
framework for the regulation of economic flows, created after World
War II and still in place today, was established by nation-states and
remains dependent on them.

Yet the fact that economic globalization relies on the nation-state
system does not mean that global market exchanges have uniform
effects on all nation-states. Although international rules and structures
enforced by these regulatory institutions inevitably limit the scope of
decision making at state-level, their ability to influence individual states
varies considerably. Powerful nation-states of Western Europe, as well
as Japan and the US, have far more power to regulate transnational
economic flows to their own advantage, as well as influence the decision-making within transnational regulatory bodies (ibid.: 82). It is
therefore not a surprise that these regulatory bodies are often accused of
being biased in favour of Western nations committed to the liberal
market economy. These same states also serve as headquarters of major
transnational corporations, and inevitably profit more from free trade
and the abolition of restrictions on foreign investment than others.
Having accepted rather than rejected global influence, these states are
able to manipulate global forces to their advantage and enjoy a comparative advantage over those that seek to reject globalization and protect
their culture and economy from foreign influence (Tønnesson 2004).
Pushing this argument further, we could even argue that globalization is
in effect a product of the successful 'internationalization' of state capacity promoted by the world's most powerful economies (Weiss 1998).

The same applies to the realm of media economy. The growing integration of national economies into global markets has undeniably opened ways for the growth of transnational media ownership, but has done so in uneven ways: transnational media ownership is concentrated in the West. Similarly to much else that goes under the banner of globalization, these developments are not new. The unequal patterns of transnational media ownership were well established already in the nineteenth century: in 1892, over 80 per cent of telegraphic cables worldwide were owned by the USA and the British Empire (Headrick 1991: 38). Although the balance of power among Western states changed considerably over the course of the twentieth century, with the USA rising as the key player and quickly overcoming European powers, the general contours remained broadly similar to the present day: the majority of the largest and most profitable transnational media companies are based in the USA and Europe. After the dissolution of the Cold War division of Europe, these media corporations have made significant inroads eastwards, into territories previously out of reach for Western media companies. In 1997, member states of the World Trade Organization signed an agreement that opened their basic telecommunications services – previously treated as a public service provided by the state – to transnational competition, thereby turning them into commodities (Blouin 2000). By the end of 1998, over 45 per cent of the basic telecommunications services market was open to international trade (Marko 1998).

However, the existence of transnational media does not mean that these are independent from nation-states and national economies. To start with, global media corporations still rely on nation-states, at the very least to provide a stable environment (Holton 1998). Due to that, media corporations and nation-states are often collaborators rather than adversaries (Thomas 2001). Secondly, national governments continue to impose restrictions on foreign media ownership despite publicly championing the free flow of information. For instance, the impact of the WTO basic telecommunications agreement differs significantly from country to country, and depends on institutional environments in particular countries (Zhang 2001). A report issued in 1999 revealed that over one-third of the WTO members that signed the basic telecommunications agreement have retained some restrictions on foreign ownership (Wang 2002: 211–13). The list of countries that retained foreign ownership restrictions included several that are normally among the most vocal supporters of free trade, such as the USA, France and Japan. Furthermore, even countries with no formal restrictions on foreign ownership can still find ways to limit competition, for example by demanding that foreign buyers fulfil certain conditions.

Similar patterns emerge if we look specifically at the economic development of the Internet. A comparative study of seven countries – France, Germany, India, Japan, Sweden, South Korea, and the USA – demonstrated that Internet business practices, originally rooted in business models created in the USA, vary significantly from country to country (Kogut 2003). The roots of this variation lie in the particularities of national economies, their systems of regulation and legislation, business networks and technological legacies, all of which necessitated a departure from the original US business model. The national specificities of course did not go unchanged, yet they were also not simply swept away by the onset of a global Internet economy.

If the particularities of national media economies are persisting despite the growth of transnational media ownership, then we need to ask what changes, if any, globalization is bringing to the realm of media economy. Rather than erasing boundaries between national economies and integrating them all into a seamlessly global market, the new communication technologies seem to encourage a reshuffling of established relations between states, markets and the media. These shifts do not necessarily end up profiting transnational players – or at least not exclusively so – but can also lead to a different, more widely spread distribution of advertising revenues among national actors themselves. This is particularly evident in the realm of broadcasting, where the rise of satellite and cable television challenged established balances of power between states, advertisers and broadcasters.

For instance, in India, the advent of digital broadcast satellite (DBS) television services in the early 1990s ultimately provoked the decline of established monopolies over advertising revenues and abolished privileges enjoyed by state-owned broadcasters (Pashupati et al. 2003). DBS provided advertisers with an alternative platform for advertising, and therefore presented a threat to state-owned broadcasting networks. Soon the advertising revenues of the national broadcaster Doordarshan dropped. Doordarshan was forced to change its programming policies to keep its audiences: it introduced more entertainment programmes and turned for inspiration to Latin American and US fiction (Mankekar 1998: 35–37). However, these changes did not lead to a surge in the quantity of imported programmes. Rather, the most popular programmes were inspired by foreign genres, but produced domestically, and adapted to local meanings and values. We will return to these issues at a later point in this chapter, when examining the cultural aspects of media globalization.

Finally, we need to keep in mind that economic institutions, including transnational media corporations, are often themselves interested in contributing to nation-making, as long as they assume that this will make their products more attractive to consumers. This is particularly important when trying to assess the relationship between globalization and nationalism in states with poorly developed cultural and media infrastructures and limited capacity to manage the influx of foreign media products or counter it by encouraging domestic production. In such contexts, we need to look beyond the state for processes and agencies involved in nation-making, and for instance take into account the role of globally distributed, mass-mediated commercial culture. As Robert Foster's (2002) study of nation-making in Papua New Guinea suggests, individual possession or consumption of goods that are considered as parts of national culture can constitute a powerful instrument of nation-making, even when the goods in question are imported. Foster demonstrates this by examining a TV advert for Coca-Cola, which shows a traditionally dressed man in a local village drinking a can of Coca-Cola together with a young boy. By joining an iconic global product and traditional dress, the elderly and the young, argues Foster, the advert sends a powerful message about the mutual compatibility between the global and the national, the modern and the traditional:

> Papua New Guineans can determine themselves collectively – as a collective individual – not by breaking free from tradition and joining an international youth culture, but rather by staying put, incorporating and domesticating the material culture brought in – no matter what the obstacle – from the outside. (Foster 2002: 170)

Cultural industry actors involved in the global distribution of cultural products are acutely aware of the tight link between national culture and consumer preferences. At trade fairs, attention is increasingly paid to cultural differences, which can help tap into hitherto unexplored niche markets (Bielby and Harrington 2008: 163–64). This is visible also at the level of business practices: executives of transnational media corporations do not conduct business as global citizens, but continue to behave as members of particular nations (ibid.: 164). As we will see later on in this chapter, such behaviour is closely tied to the pursuit of economic profit: as numerous cases from around the world demonstrate, global products will fail to attract audiences unless they are carefully tailored to suit local national preferences.

Globalization, Nationalism and Politics

At a political level, nation-states are proving equally resilient as in the realm of economy, and are far from 'coming apart at the seams', as the Tokyo-based business adviser and corporate strategist Kenichi Ohmae predicted in 1996 (Ohmae 1996: 8). Rather than being in conflict, global political institutions and nation-states are mutually interdependent. Nation-states have themselves given rise to the global political order, and the effectiveness of some of the key transnational political actors, such as the UN, remains dependent on support from nation-states, at least the most powerful ones. And vice versa, the sovereignty of nation-states is reliant on recognition in international arenas. States that do not play the game and reject international organization membership are rather weak (Hedetoft 1999: 77).

With some exceptions, social scientists today tend be critical of 'strong' theories of globalization such as Ohmae's, and sometimes even reject the notion of the powerless state as a mere myth (Weiss 1998; Hafez 2007). It is of course undeniable that the nature and scope of state sovereignty is changing, ether due to the challenges coming from the global economy and international regulatory and legal frameworks, or due to the demographic and environmental problems that cannot be managed by individual states. However, similarly as in the realm of the economy, the impact of these challenges on nation-states differs significantly depending on the state's size, level of political power, geographic position, type of political system and so on (Mann 1997). While critics of globalization often point to its adverse effects on the welfare state, research suggests that in the industrial powers of Western Europe, the USA and Japan, government welfare spending has steadily grown alongside the growth of international trade and capital flows. In poorer economies, however, the picture is very different: faced with the pressures of globalization, workers are less able to defend their welfare benefits, and state support for welfare services – already at the outset lower than in richer states – is declining even further (Rudra 2002).

This suggests that we should not focus on whether and to what extent national sovereignty is being undermined, but rather on 'how it is being defined and redefined' in response to a new, more complex global environment (Wang 2002: 220). Instead of being the key political actors in the world arena, nation-states now have to interact with transnational bodies such as the World Trade Organization, the World Bank, the UN or the EU, as well as with various non-state actors ranging from multinational corporations to transnational environmental groups (Higgott et al. 2000). The global polity thus no longer operates through intergovernmental interactions, but through a multiplicity of cross-border exchanges that involve nation-states, transnational regulatory bodies, non-governmental organizations, as well as social movements and individuals (Holton 1998: 131).

The general patterns identified above apply also to the realm of media policy and regulation. Even when it comes to telecommunications policies in states that are all subject to the same transnational regulatory frameworks, national differences persist. For example, Norway, Denmark and Ireland are all subject to the same EU regulations and are part of the single market, yet their communications policies in the early twenty-first century remain distinct, and these differences can be linked to different institutional legacies, including different welfare systems and different political cultures (Storsul 2008). Furthermore, successful regulation of national media systems is often crucially dependent on the existence of transnational media organizations and agreements. The history of international broadcasting associations in Europe provides a good example of this interdependence. The International Broadcasting Union (IBU), established in Geneva in 1925, was formed shortly after the development of the first public radio programmes across Europe, and was charged with the task of imposing a national order of things onto the chaos of early radio broadcasting, as well as with the task of facilitating cooperation between different (national) stations (Mihelj 2007).

Similar patterns of relations between the national and the global can be discerned in the realm of the Internet. From its very beginning, the development of the Internet was closely intertwined with boundary-making practices of national states, and therefore acted as a crucial tool and platform for the articulation of ideas of Self and Other (Everard 2000). The domain name system (DNS) was initially developed without national boundaries in mind, and top-level domains – ending with .gov, .int, .com and the like – were function-specific rather than nation- or state-specific. However, with time, function-specific top-level domains gave way to the national grammar and opened the door to country-specific domains. Even the most widely used websites today, such as Google, have adapted to this logic, and in many countries, country-specific versions of Google are more popular than the original one ending with .com. In some parts of the world, national and regional variants of 'global' websites are proving to be serious competitors to their .com counterparts. For instance, in Eastern Europe, the most popular social networking sites are often national or regional (Imre 2009: 16–17). Also, even the 'global' social networking facilities such as Facebook are often used to create national networks.

While acknowledging the pervasiveness of the national grammar of the Internet, we need to keep in mind that the power of individual states to influence the development of Internet infrastructure remains very uneven. The functioning of the DNS is inherently political. Particularly because the system is managed centrally, it constitutes 'a significant source of political power due to its function of allocating, storing and retrieving Internet addresses', which also entails deciding 'who exists in cyberspace and under what identity' (Ermert and Hughes 2003: 127). This power resides in the Internet Corporation for Assigned Names and Numbers (ICANN), a private non-profit corporation established by the US government in 1998 to oversee the allocation of Internet domain names and addresses. Other countries need to accept the rules of the game developed there, or opt out and create an alternative DNS root. To date, several alternative DNS roots have been launched, but with very limited success, and there were several attempts to transfer the function of domain registration to individual states. Generally speaking, then, little is new here. As with other information and communication technologies before it, the Internet achieved its global status by means of a global spread of the domain name system that matches the world of nation-states, and, yet again, this system was created in the West.

Globalization, Nationalism and Culture

Early scholarly work on the cultural dimension of globalization was inclined to interpret global media flows as the cultural equivalent of economic and political imperialism, and predicted that they will ultimately lead to cultural homogenization (Schiller [1969] 1992; Nordenstreng and Varis 1974; Katz and Wedell 1977). Such cultural homogenization or Americanization, it was argued, was going hand in hand with the gradual diffusion of commercial media systems, and thereby contributed to the spreading of capitalist economies and reinforced the dominance of advanced industrial nations (Schiller [1969] 1992). Theories of cultural imperialism struck a powerful chord among cultural and political elites globally, who were faced with the rising popularity of US cultural and media products among domestic audiences, and were concerned about its effects on national cultural production as well as on popular political preferences.

Not everyone, however, concurred with these assessments. While agreeing that the global dominance of American film, television and print media was indisputable, some observers insisted that their influence was beneficial not only to the USA itself, but also to foreign consumers (Reid 1976). The emphasis on economic factors and, in particular, the logic of the market was disputed as well. The roots of the worldwide success of US imports, it was argued, were not only in the logic of market expansion, but also in the ability of the US cultural industry to develop cultural forms that were genuinely transcultural, and had the potential to appeal to audiences worldwide (de Sola Pool [1975] 1998). Finally, some suggested that the worldwide popularity of US cultural products was only temporary, and predicted its gradual erosion. Sooner or later, argued these authors, domestic producers will be able to counter foreign media flows with domestically produced programmes, modelled on imported media genres yet adapted to suit local and national tastes and preferences (de Sola Pool 1977).

The shifting patterns of cross-border cultural flows over the subsequent decades confirmed that the early fears of American-led cultural domination were indeed somewhat misguided. As the worldwide popularity of US imports started to wane, theories of Americanization and cultural imperialism gave way to more complex accounts of cultural globalization. These theories acknowledged that the patterns of global production, distribution and consumption of cultural products were much more multipolar and multilayered than initially predicted (Tomlinson 1991; Straubhaar 1991; Tunstall 2008). It became increasingly apparent that transnational patterns of media ownership and exchange did not directly translate into an obliteration of national and local differences. Instead, transnational media flows gave rise to two interlinked cultural developments, one pulling in the direction of greater diversity, the other pushing down the route of greater standardization. On the one hand, imported content was always appropriated to suit domestic tastes, and its very presence could prompt significant diversification of domestically produced content and stimulate the rise of regional and local production. Yet, on the other hand, cultural products worldwide, both imported and domestically produced, were becoming more and more alike: regardless of the specific cultural preferences they sought to address, they were increasingly modelled on consumerist imagination.

The domestication of imported media content has been studied over a range of genres. Already the earliest forms of transnational news exchange, established by the European Broadcasting Union in 1959, were subject to national appropriation and 'indigenization'. Chosen events varied from country to country, and selection was based on national framing: for instance, a historical connection with the country where the event has occurred (e.g. France was more likely to pick up a story about an event in one of its former colonies) or a structural similarity between the event in question and domestic events (e.g. news of activities of separatist terrorist groups were most interesting to countries that share the problem). When selected events had no clear connection with the domestic sphere, they were normally accompanied by commentary that was provided by domestic experts (Bourdon 2007: 267). Similar patterns were identified in foreign news reporting more generally. Foreign events and trends are often edited and interpreted in view of the impact they may have domestically, or compared to domestic events (e.g. Cohen 2002; Clausen 2004). This suggests that the cross-border traffic of news contributes simultaneously to the process of globalization and to the process of national construction, building an awareness of the larger world yet doing so through a particular, national lens (Boyd-Barrett and Rantanen 1999).

The same is true of the mediation of sports. Even the reporting of global sports contests and the mediation of transnational sports stars whose lives stretch over several states are powerfully shaped by national imagination. Both the Chilean-born footballer Iván Zamorano, who has been living outside Chile since 1989, and the Canadian-born hockey-player Wayne Gretzky, who spent most of his career living in the US, are perceived as national stars in the countries they come from (Wong and Trumper 2002). Similarly, the Olympic Games typically achieve their worldwide appeal by means of mobilizing the waves of competing nationalisms across the globe. Not only are the games differently interpreted in different national contexts (Puijk 2000), but the participation itself is usually seen as a grand opportunity for national self-promotion and legitimation on a global scale (Bourdon 2003: 73). While the games certainly draw nations together, they also, inevitably, separate them (Real 1989: 240–47). For instance, the South Korean media coverage of the opening and closing ceremonies of the 2004 Athens Olympic Games promoted both global and national belonging at the same time: it fostered global fraternity while at the same time invoking anti-Japanese sentiments and igniting Korean nationalism (Lee and Maguire 2009).

The numerous national adaptations of global television formats provide another case in point. For instance, the Finnish version of the reality TV show *Survivor* repeatedly highlighted the difficulties experienced by contestants when having to part from their mobile phones, thereby contributing to the stereotypical portrayal of Finland as a 'high-tech nation'. The contestants also regularly engaged in typically 'Finnish' activities such as going to the sauna, fishing and picking mushrooms, and conformed to national conventions of conversation and behaviour (Aslama and Pantti 2007). The studies of the TV quiz show *Weakest Link* and its different national versions point to similar conclusions. In both the British original and the Flemish adaptation, questions often included references to the home country and other countries, thus 'creating a world of nations rather than one of global culture' (Van den Bulck and Sinardet 2006: 153). The Taiwanese version, in contrast, failed to attract audiences because it proved to be out of tune with domestic cultural sensibilities. The finger-pointing and aggressive behaviour of the presenter did not fare well with local audiences: public embarrassment of this kind was considered entirely inappropriate (Bielby and Harrington 2008: 213, n.48).

The incentives for domestication of imported news and other genres vary. First, as the Taiwanese experience with the *Weakest Link* suggests, national framing and adaptation to local tastes can be driven by market imperatives and therefore audience preferences. Most national TV systems are making their own TV shows, soaps and reality programmes to make global formats appealing to national audiences (Tunstall 2008), and while foreign imports continue to occupy a prominent role and often account for the majority of total programming, the most popular prime time shows are usually of domestic origin (Esser 2009). This is confirmed by the changing patterns of media imports and audience preferences in Central and Eastern Europe over the past two decades. After an initial surge in foreign media imports in the early 1990s, domestic programming has seen a comeback: the most popular reality TV programmes, variety shows and soap operas tend to be produced domestically, although they are often inspired by imported formats (Štětka 2009).

Second, adaptations of global genres and products can also be spurred by local policies and restrictions. In order to gain access to the Chinese market, global media corporations and agencies such as McCann Erikson, AOL Time Warner, News Corporation and MTV were forced to adjust their products to Confucian and socialist values, minimize explicit violence and sex, and more generally display appreciation for traditional Chinese culture (I. Weber 2003; Sinclair and Harrison 2004). The soap opera *Love Talks* (1999), produced in collaboration between the Hong Kong-based United Media and the multinational agency McCann Erickson, is a good case in point. The plot follows the story of Qu Ying, a young woman of modest background who is trying to make a career in an international advertising agency and ends up falling in love with the well-to-do advertising executive Hu Bing. The plot is driven by traditional Chinese notions of fate and love, but is at the same time organized around the central contest between tradition and modernity, symbolically represented in the contrast between the dirty, poor and cramped daily life of Qu Ying and the comfortable, wealthy existence of Hu Bing, associated with the pleasures of global consumer products (Sinclair and Harrison 2004).

While stimulating the production of hybrid media forms and the blending of global and national imagery, the intensification of cross-border flows also contributes to important shifts at sub-state level. As argued earlier, the rise of transnational media, in particular satellite television, presented a challenge to state-owned broadcasting networks, and endangered the established state monopoly over national broadcasting. Satellite channels provided advertisers with an alternative way of reaching potential consumers, and gradually untied the knot that anchored national broadcast cultures to the state. However, rather than leading to a weakening of national imagination and a 'cultural invasion' from beyond the state, this shift opened up the communicative spaces to a multitude of different projections of nationhood from 'below' the state, and an intensified contestation of official, state-supported ideas of belonging.

The transformation of the broadcast landscape in India over the past two decades provides an excellent example of the link between transnationalization and diversification. The growth of satellite broadcasting prompted the proliferation of commercial Indian channels, including channels broadcasting in languages other than Hindi (McMillin 2001). The Tamil-language Sun TV, the Kannada-language Udaya TV and many other broadcasters started providing language-specific programming adapted to regional tastes, thereby luring audiences away from Hindi- and English-language competitors. These regional broadcasters were reaching out to those audiences for whom the Hindi adaptations of global shows proved insufficiently attractive, and who instead demanded more 'authentic' programming attuned to local dialects and cultural environments (ibid.: 64). As a result of this sub-state diversification, Indian television was turned into a battleground for competing visions of community, which made it impossible to talk of a single Indian community of television (Kumar 2006). Instead of resulting in cultural homogenization, transnationalization thus contributed to greater diversity, and fostered the mediation of cultural identities that hitherto received little space in the national media system.

However, we need to be careful not to overstate the link between globalization and diversity, and keep in mind that the adaptation and appropriation of global influences is taking place in the context of unequal relations of power. First, while produced domestically and adapted to suit local preferences, some of the most popular prime-time shows are based on Western formats and genres, and therefore benefit media corporations based in the West. National and cultural differences may well be persisting and even multiplying, yet, at the same time, media ownership is becoming increasingly concentrated (Boyd-Barrett 2006). Second, while US dominance over transnational media and cultural flows has been successfully challenged by products originating from Latin America, India and Hong Kong (Straubhaar 1991; Sinclair et al. 1996), the USA still remains the biggest global player (Sparks 2007). It is of course important to note that some countries have been able to turn into 'little cultural imperialists' themselves, and are dominating the transnational cultural and media flows at regional level. This is the case with India, whose media products are popular across South Asia as well as among South Asian diasporas in the West (Sonwalkar 2001). Yet not all countries are equally well equipped for countering media and cultural flows from abroad with domestic programming. The ability to retain control over domestic audiovisual production depends on the size of national economies, television advertising expenditure and/or the proportion of gross domestic product spent on broadcast media (Dupagne and Waterman 1998; Štětka 2009). While local audiences may well prefer domestically produced programmes that speak to their cultural tastes, only wealthier countries with stronger economies and larger audiovisual markets are able to respond to such audience demand and profit from it.

Finally, we should also note that while allowing for and indeed demanding national diversity, the global expansion of the market economy model is premised on the standardization of the basic grammar of collective imagination. Increasingly, audiences worldwide are being addressed as imagined communities of consumers, thereby displacing alternative forms of national imagination. It is not by coincidence that some of the most prominent examples of successful local adaptations of global culture come from the realm of advertising – as in the case of the Coca-Cola advert from Papua New Guinea – or involve fictional content centred on urban, affluent, consumption-driven environments – as in the example of the Hong Kong-produced soap opera *Love Talks*. Financed predominantly through advertising, commercial media need to appeal first and foremost to potential consumers, and the symbolic worlds they create will inevitably be more familiar and more easily accessible to those with greater purchasing power. For the poor, however, the symbolic universe of national consumption is bound to remain a distant ideal, powerful in structuring their desires and aspirations, but far removed from their everyday lives. While allowing and often even demanding national and cultural diversity, the imagined communities of consumers fostered by commercial media therefore inevitably bring about their own forms of exclusion, organized around the division between the wealthy and the poor.

To untangle these changing relationships between media nations and the communication of identity and difference, we need to move beyond the key concerns of the globalization debate and turn to other ways of theorizing social change. In particular, we need to turn to theories that will allow us to better capture the changing nature of mass communication and nationhood, both historically and today, and complement the understanding of the relationship between homogenization and diversity with an appreciation of the multiple forms of inclusion and exclusion, tied not only to the cultural structures of nation-states, but also to the interlocking forces of economy and politics. As the following two chapters seek to demonstrate, a useful analytical framework can be found in theories of multiple modernities.

3

Media Nations and Alternative Modernities

There is little doubt that nations and the mass media alike are creatures of modernity. Although both had their historical predecessors, neither could have become the powerful actors they are today without the simultaneous transformation of economic production, the political order, cultural sensibilities and social relationships that first coalesced in the eighteenth century. Within the realm of politics, the new conception of the nature of power and the increasing dependence on 'the will of the people' as the source of legitimacy fuelled both the proliferation of nationalist imagination as well as the growth of the 'public sphere' and the modern mass media as an autonomous force in politics and society. The creation of the public sphere was aided by parallel developments in the realm of economy, where the growing commercialization of cultural production opened doors for the production and dissemination of messages that did not depend on government support. At the same time, the logic of the market and its incessant search for new audiences also contributed to the flourishing of print cultures in languages other than Latin, and hence also to the formation of national languages and cultures. Finally, among cultural factors, the Protestant Reformation, the ensuing European religious wars of the sixteenth century and the process of secularization have all stimulated political contestation and created the conditions for the growth of the public sphere, while at the same time making room for secular forms of collective identity.

This description of modernizing developments and their involvement in the rise of mass communication and nation-building is a familiar and compelling one. However, it is also overwhelmingly Westocentric: it leaves little room for the specificities of modernization in the rest of the world, and brushes over divergent developments within the West itself. To account for these alternative forms of modernity, mass media and nationhood, both within and beyond the West, we need to depart from the standard account in three ways.

First, we need to acknowledge that the economic, political and cultural factors mentioned above were not equally influential in all parts of the world, and that their encounter with local factors often led to divergent outcomes. The new conception of sovereignty, for instance, has been at the root of remarkably different political ideologies and systems – ranging from liberal democracies to state socialism – each claiming to represent the true embodiment of popular will. Levels of industrialization and commercialization around the world were and remain noticeably different, and so does the potential for the development of commercial media. In many cases, states have endeavoured to limit the scope of commercial media and retain a measure of control over their content. Often, the commercial logic itself has ended up working to the detriment of media autonomy, introducing forces of indirect censorship not unlike those resulting from state control.

If the constellations of political, economic and cultural factors that contributed to the rise of the modern media and nationalism were diverse, it is reasonable to expect that the types of media systems and their involvement in nation-making varied as well. For instance, in countries with relatively low levels of industrialization and limited commerce, the formation of national media was probably dependent primarily on conscious state policies and deliberate efforts by cultural elites rather than on the incessant search for new markets fuelled by the logic of print capitalism. Recent comparative research on media systems suggests that these initial settings exert lasting influence. To this day, media systems in Western Europe and the USA vary significantly with respect to the relative balance of market and state influences, and these differences can be traced back to divergent patterns of early political and economic modernization (cf. Hallin and Mancini 2004a). Journalistic conventions at work in news reporting follow similar patterns, with US journalism being characterized by information-oriented, analytical and politically neutral reporting (Schudson 1982) while for instance Italian reporting is far more prone to commentary and political partisanship (Hallin and Mancini 1984). It is quite possible that forms of national imagination vary accordingly, and that commercial media, dependent as they are on sales and advertising, foster different forms of national belonging compared with the media that rely on state subsidies, political support or benevolent censors.

Second, we need to avoid assuming that modernization necessarily entails the rise of nation-states. While many modernizing states have indeed embraced the nation-state ideal as the sole legitimate model of socio-political organization, the persistence of cultural heterogeneity, fuelled by the contemporary reality of migration flows, have prevented this ideal from being translated fully into reality. In 1971, when the term 'nation-state' was already well entrenched in everyday talk, political debate and scholarly discussion, only about one-third of all the states in the world contained a nation that accounted for more than 90 per cent of the total population (Connor 1994: 89–117). Four decades later, little has changed. As a result of the break-up of multinational socialist federations, the total number of would-be nation-states increased, yet the vast majority still contain at least one significant minority. This is not to say that the nation-state is not a powerful political ideal or that it did not exert influence in its own right. The point is that its trajectory in modernity was fraught with difficulties, and that it was entangled with other, equally modern forms of socio-political organization, such as empires and multinational federations (Chernilo 2007).

A similar argument can be made for national communicative spaces and their ties with states. The creation of national communicative spaces, congruent with state boundaries, was a goal pursued by the political and intellectual elites of many countries, but was not accepted universally. These departures from ideal-typical, territorially enclosed national public spheres are most clearly apparent when we take into account long-established multinational and multilingual media systems such as those of Switzerland and Belgium (e.g. Erk 2003). The media systems of the multinational federations of socialist Eastern Europe – the Soviet Union, Czechoslovakia and Yugoslavia – were also far from resembling the ideal-typical, internally homogeneous national spheres (Mihelj 2007: 446–47). The construction of territorially circumscribed national communicative spheres was therefore definitely not the only available option, and instead had to compete with alternative configurations of nationhood, state and communication.

And third, we need to acknowledge that the rise of modern nationalism and mass communication does not always go hand in hand with secularization and the retreat of religion into the private sphere. The persistence of religious practices and beliefs in virtually all contemporary societies has driven many scholars to rethink the ahistorical and Eurocentric binary opposition of modernity and tradition, as well as the concomitant understanding of the relationship between religion and nationalism (e.g. Juergensmeyer 1993; Smith 2003). While the period of European revolutions was indeed followed by a proliferation of secular nationalisms that demanded a disentanglement of religion and politics, it is also clear that this disentanglement often remained a political ideal rather than a reality. Instead of being wiped out, religious understandings of nationhood often coexisted with secular ones and entered a range of different relations with them (e.g. McLeod 2000). While some established themselves in opposition to the secular state, and sought to 'rescue the nation from the profane Western "nation-state" and its materialist corruptions' (Smith 2003: 415), others were prepared to acknowledge – though do not necessarily approve of – the existence of secular states, and abide by their rules (Mihelj 2007).

Parallel developments can be found in the realm of the media and the public sphere. Historically, the genesis of the national public sphere and modern communication was not dependent on the parallel retreat of religious institutions and sentiments into the private sphere. Some of the key premises of secular journalism in the USA can be traced back to religiously inspired campaigns for freedom of expression among Protestant preachers and proselytizers (Underwood 2002). Similarly, the early development of a free environment for public discussion in colonial India was dependent on the activities of Christian and Hindu religious groups demanding state neutrality and free speech (Van der Veer 2001: 14–29). In many Western societies, most notably in the USA, religion continues to exert significant influence on the public sphere, sometimes by being instrumental in opening up public debate, on other occasions acting to close it down (Casanova 1994). In Britain and France, where traditional denominations have undergone a sharp decline in public influence over the course of the twentieth century, religion has again become an important public player, this time due to immigration and fears over the perceived incompatibility between Muslim immigrant lifestyles and the secular outlook of mainstream societies (see e.g. Bowen 2006).

To capture these alternative configurations of nationhood and the media and their various ways of interlocking with states, markets and religions, we need to start by broadening our understanding of modernization. Instead of constructing a single account of modernity and its links with nationalism and mass communication, we need to acknowledge that, from its inception, the meaning of being modern was internally contested. This contestation gave rise to multiple political projects of modernity and therefore also multiple configurations of nationhood and mass communication. This chapter and the next one develop an analytical framework for exploring these multiple constellations, and do so by drawing on three key bodies of work: the theory of alternative modernities, comparative media research and historical research on nation-building.

Alternative Modernities

Ever since the formulation of classic ideas about social evolution in the nineteenth century, scholarly discussions about social change have been plagued by ethnocentric, teleological and ahistorical models of thinking. Theories developed by August Comte, Herbert Spencer, Émile Durkheim, Ferdinand Tönnies, Friedrich Engels, Karl Marx, Max Weber and their contemporaries sought to provide a universal narrative of human history, and saw change as unidirectional, organic, cumulative and irreversible (Sztompka 1994: 101–12). Although marked by fundamental disagreements over the relative weight of, and relationships between, cultural, economic and political forces, all of these authors shared the fundamental presuppositions of their epoch, and conceived of human history as a natural process that follows regular patterns than one can uncover by means of logical reasoning. After the devastating experiences of the two World Wars, these evolutionist modes of thinking were reinvigorated, now often inspired by the urge to explain the perceived aberration of Nazi Germany, and motivated by the intensifying contest between the Soviet Union and the United States. Unlike the more abstract social theories of nineteenth-century thinkers, the new wave of theorizing modernization was increasingly often coupled with systematic empirical research including quantitative measurements and testing. Broad theoretical and descriptive accounts nevertheless remained common as well (ibid.: 113ff).

Enmeshed in the foreign policies of the Cold War and the global competition for influence over former colonies in Latin America, the Middle East, South Asia and Africa, these new theories of social change were meant to offer more than mere explanation. They were also expected to provide normative guidelines that would help the USA maintain and enhance its leading role on a global scale and, most of all, its advantage over the rival project of modernity advanced by Soviet communism (Letham 2000; Gilman 2007). As such, the theories advanced by US political and social scientists such as Walt Whitman Rostow, Lucian Pye, Daniel Lerner and Talcott Parsons shared many of the weaknesses of the nineteenth-century evolutionist theories (cf. Sztompka 1994: 113ff). They were premised on a black-and-white opposition between 'tradition' and 'modernity' and saw modernization as a uniform, unilinear process bound to culminate in the forms of society, economy and politics known from the industrialized West, and the United States in particular.

These approaches had already come under severe criticism in the 1960s, and were effectively discredited by the 1970s (Gilman 2007:

203–40). While some advocated a complete abandonment of general modernization theory (e.g. Tipps 1973), others insisted on putting it on a firmer empirical grounding and replacing it with a more context-sensitive, less value-laden and ethnocentric approach (e.g. Moore [1966] 1993; Eisenstadt 1974). This second, reformist route gave rise to theories of alternative or multiple modernities, which envisage modern history 'as a story of continual constitution and reconstitution of a multiplicity of cultural programs', carried forward by specific social actors and movements holding different views on what it means to be modern (Eisenstadt 2000: 2). Rather than treating modernity as a bounded system with a fixed, unchangeable array of basic elements, this approach sees modernity as a 'loosely structured constellation' compatible with different visions of modern times, different socio-economic and socio-political constellations, and different pre-modern legacies (Arnason 2000: 64–65).

These alternative modern constellations certainly have a lot in common. At the level of social structure, all modernities are characterized by a tendency towards greater differentiation between particular social arenas – a trend noted already by Durkheim in his *The Division of Labour in Society* ([1893] 1984) and amply discussed in the post-World War II decades. At the ideological level, the different visions of modernity all share a particular conception of time, which involves a reflexive attitude to the past and the present and a general orientation towards the future (Therborn 2003). To put it differently, central to all the different projects of modernity is the idea of progress, whether conceived in terms of revolutionary change or rebirth. This shared conception of time also constitutes the basis of identity construction common to all visions of modernity, namely the opposition between the modern, civilized Self and the underdeveloped, backward and primitive Other (cf. Pickering 2001: 51ff). Despite this, we should also take note of important differences. The ways in which the particular social arenas – economy, politics, mass communication, religion and others – are organized and interconnected can vary significantly from society to society. Similarly, the criteria for judging the past and the present and defining what counts as progress can differ considerably, and can lead to completely divergent institutional solutions, and completely different projections of collective identity. In short, the revised theory of modernization was 'purged' of all its evolutionist and Eurocentric undertones, and abandoned any assumptions about a necessary, universal or irreversible itinerary of change (Sztompka 1994: 136–41).

When identifying the divergent paths into modernity, and looking for explanations capable of accounting for this diversity, theories of multiple or alternative modernities have pointed to a range of factors. Barrington Moore's groundbreaking *Social Origins of Dictatorship and Democracy*, first published in 1966, distinguished between three 'routes to modern society' – the bourgeois revolution, the revolution from above and the revolution from below – that eventually led to the formation of three main types of modern political regimes – liberal democracy, fascism and communism. Broadly speaking, the main thrust of Moore's argument was to explain the different routes to modernity with reference to a set of socio-economic and (though perhaps somewhat less prominently) political factors. Key among these was the extent of commercialization and industrialization and, as a consequence, the relative strength of classes with an independent economic base. Together with the constraints of the state bureaucracy, this factor was influential in determining the role played by the other two key actors in modernizing process, namely the peasantry and the landed upper classes, and the extent to which the bourgeoisie, when seeking to subvert existing hierarchies of power, would have to seek alliances either with the former (which would lead to the communist route) or with the latter (leading to the fascist route).

From early on, *Social Origins* was criticized for its neglect of non-economic factors, in particular the independent causal role of ideas and culture, and to a lesser extent political structures, although critics acknowledged that the approach adopted in the book represented a decisive departure from the classic Marxist type of economic determinism. (For an overview of early criticisms, see Wiener 1975.) It is also worth pointing out that Moore was notoriously vague in stating his general hypotheses, which often led his interpreters to very different, if not entirely contradictory conclusions (cf. Smith 1983: 104–7). Given that my analysis is chiefly concerned with nationalism and mass communication – both of which fall into the domain of culture – it is worth pausing to consider Moore's conception of the role of cultural factors a bit more closely. Moore addresses the role of culture briefly in the epilogue to his book, where he explains that while being suspicious of cultural explanations, he does not deny that existing cultural ideals and codes of behaviour do act as 'intervening variables', and should as such be taken into account when explaining the processes of modernization (Moore [1966] 1993: 485). Nevertheless, he insists that culture should not be regarded as a wholly independent factor in its own right, but as a phenomenon that arises from and is maintained by a particular historical, economic and political context, and as such requires an explanation itself. This is an important point that is often neglected in some of the recent debates about multiple modernities, which emphasize that every modernization inescapably unfolds within, and arises from, a particular cultural context, and then go on to argue that these diverse cultural starting points can, on their own, account for divergent outcomes of modernization.

How can we acknowledge the semi-independent role of culture in social change without succumbing to either a simplistic version of cultural determinism or an equally simplistic economic and political determinism? To start with, we should identify the particular socio-economic and political circumstances under which culture assumes a semi-autonomous role. There are two distinct sets of circumstances that can give rise to such a development. The first one entails the rise of a semi-independent sphere of cultural activity involving an array of new cultural forms and institutions, ranging from newspapers and novels to reading societies and coffee houses, known today as 'the public sphere' (Habermas [1962] 1989). The formation of this sphere was stimulated precisely by the socio-economic and political shifts charted by Moore, which also enhanced the need for a separate class of 'social mediators' whose role was to debate competing arguments in favour or against particular changes, and make them available to the public (cf. Smith 1983: 103–4). In so far as these mediators had an independent economic base – provided for instance through the sales of their newspapers, books or through theatre ticket sales – they could inflect the debate in ways that were not wholly determined by existing balances of power between social classes. Or, as Habermas would argue, this was a sphere within which both the laws of the state and the laws of the market could, at least temporarily, be suspended.

The second way in which culture can assume a semi-independent role entails a more conscious effort on the part of the elites to use 'culture' – conceived as a clearly delineated and static set of values and norms belonging to a particular (often national) community – as an independent force that shapes the process and outcome of moderniza-tion. Using culture in this way, the modernizing elites can for instance argue that certain elements of existing culture should be dispensed with in order for modernization to proceed unabated, or that models of modernization developed elsewhere should be appropriated selectively in order to protect the alleged 'essence' of national culture. To be sure, the exact understanding of culture, as invoked in elite discourse, is shaped by the economic and political interests and structures they are embedded in. Yet once this particular understanding of culture becomes entrenched in legislation and institutional structures – e.g. publishing houses, theatres and cultural associations, educational establishments – cultural fictions are endowed with the power to structure the economic and political contexts they arise from in ways that are not necessarily wholly determined by the dominant balance of power and interests. As is the case with the more spontaneously evolving forms of public debate outlined earlier, this is true in particular in cases where such elite-framed forms of cultural activity have an independent source of funding to rely on.

The two forms of culture outlined above operate alongside each other and often rely on the same field of cultural activities and institutions. This generates the characteristic overlaps between the nation and the public that are often left inadequately theorized in mainstream accounts of the public sphere. Yet these overlaps do not mean that the two forms of culture necessarily coexist in a harmonious relationship. By arguing that a particular 'foreign' model of modernization will endanger domestic national culture, elites can effectively discredit some of the possible visions of modernity as 'alien', and stifle the cultural activities that are necessary for a truly public debate. As we will show later in this chapter, such encroachments on public culture are particularly characteristic of those visions of modernity – including German Nazism and Italian Fascism – that define culture in totalizing terms and consider the interests of a particular cultural community to be the key driving force of modernization.

Let us now set these conceptual distinctions to one side and turn instead to a brief account of the multiple routes to modernity as they crystallized in the West over the course of the twentieth century. Recent debates about multiple modernities often have the unfortunate tendency to assume the existence of an internally homogeneous 'Western' modernity, and contrast such modernity with alternative 'Asian' or 'African' modernities. Such discussions of multiple modernities, premised on geocultural categories, obscure the fact that territorially defined 'cultures' are not clearly bounded or internally homogeneous, but ridden with internal tensions and contradictions. Due to this internal cultural diversity and conflict, different segments of the same population will inevitably react to modernization in divergent ways. Historically, Western societies have served as battlegrounds for several competing modernizing visions, which make it impossible to speak of a single 'Western modernity' rooted in a homogeneous 'Western culture'. The twentieth century in particular was marked by a deadly struggle between rival ideologies – liberalism, fascism, communism – offering markedly different interpretations of the modern condition and its ills and wrongs. Dazzled by the outcome of the Cold War and the seemingly global triumph of liberalism, Western societies often think of themselves as uniquely predisposed to liberal democratic values. Yet, as Mark Mazower reminds us, the history of democracy in Europe was not a story of 'inevitable victories and forward marches', but rather one of 'narrow squeaks and unexpected twists' (Mazower 1998: xii).

The hopes aroused by the promises of democracy in the early twentieth century were short-lived, and soon replaced by a shared discontent with the corruption and inefficiency of parliaments, the erosion of old certainties and lack of national consensus. Catholic integralists and Protestant fundamentalists were concerned at the shattering of religious interpretations brought about by liberalism and secularization, and sought to reinstate a social order based on the infallibility of the Pope and the Scripture (Coleman 1992). Among the old elites, the dissatisfaction with the new political order was reinforced by fears over political demands voiced by the new entrants to the political field – peasants and workers. The introduction of democracy and the widening of suffrage threw into relief ethnic, class and religious divisions, making parliaments seem like a menacing lens, 'magnifying rather than resolving the bitter social, national and economic tensions in society at large' (Mazower 1998: 17). At the other end of the political spectrum, among proponents of communism, the inefficiency of democracy and the slow pace of change were lamented for different reasons, and increasingly seen as an obstacle to the proletarian revolution. While initially joined in the struggle against the old regime, liberalism and communism were increasingly parting ways. In Russia, the democratic hopes accompanying the revolutionary overthrow of the Tsar in February 1917 were quickly dispelled by the Bolsheviks' push for the proletarian socialist revolution (Fitzpatrick 2008: 40–67). Lenin in particular was well known for his disdain for anything resembling 'bourgeois liberalism' and had little patience for the slow workings of democratic institutions and the bureaucracy-heavy 'bourgeois legality' (Burbank 1995: 33ff).

These sharp divisions between liberal democracy and its ideological rivals, and the violence they unleashed over the course of the first half of the twentieth century, can easily obscure deep-seated commonalities. Despite stemming from very different ideological and social roots, these rival projects all shared a belief in progress and a general orientation towards the future, as well as a propensity for utopian visions of the future – be it the Third Reich, a Christian order based on traditional religious authority, a classless society, or global democracy. They were also all, each in its own way, endeavouring to find solutions to the same fundamental problems – the problems of modern social organization: how to balance individual and collective rights; how to foster political, cultural and ideological diversity while at the same time maintaining a level of social cohesion necessary for the functioning of a modern state;

how far social development should be managed by the state, or left to the dynamics of the market.

These key problems also provide the best starting point for describing and comparing the rival projects of modernity. To start with, modernizing projects clearly differ with respect to the balance of power between the state and the market. At one end of the spectrum, we encounter modernizing visions that advocate the benefits of an unfettered market economy, unrestricted by any form of state intervention. At the other end of the same spectrum, we find those ideas of modernity that believe in the absolute primacy of politics over the economic arena. Among modern political ideologies, the first version of modernity is advocated by economic or laissez-faire liberalism, and the second is defended by communism. In principle, all modern societies could be distinguished by the extent to which they come close to one or the other end of the market–state spectrum. While the contemporary USA is close to the market end of the spectrum, the different state-socialist systems of early Cold War Eastern Europe are near the state end of the same spectrum, with the social democracies of post-World War II Central Europe and for instance Yugoslavia with its market socialism in the 1970 somewhere between the two.

According to some authors, modern societies all give the market and the state precedence over community and culture, and it is precisely this which differentiates them from pre-modern societies (e.g. Waisman 2002: 107). If this line of reasoning is correct, the market–state axis constitutes the only relevant axis of comparison among modern societies. However, some modern political projects – most notably Italian Fascism and German Nazism, but also various forms of religious fundamentalism – maintain that both political and economic forces should be subordinated to the interests of a particular community or culture, and be put at its service. Although self-styled as distinctly anti-modern, and often excluded from mainstream accounts of modernization or treated as aberrations, these projects in fact constitute one of the possible routes to a modern society. In socio-economic terms, the fascist route is characterized by a fairly advanced capitalist economy, but also by a rather weak bourgeoisie, reliant on support from the landed classes and the state bureaucracy (cf. Moore [1966] 1993). In terms of the relative prominence of the market and the state alone, the fascist route is in some ways similar to the social democracies of post-World War II Central Europe, yet what makes it distinct is the strategic use of community or culture, conceived in essentialist, totalizing terms, and seen as an independent force that dictates the course of change.

To understand the role played by culture in the fascist route to modernity, it is important to take into account that the dramatic dislocations prompted by the combined effects of industrialization, social mobilization and democratization not only gave rise to visions of progress, but also fuelled anxieties about degeneration, social decay and the demise of civilization itself. Italian Fascism promised to avert this imminent catastrophe by offering an alternative to both communist and capitalist visions of modernity, one that would allow Italians to enjoy the benefits of modern life while avoiding its levelling effects and its alleged threats to Italian culture and its moral order (Ben-Ghiat 2004). German Nazism fed on similar fears and anxieties, and promised to avert the threat of modern anomie and chaos by using modern technology and bureaucracy to restore and maintain order, and put both to the service of the German nation (Herf 1986; Bauman 1989). German national socialists were opposed to the liberal project and believed the only way out of the social fragmentation and 'decay' of the Weimer Republic lay in the amalgamation of the *Volksgemeinschaft* (people's community) and the state, leading to the establishment of a *Völkischer Staat* (Welch 2004: 214). Finally, the various forms of religious fundamentalism around the world can also be approached as a distinct type of modern political movements: not unlike Fascism and Nazism, they are promoting an essentialized, totalizing vision of cultural tradition and are aimed at shielding it from the perceived threats of social change (Eisenstadt 1999).

To account for the specificity of these self-styled 'anti-modern' projects vis-à-vis the more self-consciously modern projects such as those advanced by liberalism and communism, it is clearly important to take into account community as one of the key principles of modern social organization, alongside the principles of the market and state bureaucracy. It is therefore possible to argue that modern societies can be differentiated not only with respect to the relative balance of state and market forces, but also with regard to how much influence they accord to the principle of community, and how they relate community to the market and the state (Figure 3.1).

This introduces two further axes of comparison. The first one runs from those visions of modernity that claim market forces should be used to further the interests of the community, to those that believe markets should serve customers as sovereign individuals. Instances of the former can be found in some of the principles underlying the economic policies of Nazi Germany: for instance, the belief that private property should be nationalized if it was not used to further Nazi goals (Temin 1991). Examples of the latter include anarcho-capitalist visions of modern society and economy, as exemplified in the ideas of David Freidman and Murray Rothbart, who saw capitalism as an entirely benevolent force

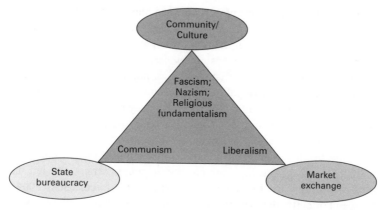

Figure 3.1 Principles of social organization and modern political ideologies

that is best left free of any intervention whatsoever (Adams 2002: 131–32).

The last axis of comparison distinguishes between those projects of modernity that believe the state apparatus should be put at the service of a particular community, and those that argue the state should abstain from interfering into community formation. If we limit ourselves specifically to the relationship between the state and religion, we can thus distinguish between cases where modernization led not only to the full separation of state and religion but also to a general decline of the latter, as in parts of Western Europe, and cases where similar processes have given rise to a successful fundamentalist reaction requiring the state to subject itself to the interests of a particular religious community, as in the case of post-1979 Iran. Midway between the two extremes are the various cases of adaptation and reinterpretation involving new forms of religious belief, including self-spirituality, pluralism and this-worldliness, which allowed religion to flourish despite the formal separation of state and religion (Lambert 1999). Also somewhere between the two poles of community and the state are the various colonial and postcolonial projects of modernization, where indigenous elites often argued for the need for a selective appropriation of 'Western' models of modernity.

A clarification is necessary at this point. Although liberalism, communism and fascism are positioned at different ends of our triadic model, this is not meant to suggest that the dynamics of any concrete society that falls into one of these categories can be explained solely by reference to a single organizing principle. Rather, in each and every modern society, all three principles are at work simultaneously; what differs is the balance of power between them. The functioning of communist societies thus cannot be reduced to political determinants and the dynamics of state-formation. Although many authors have tried to make sense of the Soviet system by seeing it either as a distinctive economic system or as a particular kind of political system, a multidimensional approach that takes into account economic, political and cultural levels provides a far more adequate way of describing its specificities (Arnason 1993: 1–5). Similarly, while the primacy of market principles in the USA is indisputable, the roots of its liberal market economy lie in key political decisions and cultural factors that have militated against state intervention into economic affairs and led the state to willingly limit its interference into market forces (Starr 2004). Most importantly, the principle of community is at work in any social context and is not confined to fascist societies. As we shall see in the next chapter, both liberal and communist modernist projects adapted to the exigencies of the principle of community, and appropriated it to suit their own ends. The gradual strengthening of (national) community as an organizing principle in communist societies is particularly telling in this respect and attests to the weakening appeal of the communist modernizing project over the course of the second half of the twentieth century and the changing socio-economic and political structures of communist societies.

Alternative Models of Mass Communication

Both the debate about multiple modernities and the triadic model of modern political ideologies find resonances in media and communication debates, most obviously in the field of comparative media research. Comparative approaches have been an integral part of mass communication research virtually from its beginnings, but in a similar way to comparative research in other areas of social scientific inquiry, comparative media research has long been plagued by Westocentrism and evolutionist thinking. For example, the widely quoted fourfold typology of the press developed by Fred Siebert, Theodore Petersen and Wilbur Schramm in their *Four Theories of the Press*, first published in 1956, was written from the normative perspective of classical liberalism and ranked the different types of the press on an evolutionary scale culminating in the press model promoted in the West. In this sense, the title of the book was a misnomer: instead of offering four theories of the press, it offered 'one theory with four examples' (Nerone 1995: 18).

As with most comparative media research in the USA at the time,

Four Theories was of course an intellectual child of the Cold War. It was shaped by the position and interests of the USA in the international arena, and measured all other media systems around the world in light of the ideals espoused by the US media (Hardt 1988). Not only was it overly normative and as such could not provide a solid grounding for comparative research but its claims also lacked firm empirical support (Christians et al. 2009). Still, despite all the shortcomings, the basic argument put forward in the book remains a valid starting point for comparative inquiries into mass communication to this day. As the authors stated in their introduction, any systematic understanding of the press has to proceed from the recognition that 'the press always takes the form and coloration of the social and political structures within which it operates' (Siebert et al. [1956] 1969: 1).

In subsequent decades, this key lesson of *Four Theories* was often forgotten, sometimes even by the authors themselves. Especially when examining the link between mass communication and processes of social change, media and communication scholars have time and again fallen prey to technological determinism, abstracting the media from the context in which they operated and treating them as an autonomous modernizing force. Mass media were thus expected to lay the ground-work needed for successful modernization: inculcate modern work routines and health habits, instil cultural attitudes favourable to innovation, cooperation and long-term effort for the common good, and lure the population away from traditional customs, fatalism and superstitions that were seen to stand in the way of progress. Wilbur Schramm was notoriously infatuated with the transformative potential of communication technologies and the good it could bring to the 'undeveloped' countries of the world. In his characteristically prophetic and moralistic *Mass Media and National Development*, the radio receiver figures as an object of almost supernatural qualities: in the hand of inhabitants of remote villages in the Middle East, it becomes 'a magic carpet' capable of carrying them 'beyond the horizons they had known' (Schramm 1964: 20).

Schramm was not alone in his hopes. For many American social scientists and UNESCO officials at the time, the media were 'great multipliers', capable of increasing the amount of information people can send and receive to unimaginable scales, and thereby speeding up processes of social and economic change and the 'catching-up' with the West in even the most remote backwaters of the world (e.g. Lerner 1958; Pye 1963). These naive beliefs were shared by the broader public, both in the West and beyond. In colonial Zambia, radio and radio-listening functioned as instruments of European, Western-style modernity, designed to help Zambians 'wake up', 'start a new life', and become 'a civilized nation' (Spitulnik 1998: 70ff, 81). It is therefore hardly a surprise that literacy rates, postal flows, newspaper circulation, and the number of cinema seats, radio and TV receivers, along with levels of media exposure, were widely adopted in post-World War II US research as indicators of modernization and development (e.g. Deutsch 1961; Rogers 1965; Deutschmann et al. 1968). Such indicators can of course provide a helpful overview of some of the common trends, yet we should be mindful of their limits. Measurements of this kind inevitably abstract the particular practices and artefacts from the social, political, economic and cultural relations in which they are embedded, and present them as discrete problems amenable to social engineering. Unless appropriately contextualized, the levelling logic that underpins them is conducive to a vision of modernization as a uniform, predetermined and unilinear process that is bound to lead to global convergence.

As Schramm would later learn himself, the early prophecies of modernization through mass communication were misguided. When experimenting with long-distance education via television in American Samoa in the 1960s and the 1970s, Schramm was forced to acknowledge that while the new technology was indeed involved in a process of change, it was not the kind of change he was wishing for. Instead of embracing the educational potential of television, students on the remote islands were attracted to the new medium primarily due to its entertainment value (Chaffee and Rogers 1997: 151). Throughout the 1960s and the 1970s, voices of caution directed against utopian visions of communication and development were gaining momentum in all quarters. It was suggested that the impact of mass media exposure varies significantly depending on age, prior level of literacy and mobility as well as level of education and social status (Rogers 1965). No longer was it believed that modernization had to proceed by means of eliminating all things traditional. To be truly effective, it was argued, modern means of mass communication would actually have to be combined with both interpersonal as well as traditional means of communication, including folk theatres and travelling story-tellers (Rogers 1974). Also important was to ensure that modern information technologies were both economically viable and adequately regulated, in a manner that guarantees control over conduit of communication is divorced from control over content of communication (Oettinger and Zapol 1974). In the 1980s, a new wave of research and theorizing put a definitive end to simplistic understandings of media effects, pointing to the crucial role of local culture in influencing audience responses to the same media products (Liebes and Katz 1993).

Gradually, the naive technological determinism of the early years gave way to more context-sensitive accounts of the media involvement in social change, and the normative models of the past were replaced with more balanced and empirically grounded comparative frameworks. When connecting the media to the broader context, the recent wave of comparative studies has paid attention primarily to the relationships between the media, economy and politics – that is, to the relative influence of the state and the market on the functioning of the media. Several different aspects of this relationship have been examined, including media ownership, the level of politicization or political parallelism in the media sector, regulation of media content and ownership, the relationships between political systems and election campaigning techniques, the impact of commercialization and politicization on the nature of news coverage and others (e.g. Swanson and Mancini 1996; Esser 1999; Hallin and Papathanassopoulos 2002; Hitchens 2006; Benson and Hallin 2007; Winseck 2008).

In an influential study that compares the media systems of Western Europe and Northern America, Hallin and Mancini (2004a) argue that these diverse dimensions do not map neatly onto one another, and that it is therefore better to keep them analytically distinct. Nevertheless, their threefold typology essentially distinguishes the different media models with respect to their relative proximity to, and type of involvement with, two key factors: the market and the state, or economy and politics. These are two of the three key factors that, as we have seen earlier, also help describe the similarities and differences between various political ideologies and corresponding visions of modernity. At one end of the spectrum is the liberal media model, which finds its best approximation in the media systems of the USA and Canada and is characterized by (a) medium-sized press markets, (b) low politicization, (c) a high level of journalistic professionalism, and (d) the dominance of market principles. In contrast, the polarized pluralist model, exemplified in the states of Southern Europe, is marked by (a) small press markets, (b) high politicization, (c) a low level of professionalism, and (d) strong state intervention. The third media model identified in their scheme, the democratic corporatist model, dominant in Central and Northern Europe, falls midway between the two on all four counts.

The three ideal-types can be mapped neatly onto our scheme of modern political ideologies. The liberal media model, with its low level of politicization and state intervention and dominance of market principles corresponds to the liberal modernizing project, especially in its economic, neo-liberal variant. In contrast, both the polarized pluralist and democratic corporatist model are characterized by a relatively greater involvement of the state and politics, and therefore fall somewhat closer to the state/politics end of the axis. We can easily envisage Hallin and Mancini's scheme being extended to include the communist media model, which corresponds to the communist modernizing project and envisages mass communication as an instrument of social revolution led by the communist party-state on behalf of the proletariat. Using Hallin and Mancini's analytical framework, and drawing on existing literature on mass communication in communist states (e.g. Siebert et al. [1956] 1969: 105–46; Hopkins 1970; Altschull 1984: 195–226; Mickiewicz 1988: 3–30), we could summarize the key tenets of the ideal-typical communist media system as follows: (a) predominance of elite politically oriented press, historically low newspaper circulation boosted by state subsidies after the communist seizure of power and historically late development of mass-circulation press; (b) a high level of political parallelism with a clear predominance of commentary-oriented genres aimed at mass mobilization for the communist project; (c) low levels of professionalism, as journalists are expected to aid the attainment of goals set by the party and act as 'agitators'; (d) high levels of party-state intervention in the form of party-state ownership and either direct or indirect censorship of non-communist voices; and (e) low presence of market mechanisms. It is worth noting that the communist media model does not literally require the media to be subjected to a strong state. Rather, the media are expected to be vigilant against the excesses of a bureaucratic state, and state intervention is required and tolerated only in so much as it operates as an instrument of party interests. In other words, both the state and the media, along with the economy, are subordinated to the interests of the party.

So far, we have found existing media scholarship rather useful for explaining media involvement in competing projects of modernization. Yet, when we turn to the relationship between the fascist ideology and the media, attend to the recent resurgence of racism in the Western media, or more broadly seek to understand the role of community and culture in shaping modern media systems, recent comparative media research offers fewer clues. A partial exception can be found in the literature on the 'communitarian' media model (e.g. Nerone 1995: 63–87; Christians 2004), which seeks to explain the characteristics of community, ethnic and minority media. However, the debate about the communitarian media model is of little help for understanding historical links between the media and fascism. As with most scholars engaged in recent research on comparative media systems, Hallin and Mancini have relatively little to say on the matter, and prefer to discuss historical links between the media and fascist parties or religious organizations as examples of political parallelism. The historic influence of Catholic-owned newspapers in

Southern Europe – *Ya* in Spain, *La Croix* in France, or *L'Osservatore Romano* in Italy – is thus presented as yet another instance of the predominance of politics over economy in polarized pluralist media systems (Hallin and Mancini 2004a: 90–97).

This is entirely in line with the narrative plot that underpins Hallin and Mancini's account of historical developments more generally. Their story is organized around the clash of two main types of historical forces, liberalism and 'traditional conservativism' (ibid.: 62–63), while the organizing principle of community is subsumed under the latter. It is important to note that this merging of culture and politics has its roots in the authors' historical focus as well as in the character of their empirical data. While reaching back to the nineteenth century and beyond, their main arguments revolve around developments in the second half of the twentieth century, and the bulk of empirical data comes from this period. Their narrative framework, centred on the clash between market forces and political powers, provides an adequate instrument for analysing this particular historical period. The post-World War II decades were the time when the fascist vision of modern society was pushed to the margins, and the major ideological battles were fought between the rival projects of communism and liberalism. Yet as soon as we turn to the history of media systems before 1945 and after the end of the Cold War, Hallin and Mancini's framework proves to be insufficient.

This can be illustrated by examining the authors' discussion of the impact of commercialization on the relationship between the media and national culture. Taking as an example the commercialization of European broadcasting from the 1980s onwards, they argue that the decline of state influence over broadcasting 'is now [...] disrupting the connection between broadcasting and national systems, submitting elec-tronic media to globalizing forces similar to those that prevail in other industries, and spreading cultural forms and professional practices, including those of electronic journalism, that developed originally in the West' (Hallin and Mancini 2004b: 39). On the face of it, this sounds like a compelling argument, well attuned to the commonly held convictions about globalization and its relationship to nationhood discussed in Chapter 2. Yet it is only partially correct, since it wrongly assumes that national identity maintenance pertains exclusively to the domain of the state and politics, and fails to consider the role of market forces.

Economic factors have played an integral part in the spreading of national imagination from its very beginning (Gellner 1983; Anderson 1991), though their influence differed from country to country, depend-ing on the balance of power between the market and the state. Where state infrastructure was weak or where the state willingly limited its interventions into cultural affairs, market forces and commercial media played a greater role in consolidating national identity. Such was the case of Papua New Guinea, where the consumption of goods and services advertised as markers of national identity – rice, betel nut and even Coca-Cola – occupied a prominent position in the construction of modern national attachments (Foster 2002: 63–127). Research on media populism in Western Europe, Latin America and India brings us to a similar conclusion, pointing to the key role of commercial competition in stimulating the growth of populism in elite media (Mazzoleni et al. 2003).

Given that the principle of community can interlock equally well with both political and market forces, we cannot analyse its impact adequately if we subsume it under the principle of state bureaucracy. Instead, it makes sense to treat it as a separate principle of organization at work in the media, and link it to an ideal-typical fascist media model (Figure 3.2). While the post-World War II decades saw this principle subordinated to the commercial logic and/or the power of the state apparatus, it played a much greater role in the pre-war decades and during the war itself, as well as after the end of the Cold War.

Some of the clearest examples of media systems organized primarily around the interests of community can of course be found in Nazi Germany. Under Nazi rule, film and other cultural forms were not solely aesthetic artefacts, but were expected to function as integral elements of *Volkskunde* ('people's' or 'national' culture) and provide artistic expression for the *Volksgemeinschaft* (Welch 1995). The ideological notion of *Volksgemeinschaft*, an egalitarian community of the German people undivided by ethnic, class, religious or gender lines, was central to the

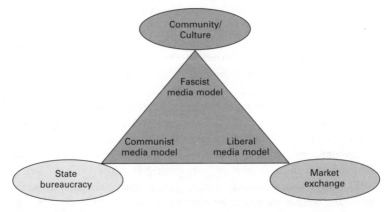

Figure 3.2   Principles of social organization and media models

Nazi project, and Nazi propaganda was expected to help bring this mythical unity about by projecting its symbolic image (Welch 2004). The key themes that shaped the cultural and artistic forms fostered by Goebbels' Ministry of Popular Entertainment and Propaganda were of course rooted in ideological patterns that long preceded the Nazi seizure of power, and stemmed from nineteenth-century *völkisch* ideologies (Mosse 1964). However, Nazi cultural policies helped these ideas achieve an unprecedented public prominence by bringing cultural production under close state supervision, and thereby also foreclosing the opportunities for a truly public debate. In other words, and drawing on the conceptual distinction proposed earlier in this chapter, public culture was reduced to national culture, conceived in totalizing, essentialist terms.

Radio in particular was seen as a key instrument of the 'social revolution' envisaged by the Nazis, one that was expected to bring about a quasi-egalitarian, racially pure German nation (Bergmeier and Lotz 1997). The new Reich radio law, passed in 1932, not only brought German radio in line with state bureaucracy, but also implemented new principles of operation, which demanded that radio programmes be both apolitical and non-commercial (von Saldern 2004). This shift stimulated radio programme makers to look for suitably 'neutral', apolitical subjects, such as *Volk* and *Heimat* (home or native country). In the context of the Great Depression, soaring rates of unemployment and the increasing polarization, fragmentation and militarization of the public space, ideas of a *Volk* community functioned as a symbolic rescue, promising to restore national harmony and unity. Radio was seen as an important instrument that should help bring about this communal harmony. In view of one of the regional radio producers, *Heimat* culture programmes would foster the 'rebirth of the German spirit' (quoted in von Saldern 2004: 326).

To ensure that the Nazi propaganda effort would reach into each and every corner of Germandom, the authorities provided subsidized radio receivers – dubbed 'people's receiver' (*Volksempfäger*) – and installed loudspeakers in public spaces (Bergmeier and Lotz 1997). These efforts are encapsulated in the often mentioned poster from 1936 featuring a gigantic radio receiver surrounded by a vast crowd of people, accompanied by the slogan 'All Germany listens to the Führer on the people's receiver' (Figure 3.3). Of course, we should be wary of assuming that German audiences embraced the exclusive national community promoted by the propaganda machine without any resistance, or that they were eager to accept all of its premises. Nevertheless, by combining symbolic forms of persuasion with ruthless suppression, Nazi

Figure 3.3   German World War II poster promoting the use of the *Volksempfänger* (1936) Bundesarchiv, Plak 003-022-025 / Designer: Leonid

authorities to a large extent managed to turn the population into a passive, politically indifferent mass, prepared to turn a blind eye on the regimes' excesses (Welch 2004).

The Italian Fascist project and its cultural policies differ in important ways from those characteristic of Nazi Germany. The regime's grip of the cultural field was less tight than in Germany, mostly due to the fact that the Fascist systems of control were not as extensive and effective as their German counterparts (De Grand 1995). This was particularly visible in the film industry, where the state had long abstained from implementing an effective system of censorship and allowed the market to be dominated by imports from Hollywood. As Marcia Landy argued, the main concern of the Italian film industry at this point 'was profit rather than strict ideological conformity' (Landy 2000: 9).

Nevertheless, the Fascist authorities gradually became more closely involved in the shaping of the industry. Step by step, film was transformed into an instrument of national integration, emphasizing ideological unity and downplaying the markers of gender, region and class. One of the first significant interventions into the film industry was a decree enacted in 1927, which was not particularly successful in stemming the import of foreign films but managed to institute new practices that greatly enhanced the industry's nation-building capacity. One of these was the practice of dubbing foreign films into Italian, which was expected to protect national culture from foreign influence and 'purify' the country's cinematic landscape (Ricci 2008: 60–62). From the early 1930s onwards, the Fascist authorities intensified their control over the film industry: they dramatically reduced the import of foreign films and imposed new requirements onto domestic producers, requiring them to film in Italy, employ only Italian actors, and avoid the use of regional dialects (ibid.: 65–68).

A more recent example that shares some of the key traits of the fascist media model can be found in post-1979 Iran. These are normally discussed in terms of an 'Islamic media model' (Mowlana 1997; Khiabany 2007). The Iranian constitution makes it very clear that the principal duty of the media is that of safeguarding Islamic values, and that this duty overrides any other functions the media might have. As the constitutional document states: 'The freedom of publicity and propaganda in the mass media, radio and television, shall be ensured on the basis of Islamic principles' (quoted in Mowlana 1997: 205). This definition of the media's role in Iranian society provides the basis for the institutional regulation of the media sector. Most means of mass communication are regulated through the Ministry of Islamic Culture and Guidance, while television – being a medium with the greatest social impact – is under direct supervision of all branches of the government. As the state and religion are not legally separated, and the sovereignty is derived from Allah rather than from the will of the people, media content is judged according to Islamic codes, and regulatory media bodies typically include Islamic legal experts (ibid.). The Islamic model of communication, as adopted in Iran, thus gives primacy to culture over economy and politics, and effectively aims to reduce public culture to religious culture.

While far more could be said about each of these examples, these brief sketches should be sufficient to demonstrate that the fascist media model deserves to be treated as a separate ideal-typical model alongside the liberal and communist ones. If we limit the examination of this model solely to the dimensions included in Hallin and Mancini's framework, the fascist media model is rather similar to the communist one, except that it tolerates the existence of commercial media. It is characterized by historically low newspaper circulation, weak professionalization and high levels of state intervention. The only problem arises with defining the level of political parallelism – the fascist media model aligns the media not with the political field, but first and foremost with the cultural field. The media are expected to act as instruments for expressing cultural values and identities – defined in terms of religion, nation, race, or other cultural markers – and any political diversity within particular cultural units should be subordinated to those or erased altogether. This kind of parallelism can best be described as 'cultural parallelism' and seen as orthogonal to political parallelism. On this dimension, the fascist media model scores very high, while both the communist and the liberal media models are characterized by a low level of cultural parallelism.

As with political ideologies and systems, the three principles of social organization underpinning the three media models never operate in isolation from one another. Rather, they are present simultaneously in every society and hence in every media system. While the three ideal-typical media models may exist on paper and in the minds of those designing media policies, they never quite correspond to the messy reality of mass communication on the ground. The three media models identified here therefore should not be treated as clearly distinct and mutually exclusive categories, and we should resist the temptation of fitting every single media system into one – and only one – of the categories. Most historical and contemporary media systems are likely to fit somewhere between the three ideal-typical models. For instance, the media systems of many communist states gradually moved away from the ideals of a communist media model, became increasingly centred on the interests of a particular (national) community, and could thus be positioned somewhere midway towards a fascist media model. On the other hand, the different forms of ethnic or community media, which seek to balance individual interests with collective ones, are positioned somewhere between the two extremes of liberal and fascist media models.

Even the Italian film industry under Fascist rule was far from being simply a propaganda machine designed to promote the Fascist doctrine; it also functioned as a cultural industry driven by market mechanisms and profit interests (Landy 1986). Similarly, the various media systems of the Middle East certainly cannot be reduced to an ideal-typical Islamist media model, within which every aspect of mass communication is subjected to the interests of the *Ummah*. When we look more closely at the actual economic and political contexts within which the Middle Eastern media operate, it becomes clear that even in the case of Iran, where the functioning of the media perhaps best approximates the Islamist model, the media are deeply marked by tensions between 'the imperative of the market and the straitjacket of Islamism' (Khiabany 2007: 3). Elsewhere in the Muslim world, the prominence of commercial imperatives is equally if not even more apparent. In Egypt, the media contribute to the commodification of Ramadan rituals, linking morality to consumerism in ways reminiscent of Christmas celebrations in the West (Armbrust 2006).

Another caveat to keep in mind is that neither societies nor their media are homogeneous. Rather, different segments of societies and media systems can be governed by different principles of social organization. In the same society, we can easily find publicly funded broadcasting coexisting with commercial broadcasting and the press as well as religious and party-aligned publications. This is clearly the case in Britain, where the publicly funded BBC coexists with commercial television and radio stations and the commercial tabloid press, as well as with elite newspapers with distinct political preferences, religious publications, ethnic and community media. Existing comparative research that takes culture seriously as a factor explaining the diversity of media output often fails to appreciate this internal plurality, preferring to treat media systems as rooted in internally homogeneous and clearly bounded cultures. Such literature often takes such cultural elements as an entirely independent factor, and fails to examine how they are themselves shaped by economic and political constraints. This is particularly evident in comparative research on advertising and cultural values, which draws on the work of Geert Hofstede (2001) and typically links cultural traits visible in advertising to patterns of cultural values deducted from public opinion surveys (e.g. Albers-Miller and Gelb 1996; Lin 2001).

4

Mediated Grammars of Nationhood

Two key questions were left unanswered in the previous chapter. First, we have not yet explained how the divergent routes to modernity and the different types of media systems associated with them shape the particular forms of nationalist discourse and imagination. For instance, if nation-formation is taking place in a society characterized by a liberal approach to economy and minimal state intervention, and within the context of a predominantly liberal media system that depends on advertising revenue rather than state subsidies, how does this affect the prevailing markers of national belonging and exclusion? We do not need to look far for the main building blocks that will help us answer such questions: the issue of the relative weight of economic, political and cultural factors in the historical rise of modern nations and nationalisms has been at the core of nationalism studies ever since the end of World War II. In the first part of this chapter we will survey a range of nationalism theories to identify the various factors that can potentially contribute to nation-building and thereby to the formation of national imagination. Based on this we will be able to distinguish between different routes to nationhood, establish how those relate to the facilities of mass communication, and identify the main traits of the different grammars of nationhood they give rise to.

Second, we should address the question of whether and to what extent the triadic scheme outlined in the previous chapter is of relevance to contemporary developments. At first sight, the key events of the twentieth century have put an end to the struggle over the definition of modernity by eliminating both of liberalism's key competitors. The Allied victory in 1945 and the devastating consequences of Nazi policies discredited the fascist alternative and expelled racist views from the domain of legitimate political debate. The end of the Cold War in 1989 eliminated the other remaining alternative modernizing project, and brought the gradual integration of all societies into a capitalist modernity (Dirlik 2003). The changes undergone by the Western European and North American media system since the end of World War II follow similar patterns: their differences have been diminishing over time, and both democratic corporatist and polarized pluralist systems have increasingly come to resemble the liberal model (Hallin and Mancini 2004a: 251–95). However, as we will attempt to show in the final section of this chapter, even some of the very recent shifts in mediated communication and national imagination can still be accounted for using our triadic analytical framework.

Explaining Nationalism: Economy, Politics, Culture

In the field of nationalism studies it has become customary to distinguish between three broad groups of approaches to nationalism: economy-centred, state-centred and culture-centred (e.g. A. D. Smith 1998; Özkırımlı 2005; Hearn 2006). A classic example of an approach that gives pride of place to economic processes can be found in Ernest Gellner's *Nations and Nationalism* (1983). In short, Gellner maintains that homogeneous cultures, coterminous with the borders of a centrally organized state, are a functional necessity of modern industrialized economies. An industrial society requires a mobile population – mobile both socially, in the sense that its members can move across different social occupations and strata, as well as geographically, meaning that they are capable of migrating, should the needs of the job market so require, from one end of the state to the other. The basic prerequisite for such mobility, argues Gellner, is a common mass culture, shared both territorially, across all regions and locales of the state, and socially, across different social strata – in short, a national culture that coincides with the limits of the polity. It is this shared culture that allows the members of the industrialized society to understand the requirements of their occupation wherever they go, and perform their duties regardless of the region or social environment they find themselves in. Or, in Gellner's own words: 'the mutual relationship of a modern culture and state is something quite new, and springs, inevitably, from the requirements of a modern economy' (1983: 140).

A similar pattern of explanation, based on the conviction that nationalism ultimately arises out of economic necessity, can be discerned in two other influential analyses, namely Michael Hechter's *Internal Colonialism* (1975) and Tom Nairn's *The Break-up of Britain* (1977). In contrast to Gellner, both authors seek the roots of nationalist sentiments in capitalism rather than industrialization, and put greater emphasis on the uneven growth of capitalist and colonial relations than on the characteristics of capitalist economy as such. In their view, the development of capitalism, both domestically and globally, proceeded in an uneven manner, prompting a complex web of colonial dependencies and centre–periphery dynamics. These locked peripheral regions and states into permanent backwardness, reducing their roles to the provision of cheap labour and raw materials for the advanced economies in the imperial cores. These relations of domination in turn gave rise to discontent and resentment among peripheral groups and stimulated the development of nationalist projects, usually codified by the peripheral elites. Again, we have an acknowledgement of both cultural and political factors, yet both are believed to arise, in the last instance, from economic developments.

A very different account of the rise of nations and nationalism can be found in the works of authors such as John Breuilly (1993, 1996), Reinhart Bendix (1964), Charles Tilly (1975) and Paul Brass (1979). Central to their accounts are transformations in the realm of politics, and the key agent is typically the modern state. If Gellner, Hechter and Nairn maintained that nationalism arose out of the functional necessities of modern economies, these authors prefer to see it primarily as an ideological prerequisite for the functioning of modern politics. More specifically, from their point of view, nationalism arose due to three interlinked transformations: (a) a shift in the nature of political authority and the concomitant changes in the legitimation of power; (b) a change in the nature of social differentiation, paralleled by a growing separation of private and public domains, and thus of society and state; and (c) the growing frequency and intensity of inter-state competition and conflicts, resulting in the progressive militarization of modern states (A. D. Smith 1998: 70–96).

While earlier forms of political power followed hereditary lines of succession and derived their legitimacy from divine sources, the rule of the modern state was perceived as legitimate only in so far as it was based on the will of 'the people' (Bendix 1964). This transformation prompted an intense politicization of cultural identities, as different elite groups struggled for power and prestige by advancing competing definitions of 'the people' and claiming to defend their unique interests (Brass 1979). Central to the exercising of these new forms of power was the formation of modern, functionally differentiated state bureaucracies, capable of providing a common framework for functionally differentiated societies (Breuilly 1993). Such societies were a result of a parallel process that involved a profound shift in the nature of social organization: social needs were no longer serviced by polyfunctional corporate institutions acting on behalf of particular groups such as religious congregations, guilds, local communities and the like, but by function-specific organizations such as schools, political parties, retail industries, museums, theatres, and the entertainment industry, aimed at a broader society.

The level of integration necessary for the functioning of such complex societies could not come from the common bureaucratic framework alone. This framework had to be complemented by the ideological 'glue' of nationalism, which could 'maintain some harmony between the public interests of citizens and the private interests of selfish individuals (or families)' (Breuilly 1996: 165). Nationalism provided an effective instrument for fostering this harmony: it encouraged individuals to be loyal to the nation and feel obliged to 'serve and be served by the state', and thereby solidified the bonds of legitimacy between the state and its population (Marx 1998: 4). At the same time, the nationalist 'glue' also served as a convenient instrument that could be exploited in the context of inter-state relations. Due to increasing inter-state competition and conflicts, modern states were eager to expand and professionalize their armies. The most effective way to achieve this goal involved extending the franchise to ever broader segments of the population in exchange for military service and taxation (Tilly 1975). To justify this expansion of citizenship and the increasing encroachment on the private lives of their subjects, states had to turn to nationalism and explain both the benefits and sacrifices in the language of national interests and loyalty. In other words, nationalism 'serviced' the needs of the changing political system both domestically and internationally.

Both groups of nationalism scholars discussed so far – those who believe nationalism arose as a functional necessity of modern economy, and those who maintain its rise was prompted by the exigencies of modern politics – share a key common conviction, namely the belief in the modernity of nations and nationalism. In their view, nationalism and nations simply could not exist outside of the context of modern societies. In contrast, scholars who emphasize the cultural sources of nationalism – as opposed to political and economic ones – are less unanimous when it comes to 'dating' nations and nationalism.

On the one hand, we find authors such as Anthony Smith and Adrian Hastings who both emphasize the continuities between modern nations and pre-modern ethnic communities, and locate these continuities primarily in the realm of culture. For Smith (1986), the links between modern and pre-modern communities are found in common myths, symbols, values, historical memories and a shared link with a historic territory. In a complementary argument, Hastings (1997) emphasizes the role of spoken language, vernacular literature and the Judeo-Christian tradition as the key building blocks in the historical construction of nationhood. Along with other authors typically associated with the ethno-symbolist or primordialist approach to nations and nationalism, both Smith and Hastings leave ample room for political forces, but insist on the relative autonomy of cultural factors, and on their pre-modern roots.

On the other hand, authors such as Elie Kedourie, Benedict Anderson and Eric Hobsbawm maintain that the cultural forces that gave rise to nationalism are distinctly modern. As with the ethno-symbolists, these authors believe that culture should be treated as an autonomous factor contributing to the formation and maintenance of nations and nationalisms, but consider it to be fundamentally different from the complexes of pre-modern myths, symbols and rituals. For instance, Kedourie ([1960] 1996) seeks to explain the development of nationalism by examining the rise of characteristically modern ideas: the Enlightenment notion of human beings as autonomous, the romantic idea of organic social units defined by a distinctive culture, the principles of popular sovereignty and egalitarianism, and others.

Anderson and Hobsbawm go a step further and make an attempt to clarify the ways in which modern cultural forms and ideas interact with political and economic processes of modernization. Hobsbawm (1990) links the rise of invented traditions, such as public ceremonies and rituals, public monuments and national heroes, to the rise of popular sovereignty and the emergence of mass politics. In his view, this new form of politics necessitated new cultural forms that could symbolize societal cohesion and establish bonds of loyalty between the masses and the political elites. Invented traditions achieved this by projecting symbols of national unity and instilling the language of national interests. In a similar vein, Anderson (1991) demonstrates that the capitalist mode of production and distribution of the printed word could not have succeeded without the simultaneous emergence of modern imagined communities (nations) and modern cultural forms (newspapers and novels).

Each of these diverse modernizing processes – economic, political, cultural – also gave rise to potential sources of conflict and exclusion, which often exerted an important influence on the particular trajectory of nation-formation (Hewitson 2006: 340–53). In other words, modernization not only demanded new forms of collective identity and inclusion, but also simultaneously stimulated new forms of internal segregation and exclusion. Although equality and unity, beyond and above sub-national cleavages, is central to national imagination, this unity is often established with the help of internal exclusion and segregation based on race, class, gender, religion and so on (Marx 1998: 275). For instance, in the realm of the economy, the new mode of economic production brought new forms of social segregation and exploitation, and stimulated the formation of class identity alongside national identity, pitching workers against industrialists, manufacturers and merchants (Hobsbawm 1983; Mann 1993).

Democratization often had similar consequences, giving rise to internal divisions within the nation, running along political lines, and to rival political visions of the nation's future. In areas of mixed settlement, such internal political divisions sometimes coincided with cultural, ethnic or racial divisions (Hewitson 2006: 342–45). Modern states also often purposefully fostered particular forms of internal exclusion and segregation by selectively granting citizenship rights only to one part of their populations. As a rule, such exclusive forms of citizenship emerged as a powerful instrument of national unity. For instance, by excluding blacks, both South Africa and the United States counteracted political and other divisions among whites themselves, while communist states used class exclusion to overcome ethnic and political divisions among the population (Marx 1998: 274–66).

Multiple Routes to Nationhood, Multiple Media Nations

This brief overview of course provides only a very basic outline of what are otherwise rather complex and multifaceted arguments. No matter how convinced the individual authors are of the determining impact of economy, politics or culture, none of them is in favour of a single-factor explanation, and some explicitly avoid giving primacy to one category of factors over any others. Still, many of these contending accounts remain underpinned by a lingering notion of modernization as a unilinear process and are set on developing a monocausal theory of nationalism and its rise. While forms of comparative analysis are present, they often remain underdeveloped. Gellner (1983), for instance, acknowledges the important differences in nation-formation between different parts of Europe, but still insists on industrialization as a chief explanatory force for all of them. Greenfeld's (1992) discussion of the 'five routes to modernity' adopts a more explicitly comparative approach, yet her insistence on the cultural roots of nationalism prevents her from systematically exploring the links between different cultural configurations of nationalism and the divergent constellations of political, economic and social transformations they are intertwined with. The more multifaceted comparative analytical frameworks for the analysis of nation-building, both old and new (e.g. Eisenstadt and Rokkan 1973; Tilly 1990; Baycroft and Hewitson 2006), are yet to be incorporated more fully into mainstream theories of nationalism. In short, one can only agree with Johan Arnason (2006) that comparative approaches in nationalism studies remain remarkably limited and underdeveloped.

Given the relative paucity of systematic comparative research that would bring together the economic and political analysis of nation-building with the cultural analysis of national imagination and discourse, we are bound to limit this investigation to a few general propositions, and apply those to a selection of case studies. It is worth pointing out that the main aim is not to develop a framework for analysing the diverse routes to nationhood as such, but rather one that will allow us to link these routes to diverse forms of mass-mediated communication and modernizing projects discussed in the previous chapter. To that end, we need to assume that the diverse paths of modernization, each characterized by a particular constellation of economic, political and cultural transformations, and marked by different forms of exclusion, opened different routes for the spread of nationalism. For instance, in the economically advanced Britain of the eighteenth century, the key force stimulating the early proliferation of nationalist outlooks was commercial capitalism, while in the economically less-modernized Prussia, the main agent was the state with its professional armed forces and administrators (Mann 1992: 146–50). Commercial capitalism played a prominent role also among those nations whose elites may have exerted control over the state apparatus, yet had limited resources to finance extensive nation-building through state-sponsored education and media. In such circumstances, the nation was not so much a product of state efforts, but above all a form of collective imagination that 'materialized' through mass-mediated commercial culture and consumption (Foster 2002).

In cases where nationalist movements had limited access to the state apparatus, and where they arose in the context of a weakly developed commercial or industrial economy, nation-building occurred primarily through cultural institutions such as the churches, literary and periodical media, reading circles, or educational establishments teaching in local languages. Such cultural patterns of nation-building were characteristic of the 'smaller' European nations that were formed on the peripheries of multicultural states and empires – for instance, the Czechs or the Croats (cf. Hroch 1985). Similar patterns can be found in the former African and Asian colonies, where state elites typically promoted a national community built around a particular ethno-cultural core and thereby marginalized other cultural, linguistic or religious groups inhabiting the state (Young 1976). As a consequence, nation-making and nation-main-tenance among the latter had to be more reliant on cultural institutions and, depending on availability, commercial or industrial forces.

The array of institutions and processes involved in nation-making, as well as their relative balance, often shifted over time. The peripheral nations of Western and Eastern Europe may have been initially depend-ent primarily on cultural institutions, but slowly acquired more and more control over the state administration. The new states of Central and Eastern Europe, formed in the early 1990s, provide a good case in point: virtually all of them initially functioned as 'nationalizing states' – that is, as states 'owned' by a particular ethno-cultural nation and designed to further its interests (Brubaker 1996: 103–4). The growing influence of a liberal market economy across the globe is another factor that led to important shifts in processes of nation-formation at both institutional and discursive levels. The expansion of commercial institutions weak-ened the effectiveness of state-sponsored nation-building, and often replaced it with patterns of collective belonging that departed from those fostered by the state. In the former colonies, commercial capitalism gradually penetrated beyond the urban centres dominated by the core ethnic group and stimulated cultural production attuned to local customs, languages and other cultural markers. These developments gave prominence to forms of collective belonging that rarely found expression in state-sponsored identity-building and inflected the processes of nation-making in unprecedented ways. The recent transfor-mations of media landscapes and collective identities in South Africa, post-communist Eastern Europe and India provide a particularly good illustration of this shift, and we will return to them later in this chapter.

It is feasible to argue that the relative weight of particular economic, political and cultural factors involved in nation-making, and the various forms of exclusion they create, all have an impact on the prevailing shape of national imagination. To understand that, we need to take into account the modern means of communication. Each modern institution – the state, the armed forces, commercial and industrial institutions, universities, schools, political parties and the like – creates its own facil-ities of communication, which allow for frequent, standardized commu-nication with large, territorially dispersed groups (Mann 1992). These facilities can be highly diverse and can range from the familiar forms of the periodical press, radio, television and the Internet to the variegated conduits and vehicles of communication built into the modern economy, politics and society: modern maps, factory operation manuals, commercial contracts, accounting records, army drill manuals, identity documents, university libraries, salons, pubs, coffee houses and so on. Each of these channels of modern communication inflects the national imagination in particular ways, and gives rise to different lines of inclusion and exclusion depending on the processes and institutions of modernization it is associated with (Table 4.1).

The channels of communication supported by religious or ethnic institutions will focus on sustaining an ethnically, racially or religiously defined national community and exclude those who belong to other religious or ethno-cultural groups. In contrast, communicative facilities established within the sphere of the economy, or those financially dependent on commercial institutions, will most likely foster a national community defined in terms of economic practices such as industrial production, trade or consumption. This kind of imagined community will be internally differentiated along class lines, and will most likely exclude those who are too poor to partake in specific economic operations. Finally, we can expect that the media associated with particular political parties or pressure groups will promote a vision of the nation consistent with a particular political ideology and exclude those not loyal to that vision. For instance, communist media will most likely support a national community of comrades and stigmatize those hostile to the communist project.

Communicative facilities established within the framework of the modern state or controlled by state institutions are, by definition, involved first of all in supporting a national community of citizens, encompassing all those individuals who are entitled to protection by the state and owe allegiance to it. Yet the communities of citizens have historically been imagined in radically different ways, and have entailed different forms of internal segregation, typically organized around ethnic, racial, class, age and gender lines. Due to that, state-owned communicative facilities are in principle compatible with any form of national imagination, and we can therefore expect that they will endorse the one most consistent with the prevailing balance of power among the key political, economic and cultural forces in a given social context.

As argued in the previous chapter, individual media systems differ in the relative prominence of the three key principles of social organization: community, market exchange and state bureaucracy. An ideal-typical liberal media model is organized primarily around the logic of the market; a communist media system gives primacy to the logic of state bureaucracy; and an ideal-typical fascist media system gravitates primarily around the interests of community. In line with that, we can

Table 4.1 Processes of modernization, channels of mass communication and forms of national imagination and exclusion

	Community Culture	State bureaucracy Politics	Market exchange Economy
Processes of modernization contributing to the spreading of nationalism	Rise of mass culture Politicization of culture New cultural forms New cultural idea(l)s (Enlightenment, Romanticism)	Democratization State modernization (shift to functional differentiation) Militarization	Industrialization Growth of commerce Global spread of capitalism
Channels of mass communication	Religious institutions (religious rituals and texts, religious media) Ethnic institutions (schools, cultural institutions, ethnic community media)	State (census, maps, coins, banknotes, ID documents, state media) Armed forces (written orders, manuals, maps) Political parties (party conferences, party press)	Commerce (contracts, accounting documents, advertising) Industry (written orders and manuals, contracts, accounting) Commercial media
Forms of national imagination	Nation of believers Ethnic nation Race-nation	Nation of citizens Nation of comrades/ liberals/democrats	Nation of consumers Nation of industrialists/ merchants/workers
Lines of exclusion	Excludes those of different race, religion, ethnicity and so on	Excludes those who are not loyal to the same state or political ideology	Excludes those who are poor

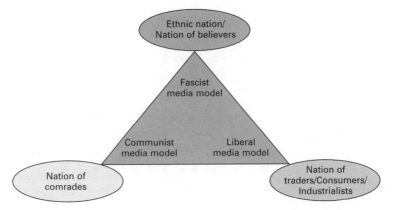

Figure 4.1   Media models and forms of national imagination

expect that a predominantly liberal media system will give preference to forms of national imagination centred on consumerism, trade, industrial production and other activities central to the market economy. In contrast, a media system approximating the communist model will favour the imagined national community of comrades, and a media system approaching the fascist media model will be inclined to support an ethnically or religiously defined national community (Figure 4.1).

We should clarify that these forms of national imagination virtually never appear in isolation. The same nation is typically constructed in several ways at once, depending on the medium and its precise links with the state, the political field, the market, and various cultural institutions. Even the prevailing representations circulating in mainstream media are likely to combine two or more of the key grammars identified above. For instance, the mediated national grammars promoted in the former communist states of Central and Eastern Europe were merging the grammar of the nation of comrades with the grammar of the ethnic nation, and the prominence of the latter increased with time. Similarly, the imagined national communities of consumers underpinning contemporary forms of 'glocal' media culture are often merged with the grammar of ethnic nationhood or religious nationalism, as for instance in modern India. On the other hand, media culture in contemporary China bears the marks of all three national grammars at once, fusing the nation of comrades and the nation of consumers, traders and investors with elements of ethnic nationhood.

We will return to some of these contemporary examples later on in this chapter. For the moment, let us turn to a historical case – that of eighteenth-century Britain. The key force stimulating the spread of national imagination and modern mass communication in eighteenth-century Britain was commercial capitalism. The commercialization of domestic agriculture and the expansion of overseas trade with the colonies created demand for both domestic and international news relevant to commercial pursuits. At the same time, the growth of commerce also established new channels for the dissemination of such news: newspapers and pamphlets, as well as different 'discussion centres' that stocked the periodical press, including coffee houses, taverns and clubs (Mann 1992: 147).

The changes caused by the growth of commerce in Britain were difficult to miss and left a clear imprint on the public imagination. Issues related to shipping, trade, stock markets and commodification were discussed not only in the periodical press, but also in literary forms of communication such as poems, novels and theatre productions, which often featured merchants and their families as main characters (Brown 2001: 53–173). Domestic and foreign observers alike were fascinated by the transformative potential of commodity exchange and praised it in many poems, pamphlets and theatrical works (cf. Griffin 2005). Marvelling at the material prosperity and the abundance of commodities in Britain, one author proclaimed that trade constitutes nothing less than the vital bloodstream of the British nation:

Free Trade the vital Streams of State supplies,
And when that Course is stopped, the Body dies.
(Cibber 1756: 11–2, cited in Blanning 2002: 304)

This is not meant to suggest that all the particularities of the British national imagination at the time can be explained solely by pointing to the impact of commerce. Civil liberties, upheld by the laws and Parliament, were an important source of national pride as well, and the severing of the link with Rome, brought about by the Protestant Reformation, contributed greatly to feelings of cultural distinctiveness (Blanning 2002: 281–322). Yet, while doubtlessly important in their own right, both political ideals and religious values were often strongly coloured by commercial imperatives. British evangelical missionaries, for instance, were convinced that spreading commerce overseas was an integral part of the nation's divine mission. Commercial superiority, they believed, was bestowed upon Britain by God, and hence the nation had the duty to use the civilizing effects of commerce to help spread Christianity across the globe (Brown 2006). Similarly, civil liberties were seen above all as a protective belt shielding the private gains of individual citizens from the state and its fiscal demands. While state administration was growing at an unprecedented rate throughout the late seventeenth and eighteenth centuries, and became highly successful at extracting taxes from its subjects, it could only do so by being highly efficient, transparent and accountable to the taxpayers. Those qualities proved essential in deflecting the criticisms of those who thought that state power equals heavy bureaucracy and authoritarianism (Brewer 1990).

The principles of exclusion at work in the British national imagination at the time were also marked by the logic of commerce. Although commercial activities and associated channels of mass communication cut across a diverse range of social groups, their reach remained restricted primarily to the propertied classes: small-town shopkeepers, agricultural traders, artisans, merchants involved in overseas trade, lawyers and members of the landed class who invested in commercial enterprises (cf. Mann 1992: 147). Stamp taxes and postal rates were among the key obstacles to the expansion of the reading public, as they pushed the prices of most printed materials outside of the reach of the vast majority of the population (Starr 2004: 38–41). Another obstacle was illiteracy: the adult male literacy rate in eighteenth-century England stagnated at around 60 per cent, and was significantly lower still among the working classes (Vincent 1993: 23–34). Gender and racial prejudice exerted an important influence as well: illiteracy rates among women and non-whites were significantly higher than among white men. Those excluded from the channels of national communication were, simultaneously, also excluded from the symbolic landscape of the national community. When featured, the labouring classes, the non-white races and women often appeared in marginal roles, or were treated as a potential threat to the harmony of the nation due to their alleged idleness (Jordan 2003).

In short, it was not by coincidence that Adam Smith, in his *Wealth of Nations*, described the British as 'a nation of shopkeepers', interested in founding an empire 'for the sole purpose of raising up a people of customers' (Smith [1776] 1999: 197). Both the patterns of modernization and the characteristics of the media system at the time were conducive to the rise of a media nation conceived primarily in economic terms, and a symbolic universe centred on the figure of the industrious entrepreneur. Those whose participation in economic transactions was limited to buying essential consumer items – the great majority of the British population at the time – remained on the margins of the imagined community drawn by eighteenth-century media, as well as outside of the remit of prevailing channels of social communication. Although significantly expanded, eighteenth-century British media were still catering predominantly for an elite public.

Economic Liberalization, Democratization and Media Nations

Having discussed the historical emergence of the multiple grammars of nationhood, it is time to ask whether the proposed analytical framework is applicable to recent changes in the mediation of nationhood. To asses that, it is instructive to look at moments of rapid democratization and economic liberalization, since these involve shifts in the balance of power between the three principles of social organization identified earlier: community, state bureaucracy and market exchange. Such moments are likely to be accompanied by the restructuring of media systems and national imagination, and it will be interesting to see to what extent these changes follow the logic outlined in our analytical framework. To answer this question, the remainder of this chapter examines three cases: post-apartheid South Africa, post-communist Eastern Europe, and post-1980 India.

Post-apartheid South Africa: From the race-nation to the multiracial nation of the wealthy

During apartheid, South Africa was a racial state, founded on the dogma of white superiority and conceived as a state owned by, and at the service of, the white race-nation. The establishment of a racial state helped overcome the political divisions among the Dutch-descended Afrikaners and the English-speaking inhabitants of British and Irish descent, and thereby played a key role in solidifying South African national unity (Marx 1998: 84–119). Both the state apparatus and the economy were structured in a way that upheld racial division while encouraging unity among whites. Whites earned several times more than blacks and were over-represented in all the key branches of the state sector, including the police and the military (ibid.: 108–9). In other words, South African nation-building was dependent on the organizational logic of community – defined in racial terms – and both the logic of state bureaucracy and market exchange were subordinated to that.

The dominance of the principle of community was clearly visible also in the realm of mass communication, which played an instrumental role in maintaining and solidifying racial discrimination throughout the apartheid decades. The South African Broadcasting Corporation (SABC) was under the direct control of the National Party, which saw the establishment and maintenance of an apartheid state as one of its key priorities. First radio and then television production were segregated into separate channels for black and white audiences, which were not only organizationally separate but also markedly unequal in access to funding and training (Krabill 2001: 577). Cinema was another important cultural institution involved in the reproduction of apartheid by presenting racial segregation as a part of normal life and thereby indirectly portraying apartheid as legitimate (Tomaselli 1989). The combined effect of the mediation of apartheid through various genres and formats was the formation of two disparate, mutually exclusive symbolic landscapes: one populated by black South Africans, the other by their white compatriots. This racial segregation was clearly visible also at the level of media use and access to communication technologies: the ownership of radio and, in particular, TV sets in black households was significantly lower than in white households, and these differences persisted also in the post-apartheid era (Barnett 1999: 278–79).

The transition from apartheid to democracy in the 1990s was accompanied by a restructuring of the media system and national imagination. Thanks to the introduction of the Black Economic Empowerment programme and its commitment to changing the unequal distribution of economic power in the country, the structure of media ownership shifted to accommodate more black media owners, and the racial composition of newsrooms started changing as well, albeit very slowly (Sparks 2009: 207–8). Aware of the dangers of unfettered economic liberalization in a racially and economically segregated society, the Independent Broadcast Authority, established in 1994, took it upon itself to promote a 'regulated pluralism' – that is, steer the commercialization of broadcasting in ways that would help empower the historically disadvantaged South Africans (Horowitz 2001: 170–74). Within the SABC, the racial segregation of radio and television channels was replaced by 'rainbow' channels providing mixed content for different language groups and the visibility of non-white South Africans increased (Barnett 1999: 290–93).

While erasing old lines of exclusion, the post-apartheid media system inevitably introduced new ones. Only two years after the first multiracial democratic elections in 1994, South Africa adopted a new economic policy, which was premised on the reduction of state intervention and aimed primarily at economic growth and the integration of the South African economy into global markets (Sparks 2009: 202). In the context of an increasingly liberal economy, the provision of basic facilities for the country's poor has slipped into background. Parallel developments could be discerned in the media sector, particularly in the realm of broadcasting and telecommunications. While state intervention as such did not diminish, its motivations and goals have changed: instead of being guided by the twin goal of democracy and diversity, state regulation of broadcasting and telecommunications was now justified by reference to economic growth (Barnett 1999: 289). The ethos of 'rainbow broadcasting' soon proved to be at odds with the new imperatives: the growing visibility of non-white audiences simply did not pay off. While the SABC's total audience ratings remained more or less the same, the proportion of poor (mostly black) viewers grew larger, which resulted in declining advertising revenue (Sparks 2009: 206).

Given these financial constraints, it is hardly a surprise that the SABC tried to remain true to its rainbow ethos by catering predominantly to the black middle class. While the newly re-imagined South African nation projected by the SABC was far more open to racial diversity, it was skewed towards the wealthy black urbanites. To put it differently: given its dependency on advertising, South African television programming 'must, of necessity, be directed disproportionately at the higher income groups, undoing much of the effort at inclusivity that had inspired broadcasting in the immediate post-transition phase' (Sparks 2009: 207). This is clearly evident in South Africa's longest-running and hugely popular soap opera, *Generations*. Aired on SABC 1 since 1994, the soap opera is situated in the urban environment of Johannesburg and focuses on the story of a wealthy black family running a successful advertising agency. Many of the key characters come from humble backgrounds, and their success is presented as an outcome of hard work, high aspirations and stubborn determination. Structural inequalities resulting from decades of apartheid, persisting racial discrimination and rural poverty remain largely invisible, leaving the impression that success and failure depend solely on individual effort (Ives 2007: 165–66). One of the main female characters, for instance, grew up in Soweto, a traditionally black, poor urban settlement south-west of Johannesburg, known for the mass protests that erupted there in the 1970s. Yet, rather than delving into her social background, the show presents her as someone who has always aspired to wealth and status and wanted to move to the prosperous northern suburbs of the city.

The conjoined processes of democratization and economic liberalization have evidently pulled the South African media system away from the principle of community and, more specifically, the ideology of racial hierarchy. The restructuring opened the possibilities for a greater inclusion of the previously disadvantaged black community both at the level of media ownership and production and at the level of media representations. However, the new, racially diverse South African media nation has its clear limits: it is, above all, a nation of wealthy and powerful city dwellers who provide a suitable target for advertisers. As the balance of power between the three principles of social organization shifted away from community and state bureaucracy and towards the market, the old, racial lines of inclusion and exclusion were replaced by new ones, which run along class divisions and follow the rural–urban split. The legacy of racial segregation of course persists: due to economic disparities consolidated through decades of apartheid, the South African imagined community of the wealthy and powerful remains overwhelmingly white. Despite this disparity, racial lines no longer coincide neatly with the income gap: instead, *inter*-racial inequality is steadily declining and is being replaced by *intra*-racial inequality (Nattrass and Seekings 2001: 47ff). Arguably, if racial exclusion under the apartheid system helped overcome ethnic and political divisions among whites, the exclusion of the poor in the post-apartheid era serves to consolidate the multiracial unity of the wealthy and powerful.

Post-communist Central and Eastern Europe: From a multinational community of comrades to ethnic nations and nations of consumers

It is instructive to compare the trajectory of South African nation-building to that of post-communist Central and Eastern Europe. Here, democratization and economic liberalization were paralleled by a similar shift towards consumerism, but had a very different impact on ethno-cultural and racial divisions. Rather than pacifying and diffusing them, political and economic changes gave cultural, ethnic and racial identities a new salience in public life, and were often accompanied by a surge in inter-ethnic tensions. All of the multinational socialist federations – Czechoslovakia, Yugoslavia and the Soviet Union – disintegrated and were replaced by states that were culturally and ethnically far more homogeneous. Even where no border changes occurred and demographic composition stayed roughly the same, newly enacted constitutions and citizenship legislation privileged one core ethnic group over others (Liebich 2007: 24–31). Media institutions and prevailing forms of mediated nationhood changed accordingly: federal media systems and transnational media flows among socialist states gradually gave way to national communicative spaces hungry for Western media products, and the multinational brotherhood of comrades was replaced by an array of ethnic nations eager to participate in global economic exchanges and competition.

The Yugoslav case probably offers one of the most dramatic examples of this transformation. The socialist Yugoslav approach to nationality and statehood was modelled on the Soviet federal system: it recognized the existence of distinct, autonomous national identities at sub-state level while at the same time promoting a common Yugoslav identity (Shoup 1968: 114ff). The joint emphasis on national distinctiveness and overarching Yugoslav union – summarized in the widely used motto 'brotherhood and unity' – was meant to guard the new Yugoslavism against any pretensions of creating a culturally unified Yugoslav nation (Jović 2003: 282–85). To that end, Yugoslav identity had to rely exclusively on common political orientations and class identities (i.e. on the communist project of modernity) and on shared working-class comradeship. Over time, the relative balance of pan-Yugoslav, communist identifications on the one hand, and ethno-national identifications on the other, shifted slowly in favour of the latter. Despite this, the basic two-layered structure of collective identifications remained in place.

This two-layered structure was replicated also at the level of the Yugoslav media system. Each of the Yugoslav republics and provinces had its own major daily newspaper, its own radio and television centre, as well as several regional newspapers, radio stations and weekly magazines. Since most republics and provinces had a clear ethno-national majority, these separate republican and provincial media systems at the same time functioned also as proto-national media systems, aimed at different national imagined communities (Vogrinc 1996: 13). These proto-national media systems coexisted with pan-Yugoslav modes and institutions of mass communication: a common Yugoslav news agency, a daily newspaper, a federation-wide system of broadcast programme exchange, and a short-lived Yugoslav television channel (Thompson 1999: 21–43). The double-layered constellation of allegiances was evident also in media texts. Particularly during the early Cold War, newspapers regularly wrote about the achievements of individual Yugoslav nations, while also emphasizing their shared support for the communist project and for the interests of the working people. One article, published in an Italian minority newspaper in 1954, described Yugoslavia as 'a community of nations with equal rights that is being transformed into a uniform organism of the working people of Yugoslavia' (*Voce del Popolo*, 19 November 1954).

The Yugoslav matrix of collective identifications and media spheres started falling apart during the late 1980s and the early 1990s, in parallel with the disintegration of the federal state infrastructure. The established pan-Yugoslav media flows were weakening, and republican audiences were increasingly served a diet of news reinforcing the positions of respective nationalist-minded republican elites. Similarly to their counterparts elsewhere in the region, Yugoslav post-communist elites treated the media in much the same way as their communist predecessors: as instruments of control belonging to the ruling party (Gallagher 2000). In such a media environment, the increased openness of public debate was a rather mixed blessing, resulting in the creation of highly exclusive public spaces (Snyder and Ballantine 1996). As the confrontations between the republics intensified and grew increasingly violent, the separate republican-national broadcasters gradually shook off identifications with Yugoslav 'brotherhood and unity', and started participating in separate nation-building projects (Mihelj et al. 2009). The new media legislation introduced by the newly independent states left little doubts about whom the media were expected to serve: in particular, the publicly funded broadcast media were seen as instruments of nationalizing states, acting on behalf of ethnically defined core nations (Mihelj 2005). As the relative balance between the principles of state and community shifted in favour of the latter, the multinational imagined community of Yugoslav comrades was replaced by a range of mutually exclusive ethnic media nations.

At the same time, consumer identities were on the rise as well, as befits the gradually advancing economic liberalization of the country. We should immediately add that market principles and consumerism were far from being alien to socialist states, even if their key characteristics differed significantly from those found in capitalist economies (Fehérváry 2009). The Yugoslav media system was particularly well-attuned to consumer identities. The doctrine of 'self-management' transformed all enterprises, including publishing houses and film studios, into 'socially owned' property and subjected their production to market demand instead of government planning. By the early 1960s, most of the print media were cut off from state funding and had to compete with each other in a relatively free market. This led to a surge in the number of local and regional radio stations, and a parallel proliferation of weekly and monthly publications catering to popular tastes (Robinson 1977: 22–25). Advertising was on the rise ever since the early 1950s (Patterson 2003) and media audiences were increasingly addressed not only as members of the multinational Yugoslav community of comrades, but also as consumers.

As 'market socialism' gave way to the full-scale market economy, the nature of consumer identities in the country changed. With the overarching Yugoslav socialist layer of identity crumbling, consumerist imagination was now becoming fully compatible with the one characteristic of the West. Gone were the socialist demands for educational, truthful and socially responsible advertising that would stand in stark contrast with the allegedly deceitful and escapist 'dream worlds' produced by Western advertisers. Members of the media audience were no longer to be treated as comrades in need of accurate information about the latest technologies and other consumer products, but as citizen-consumers hungry for an imaginary world that would help them forget the burdens of everyday existence. Everything and everyone could serve as the material for the new consumerist fantasy land. The markers of ethno-national identity, including those long marginalized due to their incompatibility with socialist ideals, proved particularly popular. Especially when trying to attract Western tourists, Slovenia and Croatia were keen to emphasize their pre-communist cultural 'heritage' and 'Europeanness', thereby disentangling themselves from the political turmoil of the Yugoslav Wars and from their socialist past (Hall 2002). Even symbols of the bygone socialist era, now steeped in nostalgic connotations, found their ways into popular culture and advertising. In several post-Yugoslav states, socialist paraphernalia and the image of Tito were used extensively to promote a wide variety of goods, ranging from cars and wine to coffee and mineral water (Volčič 2007). The transition from the multi-ethnic community of Yugoslav comrades to a multitude of ethnically defined nations of consumers was complete.

India: Commercialization and the rise of the Hindu nation

The restructuring of Yugoslav and South African media nations both involve a complex of rapid economic as well as political regime changes. However, similar transformations can occur also in the absence of radical political changes, and can be induced by the rise of commercial media. To demonstrate this, let us have a look at the transformation of the Indian media nation during the 1980s and the 1990s. For several decades, the state-controlled public television broadcaster *Doordarshan* held a monopoly over the televisual space in the country. Haunted by the legacy of partition between India and Pakistan, India's ruling elites took it upon themselves to promote national integration and sought to minimize the influence of sub-national cleavages.

The public broadcaster served as a prime instrument of this agenda: from its inception in the 1950s to the first electoral defeat of the Congress Party in 1977, *Doordarshan* was heavily centralized and its programming centred on culturally 'neutral' educational topics aimed at promoting nationwide development, such as agriculture, literacy and health (Kumar 2006: 24–31). In line with the secular convictions of the governing party, the media nation fostered by the public broadcaster was a multi-religious and multi-ethnic community, united by a common state and a common communicative sphere tied to Hindi as the official national language (Rajagopal 1993: 91–92). This official vision of the Indian nation, united in its diversity, was not left unchallenged, and in particular the privileged status of Hindi provoked rather loud protests in some parts of the country (Kumar 2006: 28–29). Yet, until the 1980s, such sub-national cleavages had little influence on the shaping of the Indian TV nation.

The 1980s were marked by profound shifts in the political economy and institutional organization of Indian television, parallel by important changes at the level of the mediated collective imagination. The geographic reach of *Doordarshan* increased rapidly, its national network was decentralized, and the introduction of commercial sponsorship prompted a rise in entertainment programming (ibid.: 31–33). Despite these changes, the state did not abstain from using television as a tool of national integration. However, instead of relying on educational programming, it now started fostering the production of domestic TV serials modelled on those produced in the USA and Latin America (Mankekar 1998: 35–37). In line with the logic of commercial media, the new forms of programming were geared towards the rising Indian middle-classes, which constituted the most attractive market for *Doordarshan*'s commercial sponsors. This had an impact on the dominant contours of national imagination in the country: increasingly, being a member of the modern Indian nation meant being in possession of particular consumer goods, including cosmetic products and home appliances (ibid.: 38). Similarly as in post-apartheid South Africa, the imagined community of Indians was above all a nation of consumers: while in principle open to all regardless of religious affiliation, caste or status, it marginalized the vast majority of the population who could not afford the advertised consumer life style.

The proliferation of consumerist imagery was soon followed by another fundamental shift in the mediation of Indian nationhood: the rise of the Hindu nation. As the reach of national broadcasting extended beyond the urban, secular elites, media producers and advertisers started tapping into popular religious sentiments. In 1987, *Doordarshan* began broadcasting a new television series, based on the ancient Hindu religious epic, the *Ramayan*. The launching of the series was a watershed in the modern history of Indian television and nation-building: it signalled the demise of the unitary, secular vision of the Indian nation. The series proved immensely popular with the audiences, leaving the streets across the country deserted during the broadcast and leading to an unprecedented surge in *Doordarshan*'s audience ratings (Rajagopal 2001: 84). Yet this rapid expansion of the viewing public was achieved in part by means of drawing new lines of exclusion, coinciding with religious divisions. This was visible in the realm of advertising: in this period, the adverts targeted at the lower middle and rural classes often drew on Hindu religious symbols to construct a collective identity that bridged the divisions between the rich and the poor (Rajagopal 1998: 23–25).

The redrawing of national imagination in the media sphere was closely intertwined with important power shifts in the sphere of politics, where the secularist vision of India's 'unity in diversity' was increasingly challenged by more sectarian forms of political identity. The roots of this shift extend well beyond the rise of Hindu nationalist political actors such as the Bharatiya Janata Party (BJP), and can be traced to a fundamental reorientation within the old political guard itself. Aware of its diminished appeal among lower castes, the Congress Party gradually shifted away from its traditional class-based politics and started tapping into communal identities and appealing to the Hindu electorate (McGuire and Reeves 2003: 102). The escalation of communal tensions in the Indian state of Punjab, the proliferation of anti-Sikh riots and the assassination of Indira Gandhi in 1984 did little to diminish the appeal of populist politics. In 1987, it was the Congress Party that sanctioned the production of *Ramayan*, counting on exploiting the appeal of religious national imagery to further its own political goals (Kumar 2006: 36). However, the legitimating power bestowed by the religious narrative was instead captured by the much more fervently nationalist BJP and its allies, which shaped the trajectory of Indian politics ever since. The fate of the old, secularist vision of India's 'unity in diversity' was sealed: in subsequent years, it was replaced by competing projections of Indianness, organized along myriad sub-national cleavages.

The final blow to *Doordarshan*'s monopoly over the mediation of nationhood, and with that to the state-sponsored secular vision of the Indian nation, came with the rise of satellite television in the 1990s. Digital broadcast satellites provided advertisers with new platforms for reaching potential customers, this time without having to comply with the particular vision of Indianness promoted by the state. This stimulated the proliferation of commercial Indian channels, including regional channels broadcasting in languages other than Hindi (McMillin 2001). The privately owned satellite and cable channels such as Zee TV, Sony TV and STAR TV did not abandon the language of nationhood. Rather, the confluence of technological innovation, global media expansion and commercialization put an end to state monopoly over broadcast national imagination and turned the Indian media space into a genuine 'market for loyalties' (Price 2002: 31ff) in which the Indian state competes with other manufacturers of national imagination. The rise of commercial media thus brought greater diversity to the Indian media sector and gave rise to a more plural form of collective imagination and public representation, drawing on a range of religious, regional and ethno-cultural differences. This diversity came at a cost: to be attractive to commercial outlets, new audiences needed to constitute viable markets for advertisers. No matter how large, they could become part of the re-imagined media nation only in if they could be conceived as imagined communities of consumers.

Mediated Grammars of Nationhood Today: Nations of Consumers

While the economic and political transformations occurring in South Africa, Yugoslavia and India gave rise to noticeably different configurations of collective imagination, we can also identify some common patterns. In all cases, political democratization and economic liberalization led to a reshuffling of existing relations of power between cultural groups, the state and the economy. Commercially funded media became important players in collective identity formation, and led to a strengthening of consumerist imagination. However, in the case of South Africa, this transformation drew the imagined community away from the race-nation, while in the case of the former Yugoslavia and India it pulled the media nations in the opposite direction: into the embrace of ethno-national communities. In other words, where ethno-cultural and racial identities were previously subordinated to other forms of identity – common political identity in the case of Yugoslavia, secular identity in the case of India – rapid economic and political changes brought religion, race and ethnicity back to the surface and allowed them to trump class and political divisions, thereby introducing a new set of restrictions on public culture. In contrast, where racial identities held sway and dominated both economic and political processes, the transformation pushed them to the background and instead gave preference to socio-economic divisions.

These three case studies provide a good illustration of the double-edged impact of media commercialization, and more broadly of market exchange as the principle of social organization. On the one hand, the logic of the market helped break the monopoly of officially sponsored imagined communities – be it socialist, secular or racial – and facilitated a greater competition over the meaning of nationhood. Hungry for new audiences, commercial media helped open doors to arguments, groups and identities that remained marginalized or invisible in state-sponsored media, or even usher in new forms of imagined communities. This process was facilitated by democratization, which initiated a similar opening up of collective imagination and representation at a political level, providing hitherto excluded collective actors with an opportunity to become part of the political process. Yet, on the other hand, the growing prominence of market principles also introduced new forms of exclusion, and, in keeping with the logic of the market, those were drawn along class lines. In other words, the abolition of old boundaries and the diversification of national imagination came at a cost: it gave rise to nations of consumers that have little consideration for the needs of the poor. In Yugoslavia and India, economic liberalization also contributed, albeit indirectly, to the instrumentalization of culture, which imposed further limitations on public culture and collective imagination.

What is also evident from the three case studies is that our analytical framework continues to provide a useful tool for a comparative assessment of recent developments. Not only do the shifts charted above follow the logic outlined in the framework, they also suggest a persistent degree of variation across cases, despite the convergence towards the liberal media model and towards national grammars organized around class distinctions. While the growing prominence of market principles and consumerist imagination is indisputable in all three cases, the relative strength of the organizing principles of state bureaucracy and, especially, community differs. It is plausible to expect that similar variations will be found elsewhere in the world, including in the West, where the resurgence of nationalist and racist movements and parties after 1989 confirms that ideas of national and racial purity continue to have their appeal today. These newly revitalized political actors tend to tread carefully when discussing issues of nation and race, preferring to package their demands in the rhetoric of liberal values – in particular, freedom of speech. Yet brewing underneath are some of the same prejudices known from early twentieth-century fascism (Copsey 2007; Richardson and Wodak 2009). The other historic competitor of liberal democracy is also not quite as dead as we may think. The recent financial meltdown and the onset of global recession has put a dent in the shiny armour of economic liberalism and brought state intervention into economic affairs back onto the agenda. The dramatic transformation of China over the past two decades also clearly shows that capitalism is not incompatible with a strong state and single-party politics, at least in the short run.

To be sure, the rival modernizing visions of yesterday have by now lost their most radical edges and accepted some of the general rules of the game set out by liberal democracy. Yet the ideological contest over the definition of modernity continues. The key problems that have preoccupied the proponents of twentieth-century fascism, liberalism and communism – the relationship between the individual and the collective, the balance of market and state forces – remain open and continue to provoke contrasting political visions. Most of these contrasting visions steer away from the extremes of community and the state, and cluster closer to the market end of our three-fold scheme. Still, it would be far too simple, if not naive, to see this as a final and irreversible triumph of liberalism. At the very least, we should acknowledge the creation of different 'varieties of capitalism', some reliant almost completely on competition and market forces, others characterized by forms of coordination that require the interaction between market and non-market actors (Hall and Soskice 2001). This variation is likely to continue to generate different forms of media nations and different shapes of mediated national imagination, despite the convergence towards consumerist imagination.

There is a further factor that is likely to keep national imagination alive in the future, one that we have not really considered adequately so far – namely, the presence of international conflicts. As the following chapter will show, this factor has the capacity to provoke similar shifts in the mediation of nationhood and similar encroachments on the public sphere everywhere, regardless of the particularities of the media system or the economic and political context.

5

Media Nations at War

For most of us, nationhood is a self-evident, largely inconsequential back-drop to everyday life – in fact so self-evident and inconsequential that one is easily persuaded that nationalism and national identity are nothing more than fading remnants of bygone times. We may be cheering our national sports teams and laughing at jokes about other nations – or, indeed, jokes about our own nation – but none of that is ever endowed with the serious-ness that the word 'nationalism' invokes. In contrast, for the many victims of nationalist violence and discrimination around the world, and for those whose family members are out on the frontlines, nationhood is not merely something that can be playfully enacted and then discarded at will. In situ-ations of conflict, being perceived as a member of a particular nation can be a matter of life and death, and a fact that needs to be reckoned with on a daily basis, whether one wants it or not.

The two experiences of nationhood – the constraining nationalist reality of the battleground and the trivial presence of nationhood away from the front – seem to be worlds apart. Living in a peaceful, stable environment, shielded from nationalist violence and bigotry, makes it difficult to fathom how something as banal as one's national belonging can ever serve as a springboard for the kind of powerful emotions that fuel nationalist conflict and genocide. The two forms of nationalism appear so far removed from each other that it seems much more plausi-ble to ascribe the propensity to aggression and hatred only to nations that are radically different from ours: nations steeped in 'ancient hatreds' and haunted by tribal traditions, or nations defined in terms of ethnicity and blood relations rather than common political structures (for a similar argument, see Billig 1995: 5–7). The stories of other peoples' wars brought to our homes by the modern media do little to dispel such perceptions, and mostly reinforce us in our beliefs that there must be something fundamentally different and irrational in those warring nations themselves (cf. Carruthers 2000: 197–243).

This is a beguiling but misleading picture. As this chapter seeks to demonstrate, the everyday forms of national imagination are not as far removed from the excesses of wartime nationalist talk as we would like to think. When faced with a sudden conflict or catastrophe, every nation tends to fall prey to similar shifts in collective imagination. Internal disagreements disappear into the background, trivial references to nationhood are replaced by loud and unambiguous declarations of national belonging, and media narratives become structured around sharp divisions between 'us' and 'them'. In other words, the loosely connected, diverse nation of citizens is replaced by an internally homogeneous, single-minded nation of warriors. The intensity and extent of these changes may vary from genre to genre, and from media system to media system, yet their main contours remain broadly the same everywhere we look.

To demonstrate this, the chapter looks at two cases of conflict reporting, taken from two markedly different socio-political and media contexts: the TV news coverage of the early phase of the Yugoslav Wars in 1991 and the *New York Times'* response to the 9/11 attacks in 2001. In the mental map of the Western world, the ex-Yugoslav nations and the American nation are poles apart: the former belong to the exotic, backward, barbaric world of 'the Balkans', the latter to the privileged club of the world's most civilized and developed nations (cf. Todorova 1997; Lewis and Wigen 1997). Social scientific typologies of nations and nationalism draw a similarly black-and-white picture: Croats, Serbs, Macedonians, Bosnians, Slovenes and Montenegrins are often quoted as typical examples of 'ethnic', inherently exclusive intolerant nations, while the USA features as a prime example of the 'civic', intrinsically inclusive and tolerant nation. Yet if we look at the mediated national imagination and the behaviour of journalists and editors before and during the conflict, the two cases have much in common.

Hot and Banal Nationalism

Before embarking on the actual analysis of the two case studies, it is worth outlining some of the relevant conceptual distinctions that can help us to better understand the dynamics of mediated nationhood in times of war and peace. For several decades, much of the mainstream debate on nations and nationalism remained centred on macro-processes fostering the rise and proliferation of national movements and nation-states: the formation of a particular ideology, the advent of socio-economic trends such as modernization and industrialization, and the development of specific institutions and infrastructures such as the modern state, compulsory education, and state-wide transportation and communication networks (Kedourie [1960] 1996; Gellner 1983; Anderson 1991; Breuilly 1993). While a lot has been said about the early periods of nation-formation, and particularly about the balance of continuity and discontinuity between modern nations and pre-modern collectivities (Armstrong 1982; Smith 1986), we know, comparatively speaking, much less about the ebbs and flows of nations and nationalisms *after* their initial rise, and about the micro-politics of nationalist mobilization and demobilization in established nations and nation-states.

Michael Billig's (1995) study of banal nationalism made a crucial step forward by providing an account of how national attachments are sustained and reproduced on a mundane basis in established nation-states, bringing to light the everyday routines and categories of nationhood that permeate the fabric of daily life. Several studies followed, building on Billig's theory to examine the multiple layers of sub- and trans-national belonging that are also anchored in everyday habits and categories alongside national ones (e.g. Beck 2002; Rosie et al. 2004). Others have shown how the mindlessly performed nation-maintaining practices enter our daily lives through a range of communication-related institutions and everyday routines such as national currencies, public phones, advertising, and consumption (Foster 2002), as well as school essays, clocks and calendars (Postill 2006).

The growing awareness of the routine rituals and everyday habits of nationhood also triggered a rethinking of established scholarly narratives of nation-formation. In standard accounts, nation-building is seen as a unilinear and irreversible process, culminating in the successful establishment of a nation-state, which is expected to attenuate and diffuse nationalist sentiments, if not eliminate them altogether. Yet, as recent literature suggests, nation-formation is not a one-way, cumulative process leading towards a final accomplishment, but rather a process that is highly uneven and 'episodic', composed of short periods of 'hot' nationalism and lengthy periods of 'quiet' or 'banal' nationalism (Beissinger 2002; Hutchinson 2005). In the protracted periods of 'quiet' nationalism, the reality of the nation is limited to seemingly innocuous, neutral conventions and routines: the habit of classifying individuals as members of nations, the tendency to narrate history as a set of parallel national histories, or the practice of thinking about culture as an ensemble of artefacts, values and norms belonging to individual nations. During the exceptional, brief periods of 'hot' nationalism, however, the nature of the nation changes. It is only in such moments that nations become what they are normally assumed to be – imagined communities that manage to capture the hearts and minds of the masses.

Between the Nation and the Public

It is reasonable to expect that the periods of 'hot' and 'quiet' nationalism will be characterized by different forms of mediated national imagination, as well as by different types of media–politics relations. Yet, at least at first sight, the established professional conventions at work in news genres appear to leave rather little room for national narratives and identification. The principles of the 'inverted pyramid' require news stories to start with a summary of key information, followed by further details in decreasing order of significance. As a result, news stories normally lack elements of narrative structure characteristic of fictional genres – for example, causal relationships, a double chronology, and typical elements of the dramatic structure such as closure and resolution (Dunn 2005: 145–46). These same elements are characteristic also of nationalist myths, which tend to recount the story of 'our nation' as an evolving drama punctuated by heroic struggles and periods of martyrdom.

Another characteristic that differentiates news genres from fictional narratives is the prevalence of third-person narration and external focalization – that is, focalization from a seemingly neutral point outside the narrative, which is not associated with any character involved in the narrative (Allan 1999: 99–101). Unlike overt nationalist narratives, which are typically written from the position of an insider who is speaking in the name of 'our' nation, news narratives adopt a more detached perspective and recount the news of the day from the position of a neutral observer who is not explicitly attached to a particular nation. Finally, the narrative plots of news genres are much less continuous and coherent than those of films, novels, or nationalist myths. Rather than providing one coherent narrative, newspapers and broadcast news offer an array of narrative segments that are internally coherent yet often only vaguely connected to other news segments in the same newspaper or news programme (cf. Ellis 1992).

The narrative conventions of routine reporting outlined above do not seem particularly conducive to the Andersonian vision of the audience as an imagined *national community*. Instead, they are meant to ensure that newspapers and news programmes provide material for a rational public debate, and are therefore tied primarily to the Habermasian vision of the audience as a *rational public* (Schudson 2003: 177–93). Indeed, much of the research inspired by public sphere theory has relatively little to say about nationalism and ethnicity, and leaves one with the impression that public debate is, or at least should be, somehow devoid of cultural identity. Yet this is at the very least empirically incorrect, if not also normatively misguided – an issue we return to in Chapter 8. To understand this, we need to keep in mind that the links between newspaper stories and the imagined national community are not dependent on explicit nationalist narratives, but on far less obvious aspects of the newspaper industry. A key source of these links lies in what Anderson (1991: 32–36) calls 'calendrical coincidence'; namely, in the fact that all stories in a particular newspaper relate to events that happened on the same day, and concern members of the same imagined community. An additional basis of imagined links is provided by the specific mode of production and distribution, which gives rise to the nearly simultaneous consumption of the newspaper by thousands or even millions of readers, who all share an awareness of each other as members of the same community, without ever meeting in person (ibid.).

The aforementioned professional codes appear to fit rather neatly with the imagined links underpinned by the calendrical coincidence of news events and the mode of production and distribution that results in simultaneous consumption of the same news items. A typical news bulletin or newspaper can be seen as a narrative about events that happened to a particular imagined community on a given day, or that are deemed important enough for all members of that community to know about. Similarly, the direct, dialogic mode of address characteristic of the television news bulletin – but appearing also in newspapers, particularly in op-ed pieces – can be seen as a manifestation of the imagined link that ties the bulletin to its intended audience. This mode of address typically involves speaking straight to the camera, as if talking to each individual viewer, and relies on dialogical, personalized forms of address such as 'Dear viewers, good evening'. This creates the impression of an intimate link between the media institution and the imagined viewer, and helps create a fictive 'we' embracing the newsreader(s) and the viewers (Allan 1999: 100). It is easy to see how this fictive 'we' can be used to refer to the imagined community of a nation, and therefore function as a banal reminder of national belonging (Billig 1995).

Nevertheless, we should be wary of jumping to conclusions too quickly. As the case studies presented later on in this chapter will demonstrate, news narratives do not necessarily explicitly define the fictive 'we' as a *national* we. In a similar vein, events reported in news bulletins and newspapers are not normally unequivocally presented as events happening to a particular nation. Although clearly compatible with national imagination, such banal reminders can in fact accommodate many competing and even incompatible definitions of collective identity, which allows the exact content and boundaries of the fictive 'we' to remain fuzzy and flexible. Sometimes, newsreaders and journalists may use the 'we' simply to refer to themselves as journalists, or to the media institution they represent (e.g. Hallin and Mancini 1984: 839). These observations are in line with one of the criticisms levelled at Anderson's theory, discussed also in Chapter 1 – namely, that it is based on a tacit assumption that the imagined community fostered by the newspaper will necessarily be a national one.

Of course, not all of the news stories are that ambiguous when referring to the fictive 'we'. In the context of war, natural catastrophe, or in moments of collective celebration – that is, in moments of 'hot' nationalism – the fictive 'we' is filled with more explicitly national content and the various events reported are unambiguously presented as events happening to a particular nation – 'our' nation. The presence of a threatening enemy drives editors and journalists to abandon the professional conventions of analytical and balanced coverage, adopt a patriotic stance and organize their narratives around the conflict between 'us' and 'them', between 'our nation' and its enemies (Hallin 1986). In the immediate aftermath of the crisis, media professionals often turn into collective therapists, share in the grief of their audiences, provide practical advice, boost morale by conveying feelings of solidarity, as well as help provide a sense of direction and reach an emotional closure (Kitch and Hume 2008). It is also important to note that this kind of reporting is normally adopted in situations of elite consensus – i.e. when events fall outside of the sphere of legitimate controversy (Hallin 1986) – and that it is meant to provide the raw materials for identity-building rather than rational public debate (Schudson 2003: 188).

Put differently, periods of hot and banal nationalism are associated with different patterns of media–politics relationships, as well as by different narrative conventions and national imagination, as summarized in Table 5.1. In a peaceful context, characterized by the prevalence of banal nationalism and elite dissensus, professional routines are observed and explicit national narratives are normally absent. Newsreaders and journalists typically use third-person narration and external focalization, identify themselves with other journalists and the media institution, and detach themselves both from their audience and from the events reported. This kind of narration is still underpinned by the assumption that all the events reported are somehow related to one another, and are of relevance to the same audience, yet these links are not explicitly presented as national and allow for the coexistence of competing definitions of reality and belonging, which is crucial for a functioning public

Table 5.1 Modes of reporting and national imagination

		Routine reporting	Crisis/celebratory reporting
Context	Political context	Peace/routine events	War/ extraordinary events
	Elite attitudes	Elite dissensus – events seen as falling into the sphere of legitimate controversy	Elite consensus – events seen as falling into the sphere of consensus or deviance
Type of nationalism		Banal nationalism – the world of nations as the invisible frame of reporting	Hot nationalism – nations as key forces and actors in reported events
Media-politics		Relative distance between political elites and the media; observance of professional norms	Overt censorship and self-censorship, political pressures on journalists and editors *and/or* unconscious self-censorship and abandonment of professional norms
Narrative conventions	Implied audience	A (national) public, divided over particular issues	A nation, united in attitudes on particular issues
	Use of deictic expressions	Mostly to refer to the journalists. National deixis, where present, used to foster internal disagreement (us, the nation, vs. the government)	Frequent use of national deixis, used to refer to both the journalists and the audience as members of the same national community; used to foster national unity

Continued overleaf

Table 5.1 *continued*

Narrative conventions		*Routine reporting*	*Crisis/celebratory reporting*
	Narrative voice and focalization	Predominantly third-person narration; external focalization	Frequent first-person narration from the point of view of the national 'we'; external and internal focalization
	Key actors	Individuals and/or groups that form part of the nation but do not share the same opinions	Nations and/or their representatives sharing the same opinions; the national 'we' (embracing the journalists and their addressees) as one of these actors
	Narrative coherence of the news bulletin/ newspaper	Open-ended array of loosely connected segments	Narrative connecting the segments into a unified whole – a narrative about the nation
	Dramatic structure	Inverted pyramid structure; dramatic structure weak, elements of classic dramatic structure missing	Dramatic structure more prominent; resemblance with the tripartite structure of rituals of passage (separation, liminality, re-integration)

sphere, while at the same time maintaining a basic overarching commonality.

In contrast, in situations of war, natural catastrophe or collective cele-bration, characterized by 'hot' nationalism and elite consensus, media professionals often abandon professional rules and the political pres-sures on the media increase. Journalists are discursively positioning themselves and their audience within the same national community, and are narrating the events from the point of view of 'us, the nation'. The individual news items are woven together into an overarching national drama that follows the structure of fictional narratives, starting with an initial equilibrium, followed by a disruption, climax, and then gradual resolution and closure. In such a context, 'the nation' continues to func-tion as a polyvalent symbol with multiple meanings, yet the scope for diversity is significantly narrower than in routine reporting. Instead of allowing for the coexistence of competing definitions of reality and a truly public discussion, such narratives serve to delegitimate and silence any form of internal dissent.

The following two sections trace these shifts from the public to the nation – or from a nation of citizens to a nation of warriors – with the help of two case studies. The first examines prime-time TV news bulletins broadcast in the socialist Yugoslavia in the early 1990s, while the second looks at the op-ed pieces published in the *New York Times* in the week before and after the 9/11 attacks. The two cases involve very different socio-political and economic contexts, different media environ-ments and different grammars of nationhood – the first one gravitating more towards the organizing principles of the state and community, the latter towards the logic of the market.

The Yugoslav Wars

The first case study focuses on prime-time TV news bulletins broadcast in the period from 21 June to 16 July 1991. Materials come from two TV stations located in two different Yugoslav republics: TV Ljubljana (TVL) in the Republic of Slovenia and TV Belgrade (TVB) in the Republic of Serbia. The period covered includes two key events that, from the point of view of the political elites in both Slovenia and Serbia, fell outside of the scope of legitimate controversy, and coincided with a period of 'hot' nationalism. The first one was Slovenia's Declaration of Independence, issued on 25 June, which was treated as a major national celebratory event on the Slovenian side, but regarded as illegitimate by the Serbian political mainstream. The second event was the so-called

'Ten-Day War' that started in Slovenia on 27 June, when the Yugoslav army made an attempt to keep the country together and maintain federal control over Slovenia's borders. The Slovenian government anticipated such developments and mobilized its territorial defence units, arguing that the Yugoslav army intervention was in fact a hostile attack of a foreign army on a sovereign state. In both republics, the political mainstream treated the events in a broadly consensual manner, and expected the media to follow suit (cf. Veljanovski 2002). Journalists and editors were often complicit in sustaining such attitudes and willingly avoided criticism. Television stations were particularly prone to governmental influence, and their positions were closely tied to the political mainstream (Bašić Hrvatin 1997). Although the elites never achieved full control over the media in respective republics, alternative voices were confined to outlets with limited audience reach.

Let us now see whether these contextual changes were paralleled by a shift at the level of news narratives. The examination of news bulletins broadcast before Slovenia's declaration of independence demonstrates that the newsreaders and journalists indeed rarely used explicit deictic references to an imagined community embracing both the narrators and their addressees. When they did use words such as 'we' or 'our', they were usually referring to themselves and their colleagues, and to the media institution they were representing. The following opening of a bulletin broadcast by TV Ljubljana after the cessation of hostilities provides a typical example:

> Good evening. The marathon-length, almost fourteen hours long, session of the Yugoslav presidency brought almost no relief. [...] Following a proposal by the Army, [the Presidency] unanimously accepted a decree consisting of six points. Before we summarize them once again ... (TVL, 13 July)

The 'we' that is about to provide a summary of the decree does not embrace the audience addressed by the bulletin. Instead, the deixis serves to establish a division between 'us, the journalists' and 'you, the viewing public'. The newsreader is not talking in the name of any imagined national community, but represents the institution of television that is bringing the latest news of the day to its viewers, conceived as a public.

At the same time, this kind of deictic positioning also detaches the newsreaders and journalists from the events they are reporting, establishes them as professional, analytical and non-partisan observers, and necessitates the adoption of third-person narration and external focalization. Such focalization does not in itself preclude or abolish the imagined link that ties the journalists, their viewers, as well as the actors of reported events, into the same imagined community. However, this link is not explicitly foregrounded in the bulletin itself by means of deictic expressions; nor does it serve as the basis for a shared point of view on events that are being reported. Rather, the nation is conceived as an imagined community of citizens with diverse attitudes and opinions. Although the reporting in this period was not entirely balanced, reporters did at the very least acknowledge the existence of diverse opinions among members of the same public, and reported them from the position of an external, third-person narrator.

The key actors of news narraties are another aspect worth examining. In routine reporting, the majority of actors consisted of named individuals, institutions and groups, such as presidents, parliaments, political parties or state officials. Individual nations and states also occasionally featured among the actors, yet journalists were deictically detached from them. All of these traits are visible in the following news bulletin opening:

> Good evening. In Belgrade, extraordinary political activity of the highest Yugoslav representatives. First Slobodan Milošević, as the host of the second round of talks between the leaders of Bosnia and Herzegovina, Croatia and Serbia, spoke to the presidents Franjo Tuđman and Alija Izetbegović. This afternoon, following the initiative of Slovenia and Croatia, Ante Marković spoke to Milan Kučan, Franjo Tuđman, Janez Drnovšek and Stjepan Mesić. [...] Later in the bulletin we provide a full report from the talk between Milošević, Izetbegović and Tuđman. (TVB, 19 June)

The opening mentions two collective actors, 'Slovenia' and 'Croatia', as well as a long list of individuals representing the respective Yugoslav republics and federal institutions. The narrator avoids using any deictic expressions that would explicitly position him closer to one or another of the named actors. Instead, he establishes a clear division between himself as a journalist and representative of the television ('we provide a full report') and the named actors participating in the narrative. The quoted excerpt also follows the typical inverted pyramid structure, starting with the key information on the who (the named actors), what (talks), when (today, in the afternoon) and where (in Belgrade) of the major events of the day before turning to further details and other events. As a consequence, the dramatic structure of the narrative is relatively weak. The same applies also to news bulletins as a whole in this period: the successive news items were only loosely connected to one another, and were not explicitly presented as pieces in an unfolding national drama.

The reporting later, however, at the time of the declaration of independence and the subsequent armed conflict, was marked by conventions that were rather different from the ones we have just outlined. To start with, the news narratives were permeated by deictic expressions that were unambiguously tied to a particular nation or state. The newsanchors and journalists of TV Belgrade, for example, spoke about 'us, the Yugoslavs' and 'our Yugoslav problem' (TVB, 29 June), and used expressions such as 'our people', 'our citizens' and 'our country' in a way that made clear they were referring to Yugoslavs and Yugoslavia. The following opening of a news bulletin provides a characteristic example:

Dear viewers, good evening. What will happen to Yugoslavia tomorrow? Several inhabitants of our country are raising this question, as do virtually all world news agencies and foreign journalists accredited in our country. [...] The country of the Yugoslavs today provides plenty of reasons for such dramatic questions. (TVB, 21 June)

By mentioning 'our country' a few moments after directly addressing the audience ('Dear viewers, good evening.'), the newsreader clearly situates himself and his audience in the same imagined community. His mention of 'Yugoslavia' in the second sentence and 'the country of the Yugoslavs' in the fourth sentence leaves little doubt as to which country this imagined community belongs to.

The presenters of TV Ljubljana were using deictic expressions in much the same way, yet tied them to a different imagined community and country: the Slovenians and Slovenia. In the following excerpt, the news presenter uses a deixis – 'we' – to include himself in the imagined community celebrating Slovenia's independence. The explicit mention of Slovenia and its independence, along with the reference to the Slovenian capital (Ljubljana) as the focus of celebrations, clarifies which nation and which country the 'we' is referring to:

Good evening. Yesterday evening, Slovenia became autonomous and independent. Today we are celebrating: in some places already the whole day, while this evening, joy and pride will burst out everywhere. The main celebrations will take place in Ljubljana. The fact that Yugoslavia already reacted to yesterday's decision should not make the evening any less pleasant, primarily because we have expected it. (TVL, 26 June)

The above excerpt can also serve as an example of how the national 'we' provided the basis for internal focalization: from the very start of the bulletin, the events of the day were narrated from the point of view of 'us, the nation'. This nation was also presented as one of the key actors of the narrative: celebrating, expecting a reaction to its celebration, and remaining in a joyful mood despite the reaction. The other key actor in the same narrative is identified as 'Yugoslavia', and is quite unambiguously cast into the role of a villain who can endanger 'our' celebrations. TV Belgrade was using the same narrative devices, but identified the key actors in a diametrically opposite way: the imagined 'we' telling the story was associated with Yugoslavia while the villain was 'Slovenia'.

It is worth noting that such use of deictic expressions and internal focalization assumes that everyone among 'us' is sharing the same attitude towards Slovenia's independence and towards the reaction of the Yugoslav Army. The opening lines of the bulletin quoted above allow no scope for members of 'us' who may not want to join in the celebrations of independence – as the newsreader states, 'joy and pride will burst out *everywhere*'. Similar patterns can be discerned in TV Belgrade's reporting in the same period. Clearly, both television companies perceived their audiences and themselves primarily as part of an imagined national community in the sense defined by Benedict Anderson: as a group of people tied by 'a deep, horizontal comradeship' (1991: 7) which exists above and beyond any inequality, exploitation, or internal dissent.

This is not meant to suggest that the deictic expressions and explicit 'flaggings' of either the Slovenian or the Yugoslav nation left no room for divergent interpretations. Although the scope for diversity was significantly narrower than in routine reporting, it was not abolished entirely. If we return again to the last excerpt, we can note that the exact nature of the relationship between 'us' and the state remains ambiguous. For example, does the 'we' include everyone permanently residing in the given territorial unit, regardless of ethnic affiliation? Is it equally open both to former communists as well as to those leaning towards the political right? Arguably, it is not a coincidence that the particular journalistic use of deictic expressions and national flags in this period avoids addressing these questions. These were, at the time, the most divisive questions among the respective political elites in each of the republics, and any attempt to address them could have undermined the appeal to national unity. Even in the period of crisis and celebration, 'the nation' continued to function as a polyvalent symbol with multiple meanings, which had the ability to mobilize different audiences who thought that they understood it in the same way (cf. Verdery 1996: 227). Indeed, the utility of national deixes lies precisely in their ambiguity, and in their associated ability 'to simultaneously carry diverse meanings to different audiences [...] while appearing to address one common audience by virtue of literally using the same words' (Rosie et al. 2004: 454).

The prominence of national deixis and internal focalization in celebratory and conflict reporting also went hand in hand with a far greater level of narrative coherence: the events of the day were explicitly presented as events happening to 'us, the nation', and were tied into an overarching national narrative. The opening of the news bulletin broadcast by TV Ljubljana towards the end of the violent confrontations provides a telling example.

> Good evening. Today was a calm day, and life is returning to our streets. This is filling us all with hope that what we have lived through in the past days will never happen again. However, things were not particularly calm for those who are now trying to settle the situation in Slovenia and Yugoslavia through negotiations and tolerant dialogue. (TVL, 6 July)

The first actor mentioned in the excerpt, which also constitutes the deictic centre and thus the venture point for internal focalization, is identified as 'us all' and embraces both the narrator and his addressees. Other actors – 'those who are now trying to settle the situation' – are described from the point of view of 'us', implying that their actions are of some relevance to 'us'. The narrative starts by relating 'our' experiences of the past few days, and situates the efforts of negotiators within the same narrative about things relevant to 'us'. Later in the same bulletin, the newsreader resumes the same deictic position on several occasions, situating the various events of the day in the context of the overarching narrative about 'our' suffering and resilience.

A final thing to note is that the national narratives weaving together the individual news items in wartime bulletins were not brought to a closure within each individual bulletin. Instead, they built upon the narratives from previous days, and extended to forthcoming bulletins. These overarching narratives, stretching over several days and even weeks, displayed elements of a classic dramatic structure typical of fictional genres. This can be demonstrated by looking at a selection of openings of news bulletins broadcast by the same channel:

> Good evening. All domestic events are, understandably, subordinated to the preparations for independence, which will be [...] declared the day after tomorrow. (TVL, 24 June)

Good evening. The attack by the invading army on the independent and sovereign Republic of Slovenia reached its climax today. (TVL, 28 June)

Good evening. [...] When will this carnage end? Unfortunately the fact is that almost 24 hours after the ceasefire one still cannot know for sure when the hostilities will really end. (TVL, 29 June)

Good evening. The arms are quiet. We hope this is for ever. (TVL, 3 July)

The openings are telling an unfolding story about the nation, country, or 'us'. The narrative starts with a relative equilibrium and expectation of change – i.e. Slovenia's independence (24 June) – then follows a dramatic climax in the form of the 'attack by the invading army' (28 June), a longing for closure (29 June), and finally a re-establishment of equilibrium (3 July). The storyline continues from one bulletin to the next, with newsreaders frequently referring to events of the past days or speculating about the future.

Arguably, this overarching narrative plot resembles the structure of the 'rites of passage' (van Gennep [1909] 1960; Turner 1969) usually associated with events that represent the key milestones in an individual's life, such as birth, coming of age, marriage, or death. Regardless of the social context, rites of passage always include three key stages: separation, liminality, and re-integration. The first stage involves a move away from the previous role or identity; the second stage is associated with a chaotic, orderless 'limbo' between the old and the new; and the third stage entails the incorporation into the new role or identity, and an establishment of new rules. The overarching narrative plot emerging from the news bulletins is marked by the same stages, yet these were associated with a collective – Slovenia – rather than an individual. The declaration of independence was meant symbolically to mark Slovenia's detachment from its old status as a federal republic within the wider Yugoslav political framework (separation); this was followed by a period of the armed conflict, when the old Yugoslav order and rules were suspended while the new Slovenian order had not yet been fully established (liminality); finally, towards the end of the conflict, a return to normalcy and order followed (re-integration). By narrating the conflict in this way, TV journalists and newsreaders were contributing to the symbolic enactment of a collective ritual of transformation, which helped transform Slovenia and its viewing public into a sovereign nation.

The 9/11 Attacks

The media–politics relationship in twenty-first century USA is undoubt-edly very different from the one characteristic of the disintegrating Yugoslavia in the early 1990s. Levels of media professionalism and independence are high, political pressures on journalists and editors relatively limited and overt state censorship virtually unheard of. Yet despite this, the American media are far from immune to ethnocentrism and ardent patriotism, particularly in times of crisis (cf. Gans 1979: 42–43, Calabrese and Burke 1992). The almost unanimous embrace of national unity following 9/11 dispelled the hopes of those who maintain that a journalistic culture rooted in a strong tradition of professionalism is able to resist the lure of patriotism. While explicit political pressures were rather rare, other forms of censorship, prompted by either public outrage or editors' sense of patriotic duty, were not that uncommon. For instance, the publishers of *The Texas City Sun* and *The Daily Currier* in Grants Pass, Oregon, fired columnists who wrote openly critical pieces on George W. Bush, and a network TV show was under threat of cancel-lation after its host suggested that the USA's foreign policy may in part be responsible for the attacks (Scordato and Monopoli 2002: 186).

At the time, the US administration showed little concern for such constraints on freedom of speech, and instead pushed for legislation that would expand the government's ability to monitor private communica-tion. Well over a week from the attacks, the White House press secretary reminded all Americans 'that they need to watch what they say, watch what they do', and suggested that this is not a time for voicing critical opinions (ibid.: 187). Within a month, the US Senate passed the now infamous Patriot Act, which imposed serious restrictions on civil liber-ties in the name of national security, with an overwhelming 98–1 vote (Hutcheson et al. 2004: 47). The establishment of the new cabinet-level Department of Homeland Security expanded the discretionary powers of the White House even further, while also limiting the ability of Congress to influence presidential policymaking. Even within the president's war cabinet itself, consultation was limited, and the most fundamental deci-sions were taken by the president alone (Crotty 2003). The combined effect of the new legislative measures inevitably imposed restrictions on the voicing of alternative opinions, and thereby fostered the establish-ment and maintenance of elite consensus.

For the overwhelming majority of American journalists and editors, the temporary suspension of professional routines and suppression of dissenting voices came naturally. The patriotic press and broadcast news across the political spectrum eagerly echoed the nationalistic, apocalyptic rhetoric of political leaders, and marginalized dissenting voices (Hutcheson et al. 2004; Domke 2004). The framing offered by the White House – the attacks as an act of evil terrorists; the USA as an entirely innocent victim – was simply too congruent with dominant cultural values to arouse any suspicion among the commentators or their sources. Faced with such a culturally congruent framing, elites outside of the administration tended to avoid contesting the presidential framing, and thereby eased its dissemination through the mass media (cf. Entman 2004: 15–25).

Given these contextual factors, it is hardly a surprise that *New York Times* journalists adopted the same interpretative frame and abandoned their professional norms and routines. In the month following the attacks, the op-ed pieces drew abundantly on mythic themes and figures, and modelled their portrayal of the 9/11 aftermath on archetypal stories familiar from ancient epics and Arthurian romances (Lule 2002). As will become apparent, the narrative patterns shifted accordingly. Enveloped in the swirl of post-9/11 events, *New York Times* columnists were prone to follow similar narrative patterns as their TV colleagues in war-torn Yugoslavia. Contrasting the week before the World Trade Center attacks with the week after, we can trace a similar shift from the public to the nation, from disagreement to unity.

In the seven days preceding the attacks, the *New York Times* in-house columnists wrote a total of eleven op-ed pieces. Many of those were dedicated to the looming economic downturn and the sudden jump in unemployment announced just days before. The commentators were on the lookout for the heroes and villains of the economic drama, and were busy debating its causes and proposed solutions. They used every opportunity to criticize the government's mistakes, including in particular the overly optimistic economic forecasts of government advisers and George W. Bush's enthusiasm for tax cuts and the missile defence system. In one piece, Bush was described as 'darker and more complex than we thought', 'seized by a desire that defies the laws of politics and physics', and obsessed by a 'self-destructive craving for his ineffectual missile shield' (Dowd, *New York Times*, 5 September 2001, p. 19). Another commentator described the budget projections of the US Congress and the White House as being 'horrendously out of whack', and harshly criticized government's responses to recession (Safire, *New York Times*, 9 September, p. 29).

All the eleven op-ed pieces followed the basic patterns of routine reporting and professional conventions identified in Table 5.1. The common thread uniting the stories was the imagined community of the American nation, yet it was a nation united in disunity, a community tied together by debate and disagreement – in short, a public in the true sense of the word. This was a nation in which Republicans were pitted against Democrats, the government against the people, one electoral candidate against another, and one part of the public against another. At the same time – and in contrast to Yugoslav TV journalists and news presenters – *New York Times* columnists were rather keen on using national deixis, and often interpreted the events of the day from the position of a national 'we'. In other words, while Yugoslav TV journalists sought to discursively establish themselves as external observers of events, *New York Times* columnists adopted the position of passionately involved insiders. These differences can be linked to divergent narrative conventions for the two genres. Op-ed pieces require an opinionated discussion rather than a balanced presentation of facts, and are prone to be more story-like than television reports. As such, they are potentially more open to elements of national imagination, including explicit references to a national 'we'.

On the other hand, it is important to note that references to the American nation appearing in opinion pieces before 9/11 were not used to build unity. As a rule, the national 'we' was pitted against the government or the economic elites, and the narrative was organized around a fundamental tension between the American people and their representatives. One of the commentators accused Bush and his supporters of being stuck in Cold War mentality, and of pushing for policies that were entirely out of touch with the real needs of the US economy and security:

> Was the USA economy so bad these past eight years that we needed a deep tax cut that has now put the whole budget out of whack? Is America really threatened by rogue missiles so much that we need to immediately unravel every arms control treaty for an untested missile defense scheme? (Friedman, *New York Times*, 7 September 2001, p. 19)

The columnist's answer to these questions was of course negative: the US economy is sound, and its old defence system entirely appropriate, yet the political leaders are unable to see the error of their ways, and are obstinately backing solutions that will prove to be detrimental to the nation's security and economic prosperity. While invoking a national 'we', the article was aimed at creating disagreement rather than unity: it mapped out an internal struggle between the Conservative leaders and 'us', suggesting that Bush and his supporters were unable to protect the nation's vital interests. Although using national deixis in different ways, and adopting different types of narration and focalization, both *New*

York Times columnists and Yugoslav TV journalists were thus constructing the imagined community of the nation in fundamentally similar ways: in both cases, this community was conceived as an internally divided public.

The sixteen op-ed pieces published in the week following the attack tell a very different story, one centred on a shocked and wounded nation united in grief and ready to act in concert. The frequency of national deixis increased dramatically and external focalization gave way to first-person narration from the position of an all-embracing national 'we'. Internal differences receded into the background and the members of the nation were assumed to share the same experiences, feelings and perceptions. As one commentator argued, '[t]housands and thousands of Americans will have a personal connection to a victim', and 'we will imagine the feelings of the passengers on those planes, knowing they were flying to death' (Lewis, *New York Times*, 12 September, p. 27).

As is to be expected, the impression of internal unity was most pronounced in those columns that were organized around the central contrast between 'us' and 'them'. The following passage, taken from a piece ominously entitled 'World War III', is a good case in point:

> [...] this Third World War does not pit us against another superpower. It pits us – the world's only superpower and quintessential symbol of liberal, free-market, Western values – against all the super-empowered angry men and women out there. Many of these super-empowered angry people hail from failing states in the Muslim and third world. They do not share our values, they resent America's influence over their lives, politics and children, not to mention our support for Israel, and they often blame America for the failure of their societies to master modernity. (Friedman, *New York Times*, 13 September 2001, p. 27)

The excerpt is a textbook case of wartime coverage, replete with black-and-white contrasts and rooted in long-standing stereotypical representations of 'the West' and 'the third world'. The symbolic map of the world underpinning the excerpt is not only unmistakably ethnocentric, but also leaves no room for those Americans and Westerners who do not subscribe to free-market values, or have misgivings over America's support for Israel. The picture of the enemy is similarly problematic and one-sided: in a typically jingoistic manner, it bundles together 'all the super-empowered angry men and women out there' who 'do not share our values' and suggests that most of them are to be found in the 'failing Muslim states' and 'the third world'.

This is not to say that critical voices were entirely absent from the post-9/11 editorials, or that all columnists were equally willing to put their professional norms aside and blow the patriotic horn. In particular, the first few pieces, published on the first day following the attacks, were rather critical of the Secret Service and the first reactions of the government. One columnist suggested that the 'images of a government evacuating and scurrying for cover' were definitely not what the nation needed in a time of crisis (Keller, *New York Times*, 12 September 2001, p. 27), while another was dismayed at the fact that the well-resourced intelligence agencies were unable to prevent the attack (Safire, *New York Times*, 12 September 2001, p. 27). A few days after the attacks, some commentators began indicating the existence of disagreements among the political elites, and suggested that Bush may be tempted to act too quickly and aggressively, and that the more measured approach suggested by Secretary Powell may be more appropriate (e.g. Lewis, *New York Times*, 15 September 2001, p. 27). The latter example suggests that even in a context of heightened national unity and crisis, the *New York Times* did provide at least some room for internal disagreement among the otherwise united national audience.

However, we should point out that many of the criticisms voiced by *New York Times* columnists after 9/11 were far from being informed by a wish for more open political deliberation. Many authors were driven by a pronounced sense of patriotic duty and were criticizing the government and the security agencies for being too soft and slow in their reactions. Instead of urging the leaders to adopt a calmer, more measured approach, and develop a response strategy based on solid intelligence and involving minimal risks for civilians, these columnists were pushing in the exact opposite direction, and argued that security measures adopted so far were too limited and could not act as an effective deterrent for terrorists. The following passage is particularly remarkable in this respect:

> Five years of investigation and trials and appeals, as after the first World Trade Center attack, deter nobody. Lobbing a few missiles at possible training sites, as President Clinton hastily and ineffectually did, is a demeaning pretense.
>
> Lashing out on the basis of inadequate information is wrong, but in terror-wartime, waiting for absolute proof is dangerous. When we reasonably determine our attackers' bases and camps, we must pulverize them – minimizing but accepting the risk of collateral damage – and act overtly or covertly to destabilize terror's national hosts. The Pentagon's rebuilt fifth side should include a new

Department of Pre-emption. (Safire, *New York Times*, 12 September 2001, p. 27)

While the commentator was clearly critical of the authorities, his criticisms were not fuelled by a drive for fact-based, rational deliberation. From the perspective of a reader familiar with the controversies surrounding the Afghanistan and Iraq wars, the language of the passage is disconcertingly familiar: the rhetorical tropes and strategies it uses – collateral damage, pre-emption, inaccessibility of absolute proof – were to become commonplace in subsequent weeks and months, and assumed a central role in legitimating the US-led 'War on Terror'.

Another line of patriotic criticism involved criticizing internal disagreements among the political elites and appealing to politicians to put their differences aside and build a unified response to the crises. Any signs of partisan politics – accepted as normal in peacetime reporting – were now portrayed in negative terms and even described as acts of national treason, as in the following excerpt:

One hopes that the White House will distance itself from this disgraceful opportunism, that it will deliver the bipartisanship it originally promised. But initial indications are not good: the administration developed its request for emergency funding in consultation with Congressional Republicans – full stop. [...] I didn't want to mention this, but now is the time to draw the line. This tragedy will only be magnified if it is exploited for political gain. Politicians who wrap themselves in the flag while relentlessly pursuing their usual partisan agenda are not true patriots, and history will not forgive them. (Krugman, *New York Times*, 14 September 2001, p. 27)

As the author himself notes, he 'didn't want to mention this' – presumably to avoid disturbing the impression of national unity in such a critical moment – yet was finally compelled to react for the benefit of a greater good. These commentators did not need anyone to remind them of their patriotic duty in a time of crisis; they were in fact more resolutely patriotic than the political elites themselves.

Finally, as with the coverage of the Yugoslav conflict in the early 1990s, the *New York Times* opinion pieces after 9/11 were marked by a more pronounced dramatic structure, and a sense of narrative coherence spanning across several days. All pieces published in the first week after the attacks were dedicated to the same basic set of events and contributed to the same overarching narrative, all of which enhanced the narrative unity of *New York Times* reporting in this period. The columnists were often referring back to columns published and events reported over previous days, establishing a sense of narrative continuity and dramatic development over time. Looking at the content of all the sixteen columns together, one can discern a clear narrative unfolding over time, starting with the initial awe and chaos, coupled with a deep sense of a historic break and transformation, moving on to first interpretations and reactions, and finally concluding with a sense of closure and restoration of order.

The main contours of this narrative plot can be gleaned from the columns' titles. On 12 September, the commentators were focused on conveying the sense of shock and confusion ('A Grave Silence', 'America's Emergency Line') along with a perception of the events as momentous, historic and profoundly transformative ('A Different World', 'New Day of Infamy'). The exact meaning of the attacks and their extent were still unknown, and so were their consequences and the reactions they would provoke. On 13 September, as the details about the whereabouts of the government became available, the events of 9/11 were beginning to acquire a clearer shape ('Inside the Bunker') and the commentators began to sketch the first broad interpretations of the attacks and their perpetrators ('World War III'). On 14 September, the columnists sent a clear signal that it is time to start thinking about appropriate responses, and about the likely shape of the world and the country in the aftermath of the attacks ('Smoking or Non-Smoking', 'After the Horror'). From 15 September onwards, authors started returning to their normal routines, although they remained concerned exclusively with the attacks: they were critically assessing the proposed political and military responses (e.g. 'Beware of Unintended Results', 'The Modernity of Evil') and debated the likely causes of the attacks and lessons to be learned, focusing in particular on the dangers of anti-Arab and anti-Muslim prejudice and the need to protect civil liberties (e.g. 'Paying the Price', 'A Look in the Mirror').

Similarly as in the case of Yugoslav wartime news bulletins, the dramatic structure emerging from the *New York Times* columns in the first week resembles the tripartite structure of rites of passage. The first day after the attack is marked by a sense of shock at the disruption of the old order (separation), the second day is characterized by an outburst of jingoistic rhetoric, calls for revenge and a clear abandonment of professional standards (liminality), while the remainder of the week is spent debating the lessons to be learned, the key values and principles that are to inform the response and the likely shape of the new social order (transition from liminality to re-integration). The gradual return to normalcy on the pages of the *New York Times* coincided with similar shifts in TV programming: by the weekend of 15 September, after several days of commercial-free disaster coverage, normal TV schedules and commercial breaks were back in place, channelling the American nation back to the normal routines of media use and consumer practices (Spigel 2004). The 9/11 coverage in the major US news magazines followed a similar tripartite structure, though the ritual cycle took longer to complete: the expressions of anger and patriotism were particularly common in the second week following the attacks, and a turn to closure and re-integration followed only in the third and fourth week (Kitch and Hume 2008: 140–48). This transformation was apparent also in the visual images used in the media. For instance, the cover of *Time* magazine published following the attacks represents a striking visual equivalent of the discursive shift to national unity that we have traced in the *New York Times* coverage, symbolized in the figure of President Bush waving the US flag, surrounded by rescue workers and accompanied by the caption 'One Nation, Indivisible'. This was followed by a cover featuring the image of Bin Laden identified as 'a target' (1 October 2001) and by a cover including an image of a gas mask accompanied by the question 'How big is the threat?' and an appeal to the 'jittery nation' that 'needs to separate reality from facts' (8 October 2001).

The basic narrative structures and forms of national imagination characteristic of peace and crisis reporting in the *New York Times* resemble rather closely those identified in the Yugoslav TV bulletins from the early 1990s. In both cases, the onset of the conflict was accompanied by a shift in the media–politics relationship, a temporary suspension of professional codes of conduct and a change in the mode of address. The audience was no longer treated as an internally divided public, but as a homogeneous, united nation. Or, to use the terms introduced at the start of the chapter, a mediated imagery centred on the figure of the informed, rational, deliberate citizen was replaced with one organized around the figure of the warrior. We should of course avoid stretching the parallel too far – the media–politics relationship in the former Yugoslavia was certainly tighter than in the USA, and the forms of control employed by the governing elites became increasingly overt and harsh as the conflicts intensified. While the narrative conventions of crisis reporting and the limitations they imposed on public debate were very similar, they were motivated by different constellations of contextual factors, and different levels and forms of coercion. Nevertheless, the existence of these similarities should serve as a reminder that the wartime experiences of nationhood and mass communication in different parts of the world are not as far apart as we may sometimes want to believe.

We will revisit the differences between routine and crisis reporting at various points in the following two chapters, and examine how the aforementioned characteristics of wartime reporting relate to the patterns of gendered national imagination and the mediation of national memory.

6

The Gendered Order of Media Nations

Familial, kinship and gender relations figure prominently in national imagination. Whether explicitly based on ideas of ethnic lineage or not, the nation is often thought of as an extended family, and nationalist discourses around the globe are structured around notions of kinship relationships and gender roles. Expressions such as 'motherland', 'fatherland' and 'mother tongue', along with references to 'our boys' in representations of soldiers at the front, all attest to how deeply engrained the slippage between family and nation is in everyday discourse. Both historically and today, political leaders have been adept at exploiting this metaphoric link, using it to construct seemingly intimate connections between themselves, their families, and the wider population. The modern media, and broadcasting in particular, served as a key vehicle for these symbolic bonds, bringing voices and images of political elites into the intimacy of the nation's family homes, and thereby tying the public world of the national family to the private spaces of individual families.

Few examples can demonstrate this interweaving of nationhood, family, mass communication and politics better than the royal Christmas broadcast. Queen Elizabeth II's first televised Christmas message, broadcast by the BBC in 1957, provides a good case in point. Sitting at a desk in her library at Sandringham House, surrounded by photos of Prince Charles and Princess Anne, the Queen opened the broadcast with the following words:

> Happy Christmas. Twenty-five years ago my grandfather broadcast the first of these Christmas messages. Today is another landmark because television has made it possible for many of you to see me in your homes on Christmas Day. My own family often gather round to

119

watch television as they are this moment, and that is how I imagine you now. I very much hope that this new medium will make my Christmas message more personal and direct. It is inevitable that I should seem a rather remote figure to many of you. A successor to the Kings and Queens of history; someone whose face may be familiar in newspapers and films but who never really touches your personal lives. But now at least for a few minutes I welcome you to the peace of my own home. (Queen Elizabeth II 1957)

By drawing comparisons between her own family and the families of her viewers around Britain, the Queen was symbolically bridging the divide between public and private spheres, and also seeking to establish a symbolic link between herself and the nation, temporarily suspending the hierarchies of power and privilege that inevitably set her own family life miles apart from the everyday life and concerns of the average British family.

In forging the intimate links and welcoming her subjects' families to the peace of her own home, the British Queen was perhaps inadvertently doing what has since become seen as a hallmark of modern political communication. Long before political communication scholars started talking about the 'personalization' of politics, Queen Elizabeth sensed how important these intimate links were for the survival of the British Monarchy. Indeed, royal family affairs would continue to feed the public interest in the monarchy for decades to come, and provide a pretext for everyday talk about a range of issues, including morality, family life, parenting and divorce (Billig 1992). In a similar vein, the personal traits, family relationships, religious and sexual preferences of politicians have become an important element of political campaigns, and are often every bit as important in attracting potential voters as their political programmes (see e.g. Stanyer and Wring 2004). Even in France, where both politicians and journalists have long been keen to maintain the separation of private and public domains, the lines of demarcation are becoming increasingly blurred. For instance, the intense media scrutiny of Nicolas Sarkozy's family saga and his relationship with Carla Bruni, and Ségolène Royal's mediated construction as a 'working mother', have both been central to their political fortunes as representatives of the French nation (Kuhn 2008).

The prominence of politicians' private lives in political communication may well have increased in recent times, following changes set in motion by democratization, the rise of commercial media and other factors, but it follows a tendency that has marked national imagination since its inception. Although the 'national family' belongs to the public domain, its well-being is believed to be firmly anchored in the quality of private relationships and domestic life. As a consequence, the morality, family relationships and sexual mores of the nation as a whole – as well as those of politicians as the nation's representatives – regularly serve as a yardstick for measuring a nation's worth and its comparative advantages over other nations. For instance, the US comic strips such as *Peanuts* were instrumental in constructing an image of Cold War America as a superior nation that allows its children to be truly free. As Lynn Spiegel (2001: 227–62) points out, the world of Charlie Brown, Violet and Snoopy was a world revolving almost entirely around exploration and play, and parents were either entirely absent or featured as 'helpers' who not only tolerated but even supported kids' naughty adventures. The liberal, permissive approach to childrearing gradually turned into a symbol of a truly 'democratic' approach to childhood, superior to the allegedly authoritarian and punishment-driven childrearing practices of the Soviet Union, as well as the austerity-bound parenting traditions of post-1945 Western Europe (ibid.).

The contemporary Western obsession with veiled Muslim women, anxieties over falling birth rates and outbursts of moral panic surrounding the sexualization of young girls all form part of the same symbolic universe within which private practices become not only a matter of public concern, but also a key marker of collective identities and differences. It is important to note that such public anxieties often converge on women's bodies, appearance or behaviour. This is not a coincidence. Within traditional nationalist discourse, women are charged with the task of national reproduction and as such provide ideal vehicles for symbolic representations of national authenticity and distinctiveness. As we will see later on, women's bodies retain this powerful symbolic function even in nations characterized by a high level of gender equality. This is why, for instance, news coverage of immigration and the Middle East in the Western media so often features images of anonymous veiled women, who are typically associated with the terrorist threat, patriarchal oppression, irrationality and exoticism (Roushanzamir 2004; Duits and Van Zoonen 2006). Presented in this way, the veiled woman serves as a powerful marker of difference between the supposedly civilized and liberal nations of the West, capable of providing 'their' women with the freedom to wear what they like, and the allegedly oppressive, patriarchal Muslim nations, intent on forcing their women to hide their bodies from public scrutiny. Even the alternative, more tolerant attitudes to female veiling that we come across in public debates can be anchored in national imagination. For instance, a recent survey of public attitudes in Australia revealed a high level of public support for hijab, anchored in normative beliefs about Australia as an inherently liberal and democratic nation (Dunn 2009).

The following sections discuss the intertwining of nationalist, familial and gendered discourses in the modern media in more detail. I start with a brief overview of general approaches to gender in nationalism theory, and then build on arguments developed in preceding chapters to examine how the gendered orders of nationhood vary depending on the prevailing vision of modernity and the corresponding configurations of media, politics, economy and culture in different national contexts. The final section of the chapter examines how the mediation of gendered forms of nationhood changes in the context of war.

The Gendered Order of Nationhood, Multiple Modernities and Media Nations

Given the ubiquity of the familial, gendered imagery in national imagination, it is surprising how little both the classic literature on nations and nationalism as well as the early writings on gender had to say on the matter. As Nira Yuval-Davis (1997) pointed out in her landmark study on the topic, the writings of authors such as Ernest Gellner, Benedict Anderson and Eric Hobsbawm are devoid of any sustained discussion of the gendered nature of nations and nationalist movements. Their accounts of the rise and reproduction of nations and nationalism focus primarily on the public – and predominantly male – domain, thereby rendering the contributions of women and family life all but invisible. Similarly, the early studies of gender were only obliquely aware of the fact that the gendered division of social life into private and public domains became central to the organization of power relationships within and between nations.

These omissions are in part due to the perception of the nation as a fraternal, inclusive community that was historically constituted to overcome the traditional social, geographic and cultural divisions. According to Benedict Anderson, this fraternity or 'horizontal comradeship' is at the centre of national imagination, and persists in spite of the actual inequality and mistreatment of some of the nation's members (Anderson 1991: 7). This definition adequately captures the tendency of nationalist discourse to put unity over difference, and conceal internal inequality and exploitation. Yet at the same time, it also overlooks the other, equally powerful part of national imagination, which focuses on a systematic demarcation between full citizens – who bear full rights and responsibilities – and part-citizens – who are believed to require protection, education or control. The latter typically include children and the elderly, but often also ethnic minority members, women, servants or the working classes. These 'bonds of dependence' as Claudio Lomnitz (2001) calls them, are equally central to modern national imagery as the bonds of fraternity. It is precisely the sense of obligation derived from such bonds of dependence that often drives individuals to commit sacrifices in the name of their nation, whether by enlisting in the army, taking on voluntary work, or accepting austere living conditions. While framed as acts performed for the greater good of the nation, these sacrifices are often motivated by concerns over the well-being of one's dependants: 'our children', 'our women', 'the sick and wounded'. Within national imagination, the ideology of fraternity is thus intimately bound with hierarchical relations of power, obligation and dependence (ibid.).

This interlocking of fraternity with hierarchy constitutes the backbone of the gendered order of modern nations. Gender and family relations are, at their core, relations of responsibility and dependence, constituted around a differential distribution of rights and duties. When articulated with national imagination, these gendered rights and duties come to be seen as something individuals have to comply with not only for the benefit of their families, but also for the greater good of their nations. Of course, the gendered division of labour within nations inevitably introduces hierarchical relations and often forces individuals into roles they may not want to accept. Nonetheless, we should keep in mind that the gendered order of nations – however unjust – also allows individuals, regardless of their sex, to be active and valued members of their nation, and provides them not only with duties, but also with entitlements. It is this particular combination of obligations and entitlements that helps explain the enduring appeal of the gendered order of nationhood among both men and women, regardless of the inequality and exploitation it engenders.

Let us take as an example the nationalist appropriation of the traditional patriarchal order. On the one hand, this order restricts the lives of women to a rather limited set of roles tied to the private domain: caring mothers, loving wives, dutiful daughters and sisters. By enacting these roles over the course of their lives, women are expected to reproduce the nation both biologically and culturally: give birth to a new generation of the nation's children and raise them as reliable members of the national community, acquainted with national values, rituals and myths (Yuval-Davis 1997; Banerjee 2003). Yet, while creating a set of restrictions and demands, the traditional gendered order also allows women to become cherished members of the national community and gives them leverage to claim certain rights and benefits from the nation and the state: physical protection, political representation and economic well-being, both for themselves and for their children. Filtered through the discourse of nationalism, these rights and benefits translate directly into duties and tasks that are expected to be fulfilled by the nation's men. Although highly restrictive, this patriarchal 'division of labour' within the nation is based on reciprocal relations rather than outright exploitation. It is this reciprocity that helps explain why so many women are willing to bang on the nationalist drum despite the subordinated position nationalist movements push them into.

How, if at all, is this gendered distribution of rights and obligations operating within contemporary nations, many of which have invested considerable efforts into countering gender inequity? Are gendered orders of nationhood in decline? Hardly so. The inclusion of women's rights among universal human rights – so central to the advancement of gender equality on a global scale today – can easily obscure the fact that women's emancipation was and continues to be fought for also from anti-universalist, nationalist positions. Today, feminists in the West tend to be resolutely anti-nationalists, yet historically, the struggle for women's rights in this part of the world was closely intertwined with nationalist movements and revolutionary struggles. *The Declaration of the Rights of Woman*, written in 1791 by the French playwright and political activist Olympe de Gouges, was unmistakably shaped by the nationalist discourse of its time. De Gouges defined the nation as 'a union of woman and man', and presented women's political participation as a necessary step in eradicating 'public misfortunes' and 'the corruption of governments' (de Gouges [1791] 1980: 89–90). Women's equality was thus seen not only as a matter of justice, but also as a necessary step in ensuring the nation's well-being. Feminists beyond the West used similar strategies, and presented women's rights as an integral element of anti-colonial nationalist agendas (Jayawardena 1986; West 1997).

Obviously, not all of nationalist movements are equally willing to include women's liberation among their goals. The preferred forms of women's participation in the life of the nation vary significantly from case to case: while some promote women's domestication, others explicitly foster their inclusion in the labour force and politics (Walby 2006). In the colonial context, feminism often came to be perceived as an alien force associated with Western imperialism; nationalist leaders felt compelled to protect female bodies from its corrupting influence, and required women to revert back to their traditional roles. A good illustration of this is the forced veiling of women in post-revolutionary Iran (Yuval-Davis 2001: 134). Communist liberation movements, on the other hand, believed women's unpaid labour at home to be an integral part of capitalist exploitation and treated women's political, civil and economic rights as an important part of their national revolutionary agendas (Goldman 1993). The success of feminist movements beyond the West often depended precisely on the extent to which the struggle for women's emancipation was conceived as an indigenous nation-building project rather than as a part of changes enforced by Western colonizers, and feminist activists were well aware of that.

This is not to say that feminists in the former colonies became nationalists simply out of pure calculation. Historically, the struggle for women's liberation outside of the West was frequently interwoven with imperial domination, and even served as a pretext for the continued presence of colonial administration. Katherine Mayo's *Mother India* (1927) provides a typical example of such colonial feminist discourse: for Mayo, the unequal treatment of the sexes is so deeply rooted in established Indian traditions that Indian women have no hope of achieving equality without the benevolent supervision of enlightened British colonizers. Due to this mixture of feminist criticism and imperial arrogance the book created serious problems for local feminists who agreed with Mayo's criticisms of gender relations in India yet opposed her imperial thinking (Hasian and Bialowas 2009). In this context, pushing for women's emancipation within the context of national liberation was thus not simply a strategic choice, but also a logical alternative to Western domination.

The divergent gender regimes promoted by different nationalist projects and underpinned by competing modernizing visions were inevitably reflected also in mediated public discourses. Women's appearance and behaviour were often at the centre of public struggles over definitions of modernity, and female bodies regularly featured in the media as symbols of national authenticity and the nation's ability to cope with the challenges of modernization, Westernization and globalization. The divergent nationalist projects also created different opportunity structures for men and women within the media industries, and influenced the spatial and temporal organization of media use in private and public realms. This diversity can be elucidated by examining the links between the mediation of nationhood and the gendered structures of mass communication in three distinct contexts: socialist Central and Eastern Europe, post-colonial India and post-9/11 USA.

Mediating Socialist Womanhood: Women's Emancipation and the Double Burden

On the face of it, state socialism brought the fulfilment of many feminist dreams. Women's emancipation was an important goal of communist revolutionary projects, and socialist constitutions all guaranteed women and men equal rights in all social spheres, including the economy, politics and culture (Łobodzińska 1995). Upon seizing power, communist authorities granted women a range of rights – including the right to abortion, paid maternity leave, state-funded childcare facilities and economic independence – that helped boost female participation in the labour force. Women's employment in the socialist media industries increased accordingly. A survey of the Hungarian film industry, for instance, showed that the numbers of women involved in behind-the-screen positions such as script writer, storyline editor and director were rising throughout the socialist period, reaching a peak in the late 1980s and the early 1990s before decreasing again in the decades after the fall of socialism (Hock 2010). In some parts of the media industry, socialist family and employment policies left a lasting legacy that continues to be felt in the post-socialist period. In the mid-1990s, the proportion of women in the news media industry was still significantly higher in Central and Eastern Europe than in Western and Southern Europe (cf. Gallagher 1995).

Given the emphasis on women's employment in socialist states, it is not a surprise that the figure of the working woman featured prominently across a range of media forms and genres. Communist propaganda posters often included images of working women in industrial and professional environments or in conventionally masculine roles, for instance as soldiers and political activists (e.g. Evans 1999; Bonnell 1997: 64–135). Particularly when comparing the successes of their socialist homeland to the achievements of the capitalist West, communist leaders were keen on pointing to evidence of women's equality. For instance, an East German journal aimed at Western readers boasted about the number of female judges in the German Democratic Republic (Herzog 2008: 85). Yugoslav newspapers published in the vicinity of the Italo-Yugoslav border were also proudly describing the benefits communism brought to local women, and sometimes explicitly contrasted the position of women in Yugoslavia to that in Italy. According to one article, the communist revolution 'swept away the shameful stains of the inequality of women and the outdated beliefs about the worthlessness of women, their subordination to men, and their inability to contribute to social, political, and economic life' (*Primorske novice*, 3 June 1954).

Some of the socialist societies also perceived themselves as having more relaxed and 'natural' attitudes towards human sexuality. The authors of a study on sexuality and love among East German youth, published in 1984, proudly argued that the improvements in women's equality in the GDR have boosted women's self-confidence and made them more sexually demanding and creative (Herzog 2008: 86–77). At first sight, the emphasis on sexual enjoyment may seem to be at odds with the legal prohibition of pornography in socialist states. Yet as Biljana Žikić (2010) points out in her study of pornography and nudity in Yugoslavia, the legal definition of pornography was rather unclear, and left substantial room for manoeuvre. As long as the images of naked bodies could be presented as 'artistic' and 'aesthetically pleasing' rather than 'vulgar', they could easily pass under the radar. In East Germany, nude photographs were also rather common, and framed in similarly positive terms – as 'artistic', 'natural' and 'clean', and as such entirely distinct from pornography (McLelland 2009).

While nude images were far from being universally approved, and often triggered concerns over public morality, a sufficient proportion of the socialist establishment was willing to concede that they might have educational and liberating potential. As one Yugoslav commentator argued in the mid-1970s, images of naked women and other elements of 'trash' culture contributed to 'a particular kind of demystification' and presented a challenge to 'traditional taboos surrounding human sexuality' (quoted in Senjković 2008: 68–69). The interpretation of nudity as progressive provided a handy tool for legitimizing the publication of soft pornography. For instance, the editors and journalists of *Start*, a popular Yugoslav magazine known for its provocative political commentaries, insisted that their photographs of naked women were aesthetically pleasing, educational, and sexually liberating, and presented a challenge to traditional bourgeois morality and the power of the Church (Žikić 2010). In this manner, soft pornography could be seen as a constitutive feature of socialist nationhood, and presented as yet another proof of socialist superiority vis-à-vis its Western neighbours.

Of course, we should beware of accepting these self-congratulatory images of socialist attitudes to gender and sexuality at face value. From the perspective of state socialism, women's emancipation was neither seen as an end in its own right, nor as a matter of free choice. Rather, support for women's equality was firmly embedded in the communist vision of modernity and progress, according to which women's liberation could be achieved only through communist revolution. The emancipation of women, as the German socialist Clara Zetkin argued in 1889, formed an integral part of the liberation of the whole of humanity, and 'will take place only with the emancipation of labour from capital' (quoted in Boxer 2007: 131). The subordination of women's emancipation to the liberation of the working classes unavoidably limited the extent and shape of feminist politics within state socialism. Communist policies not only encouraged but *demanded* women's participation in the workforce and rarely questioned the unequal distribution of labour in the private sphere, thus leaving women with the 'double burden' of both unpaid domestic work and full-time paid work outside the home (Bucur 2008). Ultimately, socialist family policies were aimed primarily at reducing the potential tensions between family and work duties, and abstained from challenging the assumption that childrearing and domestic work were, at their core, a woman's job.

In spite of the alleged equality of men and women, state socialism thus continued to perpetuate fundamentally gendered perceptions of human relations and constructed women as inferior to men. This inferior position stemmed from the belief that biological differences between men and women, and in particular women's role in human reproduction, inevitably made women weaker, more emotional and small-minded (Evans 1999: 64). Due to their deeply engrained attachment to children, women were also deemed to be less devoted to the communist cause and less reliable as workers (Fodor 2002). In line with these assumptions, women were designated as 'incomplete' socialist citizens who needed special help from the authorities to liberate themselves from the bonds of nature and tradition. Even in cases where the root cause of women's inequality was believed to lie in backward attitudes of *both* women and men – as for instance in an East German campaign aimed at improving the proportion of female workers in high-skill jobs – only women were singled out as those who needed special help in order to 'develop' into fully fledged 'socialist female personalities' (Eghigian 2008: 51). Despite the proclaimed equality of sexes, it was therefore women rather than men who were seen as primary obstacles to the advancement of socialist modernity.

Although patchy and often anecdotal, available data on media preferences and use in socialist countries reveal compatible patterns. A study of television viewers in the 1960s Soviet Union demonstrated that television viewing was, above all, a male activity, with men spending significantly more time in front of television sets than women (Roth-Ey 2007: 297). Television viewing also seemed to provoke gendered tensions over the choice of programmes, a trend familiar from studies of television audiences in Western Europe (Morley 1986; Gray 1992). This becomes apparent in an illustrated cartoon published in a popular Soviet magazine in 1960, featuring a husband and a wife happily watching different television programmes after having cut their television set in half (Roth-Ey 2007: 298). A report documenting the position of women in socialist Hungary, written for the attention of Politburo members, mentioned women who described how their husband would 'read them out from the newspaper or a book and he would explain the stories too, as she was ironing or mending clothes' (quoted in Fodor 2002: 253). This provides a telling image of the gendered structures of media consumption in socialist societies, with the husband featuring as a figure of authority 'helping' his wife to keep up to date with the wider world and thus alleviating the detrimental effects of her 'natural' responsibilities, namely domestic chores.

Public discourses surrounding women's sexuality and nude photography in Tito's Yugoslavia – although more liberal than in many other socialist states – were underpinned by similar assumptions about gender relations. Public debates prompted by the publication of nude photographs of a home-grown pop singer in the aforementioned magazine *Start* in 1979 provide a telling example. By that time, reproductions of nude photos of foreign models were a fairly regular feature of Yugoslav popular culture and, although controversial, never provoked a public outrage comparable to the one caused by naked photos of a domestic celebrity. When defending their decision to publish the photos, the editors of *Start* pointed to this apparent hypocrisy, noting that while images of foreign nudes were tolerated, 'our' women posing naked were immediately turned into national symbols, their naked bottoms and bare breasts invested with national values (Žikić 2010). Yet while attempting to 'liberate' the bodies of Yugoslav women from the oppressive embrace of Yugoslav puritanism, *Start*'s commentators were simultaneously subjecting them to a competing, libertarian version of Yugoslavism. By posing naked, they argued, the woman was taking control over her sexuality, released her hidden energies, and challenged traditional patriarchal prejudices (ibid.). To put it differently, *Start*'s editors and journalists countered mainstream socialist morality by turning the naked female body from a menacing sign of the nation's moral decay into as a symbol of its progressiveness.

Regardless of official proclamations in favour of women's equality, the gendered structures of nationhood – and, with those, the gendered patterns of media production, representation and consumption – were clearly present under socialism. There is evidence to suggest that, in some ways, the gendered division of labour was in fact growing stronger with time, and that the early emphasis on women's inclusion in the labour market gave way to a renewed emphasis on women's duties in the private sphere. From the 1970s, a number of socialist states introduced pro-natalist policies and set up restrictions on abortion in response to declining fertility rates (e.g. Legge and Alford 1986). Although these policies did not manage to achieve their stated aims, they did encourage a further feminization of childrearing and household work.

This reconfiguration of gender roles was reflected in media representations at the time. A notable embodiment of new gender ideals in post-1968 Czechoslovakia can be found in the middle-aged shop assistant Anna Holubová, the lead character in the hugely popular television series *The Woman behind the Counter* (1977). Anna was a recent divorcee who lived with her children in Prague and had recently taken up a new job at the local supermarket. Each of the twelve episodes of the series tells the story of a month in Anna's life and focuses on her efforts to cope with the manifold demands of her children, household chores and her new workplace. Through the series, Anna emerges as a true Czechoslovak 'superwoman', who carries her 'double burden' of work and family duties with confidence and pride and acts as a caring mother not only for her children but also for her supermarket collective – and through that, symbolically, for the Czechoslovak socialist nation as a whole (Bren 2010: 159–76).

This re-inscription of socialist womanhood into the domestic sphere was happening at a time when traditional forms of socialist masculinity were undergoing a severe crisis. With the decline of heavy industry and the coming of age of the post-war generations, the old anchors of socialist masculinity, such as physical strength, revolutionary zeal and military might, were declining in significance. At the same time, political engagement – another realm in which traditional socialist masculinity could be performed and confirmed – was being discouraged. In the early 1970s, following the destabilizing effects of events such as the Prague Spring and Croatian Maspok, communist authorities in several states purged their ranks of liberally minded politicians and promoted a retreat from political activity into the family realm. Devoid of their traditional roles, men appeared increasingly lost and insignificant, especially in comparison with their confident, multitasking wives. In *The Woman behind the Counter*, for instance, men were still in positions of power, yet appeared decidedly helpless, incapable of taking care of themselves and reliant on women's care and support (Machek 2010). A Brezhnev-era TV series in the Soviet Union traced a similar crisis of socialist masculinity, with male characters being portrayed as increasingly lost and displaced (Prokhorova 2006).

The sad figures of socialist men appearing in the illustrated cartoons in the Hungarian satirical magazine *Ludas Matyi* follow similar representational trends (cf. Magó-Maghiar 2010). These unattractive male characters are either overweight or unappealingly emaciated, and worlds apart from the virile, muscular communist workers known from the propaganda posters of the late 1940s and the 1950s. Yet, unlike the similarly weak, helpless men in the mainstream *The Woman behind the*

Counter, who appear alongside the super-powerful communist worker-mothers, they feature in the company of a rather different set of female figures: the unattractive, bossy, old housewife on the one hand, and the fatally attractive and sexually provocative young women on the other (ibid.). Although motivated by a different set of social and political circumstances, this double-headed female threat reproduces the typical sexist division of women into asexual, sanitized wives and mothers, and the sexually appealing yet morally disgraced young sex symbols known from Western media culture. As Magó-Maghiar (ibid.) argues, the Hungarian state's acceptance of such mildly pornographic satirical imagery formed part of the socialist sexual contract, through which the regime sought to buy the patience of its male citizens by tolerating their exploitation of women's bodies. Arguably, the relatively tolerant attitudes toward soft pornography among communist authorities in this period could be interpreted as an attempt to maintain popular support at a time when the old visions of socialist nationhood and modernity were losing their appeal.

The Mediation of Indian Womanhood: Between Modernity and Authenticity

It is interesting to compare the mediation of gendered forms of nationhood in the context of socialist Eastern Europe to that of postcolonial India. At first sight, the positioning of women within Indian nationalist discourses has little in common with the communist project of women's liberation. Indian nationalists viewed women's liberation with suspicion, seeing it as an alien and potentially corrupting process inseparable from colonial domination. Yet, instead of countering modernization as a whole, Indian nationalists conceived of modernization and women's liberation as something that can and should be made compatible with Hindu traditions. As Prathra Chatterjee (1990) argued, this was achieved by splitting the cultural domains of Indianness into two spheres: the material and the spiritual, the outer and the inner. To overcome India's backwardness, argued the nationalists, the material domain of Indian culture – its science, technology, political and economic organization – had to be opened up to Western influence, and reformed following Western examples. At the same time, the spiritual core had to be protected from outside influence, not only because its preservation was a precondition of national distinctiveness, but also because Indian spirituality was believed to be far superior to its Western equivalent.

These two domains and the associated tasks of modernization and preservation of spiritual tradition provided the basis for the gendered division of labour within the Indian nation. Being associated with familial and domestic spaces and with national reproduction, Indian women were expected to secure the survival of the distinctive spiritual essence of Indian national culture (Mankekar 1999: 108). In contrast, Indian men were charged with the task of charting the path of Indian material modernization by learning from the West. This does not mean that an Indian woman's life left no scope for public engagement, education, or acquisition of modern techniques adopted from the West. Within Indian nationalist discourse, women were often seen as active contributors to the national project, and they participated eagerly in India's struggle for independence (Jayawardena 1986: 99–107). Some nationalist leaders, including Gandhi, even believed that a woman's service to the nation could occasionally take precedence over her service to the family, and that a woman had the right to disobey her husband if he did not support her patriotic efforts (Mankekar 1999: 109). Yet, by and large, women's political participation was believed to be secondary to their roles as mothers and wives, and women were typically commended for bringing a non-violent and thus 'feminine' quality to campaigns and protests (Jayawardena 1986: 99–100).

A similar combination of progressive and conservative ideas can be detected in nationalist views on women's education. On the one hand, education was of paramount importance to the formation of the new, postcolonial Indian woman, and was believed to constitute one of the key preconditions for successful national development. It was seen as a means of cultural refinement that would enable modern Indian women to achieve cultural superiority both over the older generations of Indian women, and over Western women to whom formal learning was merely a means of acquiring material rather than spiritual skills (Chatterjee 1990: 246). On the other hand, the main goal of education was to equip the new Indian woman for her primary national tasks, namely her domestic responsibilities. Only an educated woman – literate, knowledgeable, cultured, and versed in modern techniques of childrearing and housekeeping – could provide a fitting companion for her equally well-educated husband and an adequate spiritual and moral guide for her children. In other words, education was an instrument of building a good, modern Indian wife and mother (Jayawardena 1986: 87).

The views on women's education and public participation outlined above share the characteristic perception of Indian womanhood that merges the traditional and the modern, the spiritual and the material. While keeping up with modernization, the model Indian woman has to be able to walk the thin line separating modernity from tradition, the material from the spiritual, making sure that the modern skills and knowledge are used only in so far as they can be reconciled with the preservation of India's spiritual core. This peculiar mixture of modernization and spiritual preservation is reflected in the particular virtues, skills and behaviour that modernization was expected to instil in a model Indian woman – namely, orderliness, cleanliness, literacy skills, a preference for traditional dress codes and food, as well as religiosity (Chatterjee 1990: 246–48). These postcolonial ideals of Indian femininity were interwoven with those of Indian masculinity. The aggressive, muscular and virile Indian male body functioned as a symbolic marker of Indian independence and can be interpreted as a reaction to colonial images of Bengali men as effeminate (Sinha 1995). An integral part of this gendered nationalist rejection of colonial imagery was also the performance of authority over women and the insistence on the family and household as the primary domains of Indian women (Derné 2000). This construction of masculinity remained central to Indian and in particular Hindu nationalism in the latter part of the twentieth century, with the key difference being that the colonial enemy of the colonial and early-postcolonial period was replaced by the Muslim enemy (Banerjee 2003).

Modern means of mass communication played an important role in negotiating the ideals of Indian femininity and masculinity we have just described. Television was long seen as a particularly effective means of national development, and as a universal remedy for India's backwardness, including the alleged ignorance and backwardness of its women. Indeed, it was precisely the perception of television as a tool of modernization and social education that helped legitimize state investment in the introduction and expansion of this new communication technology (Chatterji 1991: 51–53). Already in the early years of Indian television, some programmes were addressed specifically at Indian women, and aimed at mobilizing them for modern nation-building. One such pro-development television series, entitled *Nari tu Narayani* (Women are Powerful, 1983–44), was designed to improve the status of women by promoting their economic independence (Singhal and Rogers 1988: 123, n.5). Other programmes from this period were aimed at educating women about proper standards of modern life, including hygiene and the importance of using clean water (Mankekar 1999: 58), thus clearly signalling the link between women's education and their domestic duties.

The first Indian soap opera, *Hum Log* (We the People, 1984–85), which followed the fortunes of an Indian lower-middle-class family, is a particularly telling case of the mediated construction of modern Indian womanhood in this period. The plot of the series often revolved around issues of women's equality and gender relations, presenting them as examples of typical cultural tensions that the encounter between traditional codes and modern ways of life was creating in the everyday lives of Indian families (Kumar 2006: 32–33). Yet, while the series featured several female characters eager to acquire a good education and succeed in their professional careers, and displayed the misery caused by the tradition of dowry, women's equality remained circumscribed by the demands of the family and parental authority. One of the central female characters, for instance, disregards the advice of her parents, leaves for Bombay to pursue a career in Hindi films and ends up being sexually exploited, while another struggles with reconciling her political commitments with the demands of her husband (Mankekar 1999: 110–17).

Televisual portrayals of womanhood such as the one encountered in *Hum Log* also served as key points of reference in everyday negotiations of women's professional and private choices. The reactions provoked by the series *Yugantar* (1990) are a good example. The plot was set in nineteenth-century India and promoted the idea of women's education as a means of national modernization as well as an instrument allowing Indian families to acquire middle-class respectability (ibid.: 130–31). However, while featuring women's education in a positive light, the series prompted contrasting responses among audiences, and often aroused fears over the potential threat education could represent for women's traditional roles. While some respondents doubted the ability of educated, working women to perform their duties as good wives and mothers, others believed that the burden of tradition weighed too heavily on women's lives and acted as a break on modernization (ibid.: 131–37).

Films produced in this period promoted very similar notions of modern Indian womanhood. Many popular Bollywood films from the 1980s celebrated modest Indian heroines, and contrasted them with the overly liberal, immodest, and excessively 'Westernized' anti-heroines. For instance, the plot of *Maine Pyar Kiya* (I Fell in Love, 1989), one of the greatest Bollywood hits at the time, revolves around Suman, a religious, modest and traditionally dressed village girl who is highly respectful of her father, and stands in stark contrast to the anti-heroine, who smokes, wears a short haircut, mini-skirts and other 'Western' clothes, and is sexually promiscuous (Derné 2000). The central male character Prem also smokes, wears 'Western' clothes and shares many similarities with the female anti-heroine, yet is portrayed in a positive light and ends up marrying the modest, traditionally dressed village girl.

The gendered Indianness portrayed in adverts for consumer products from the 1970s and the 1980s followed analogous patterns. In particular, adverts for modern home appliances and gadgets, such as pressure cookers and TV sets, often featured traditionally dressed Indian women and were set within domestic environments. An advert for the J.K. TV set from the mid-1970s showed Farzana Habib, winner of the Miss India beauty pageant that year, crouching next to a television set in a luxurious dress, wearing large, traditionally shaped earrings, and with her hair neatly tied up in a bun (Kumar 2006: 58–59). The caption underneath the picture referred to the TV set as 'India's largest-selling TV' and lured the prospective customer by referring to its 'elegant appearance' and 'flawless performance', thus establishing a symbolic link between the modern appliance and Indian female beauty. The television advert for the laundry detergent Surf from the mid-1980s provides another example. It features the model housewife Lalitaji, played by the actress Kavita Choudry, expertly performing her household chores while explaining why Surf is her preferred choice among detergents. Although clearly excelling at domestic work and expertly assessing the pros and cons of detergents, Lalitaji is wearing a sparkling white sari, wears her hair tied up in a bun, and has a *tikka* on her forehead (Mankekar 1999: 92). Lalitaji thus embodies all the virtues of a model (middle-class) Indian woman of her time, merging the markers of tradition and modernity, spirituality and modern techniques.

The arrival of satellite television and the influx of global consumer culture in the 1990s brought some important shifts to the construction of Indian womanhood. While the images of the domesticated, goddess-like mother and wife continued to circulate, they were increasingly challenged by a very different female figure, one that was assertive, mostly urban and determined to pursue her sexual pleasures. This new Indian woman was rising to prominence across a range of media and cultural genres, including TV series, music videos, adverts and magazines. For instance, while television series from the 1980s championed the figures of modest, dutiful, asexual wives and mothers, and portrayed any sexually explicit behaviour in negative tones, the soap operas of the 1990s, often broadcast on commercial satellite channels, showed assertive female heroines who were actively pursuing their erotic desires and engaged in premarital or extramarital sexual affairs (Mankekar 2004). The new, glossy women's magazines of the 1990s, modelled on *Cosmopolitan*, *Belle Claire* and other globally distributed magazines, were marked by similar trends. For example, the magazine *Femina*, popular among middle- and upper-class women in urban India, associated Indian womanhood with the latest fashions and luxury beauty products, as well as with sensuality and pleasure, independence and self-confidence (Thapan 2004).

Yet, in spite of her newly found independence and sexuality, the new Indian woman continued to be embedded in authentic Indian values. In TV series, the newly found female sexuality remained bounded by women's family obligations and concerns over the loss of authenticity (Mankekar 2004), while magazines featured images of women who were assertive and markedly sensual or even provocative, yet also unmistakably feminine in an 'Indian' way, draped in saris and wearing traditional jewellery (Thapan 2004). Audiences were also not always equally willing to embrace the new Indian woman they saw portrayed in the media. Some viewers praised the media for providing positive role models for independent, educated and professional women, but others were concerned about the proliferation of sexually explicit images and the impact they might have on their children (Scrase 2002: 333–35). Finally, these conflicting ideals of Indian femininity also shape the lives of women working in India's thriving information and communication industry. As an ethnographic study conducted among software engineers in Mumbai and Bangalore suggests, young women in professional media jobs feel compelled to construct a respectable middle-class Indian femininity, emphasizing that despite their jobs, their families come first (Radhakrishnan 2009).

On the whole, then, the Indian woman of the late twentieth and the early twenty-first centuries continues to embody – and resolve – the characteristic tensions created by the conflicting demands of national distinctiveness and global competitiveness, family life and professional career, and she does so in ways that are not fundamentally dissimilar from those characteristic of the early postcolonial decades. This new woman, argues Rupal Oza (2006), became a symbol of the new, liberalized and globalized India: open to foreign influences and global flows, able to compete on a global scale, yet at the same time firmly anchored in Indian traditions and spirituality. As with Western colonialism and modernity beforehand, transnational television, global culture and multinational corporations are perceived as polluting forces endangering the purity of Indian culture, and, yet again, women are turned into symbolic emblems that embody and resolve the tensions between the global and the local, modernity and national tradition.

Women's Liberation, Mediated Nationhood and War

Although the previous sections focused on the mediation of gendered orders of nationhood beyond the West, this is not meant to imply that the most economically advanced liberal democracies are devoid of the inter-twining of gender equality and nationalist discourses. As mentioned in the introduction, nationalist discourse continues to constitute the back-bone of contemporary public debates over women's position in these societies, yet it is often mobilized in ways that appear, at least superfi-cially, congruent with the ideals of gender equality. Similarly to social-ist nationalist discourses, nationalist imagination in the advanced liberal economies of the West often uses images of strong, independent, profes-sionally established or sexually liberated women as badges of the nation's progressiveness.

Few media images can illustrate this better than the American comic book heroine Wonder Woman. There is little doubt that this female superhero, first created in the 1940s, is a symbol of the American nation. In all her diverse incarnations, Wonder Woman appears in costumes covered in eagles, stars and stripes in combinations of blue, red and white – all familiar symbols of the USA. She also consistently embod-ies some of the key virtues of the American nation, in particular inde-pendence, freedom, strength and belief in individual achievement. These virtues are clearly at odds with traditional feminine qualities character-istic of patriarchal nationalist imagery, and Wonder Woman was often explicitly used as a role model aimed at instilling assertiveness and a desire for independence and achievement among young American girls and women. Yet, as Mitra Emad (2006) points out, Wonder Woman never lost all of her womanly attributes; her 'feminine' skills of decep-tion and disguise were often instrumental in her success and, especially since the 1980s, her body – although always muscular – was becoming increasingly sexualized and eroticized.

This interweaving of 'masculine' and 'feminine' traits, and especially the simultaneous emphasis on strength and sexuality, is also clearly apparent in the most recent reincarnations of Wonder Woman. The close link between these gendered representations and contemporary American nationalism comes most vividly to the fore in those contem-porary images that depict the heroine in the context of allegedly 'back-ward others'. For instance, in the graphic novel entitled *Wonder Woman: Spirit of Truth* (2001), Wonder Woman ends up fighting the enemies of the people in the 'desert nations', populated by dark-skinned men and women covered in chadors (ibid: 977). Using her 'womanly' powers, she manages to sneak into the country by disguising herself as a Muslim woman. Upon arrival, however, she takes off her disguise and reveals her muscular, sexually appealing body in front of the visibly shaken local residents, among whom are many women draped in dark chadors (Figure 6.1). The contrast between the sexually liberated American

Figure 6.1 Wonder Woman faces the members of the oppressed 'desert nation'. From: Ross and Dini 2001. WONDER WOMAN™ and © DC Comics. All Rights Reserved

woman-nation and the sexually repressed Islamic women-nations could not be clearer. Yet, at the same time, the two contrasting representations of femininity are rooted in similar motivations – namely, in the drive to regulate women's behaviour, and above all their sexuality, in the name of national interest.

The onset of an unexpected crisis, armed conflict or natural catastrophe provides a particularly powerful impetus for the resurgence of gendered forms of nationalism. Regardless of the social context and the level of gender equity, the presence of a collective threat always prompts a reversal to the traditional, patriarchal gender order. The figure of the warrior is typically associated with strength, virility and, above all, masculinity, and the behaviour characteristic of soldiers – killing, torturing and destroying – are clearly at odds with the archetypal 'feminine' qualities emphasized in the patriarchal gendered order (Prividera and Howard 2006: 29–30). War discourse pushes women into the traditional, supportive roles of mothers and wives, and neglects and obstructs the contribution of women to the war effort. While it is true that women tend to be, on average, less enthusiastic supporters of nationalist militarism (cf. Walby 2006: 123), we should keep in mind that the propensity of women for peace and compassion is in part a consequence of specific opportunity structures rather than any inherent female inclinations. For instance, the tendency of women reporters to focus on the impact of war on everyday lives and for male reporters to write about high politics and dramatic battles is tied to differences in practical constraints that influence journalistic work. Lacking status in the battlefield, women have limited access to the front lines and senior political and military figures involved in decision making, and, as a consequence, often have little choice but to concentrate on everyday experiences of the general population (cf. Deacon 2008: 78–80).

The resurgence of patriarchal models of gender relations in the USA media following the attacks on the World Trade Center and the Pentagon in 2001 is a good example of these trends. The events of 9/11 fuelled fears about the consequences of America's 'feminization' and calls for the return of truly 'manly' men, able to defend American women and children in the face of the terrorist threat. In the days following the attacks, the US TV screens were full of images of (predominantly white) men taking on the role of protecting the home and the nation, and defending the American way of life, while women were largely invisible or present only as victims (Tickner 2002). In reality, women made a substantial contribution to the post-9/11 rescue operation and reconstruction efforts either as police officers and fire-fighters or as members of the rescue personnel. Yet, through the gendered lens of the media, the heroes of the rescue operations in New York and Washington were overwhelmingly male, while the most common female characters were the bereaved, helpless mothers and wives who lost their brave husbands in the attacks or rescue operations (Dowler 2002).

The influence of traditional gender norms comes clearly to the fore also in the media coverage of female soldiers involved in the Iraq war, as well as in the media images of female torturers at Abu Ghraib. The news stories featuring US women soldiers consistently focused on their feminine traits and private lives, while downplaying their professional roles and 'masculine' job tasks (Prividera and Howard 2007). Two of the three women soldiers from the 507th Ordinance Maintenance Company, for instance, were repeatedly referred to as 'single moms', while the third one was described as a 'friend', 'roommate' and 'daughter'. In contrast, male members of the same unit were typically presented as 'warrior heroes devoid of friendship or family connections outside of the military' (ibid.: 33). Traditional expectations about gender roles were also influential in shaping the coverage of soldiers complicit in the Abu Ghraib abuses scandal (Gronnvoll 2007). While male soldiers implicated in torture were discussed in non-gendered terms, and criticized for not behaving as good soldiers should, female torturers were criticized for failing to behave as a woman ought (ibid: 377ff).

The gendered nationalist symbolism in the US media also functioned as an obstacle to rational deliberation, marginalizing dissenting voices in much the same way as the nationalistic wartime rhetoric discussed in Chapter 5. As Christensen and Ferree (2008) demonstrate in their analysis of the Iraq war debate, gender binaries provided a powerful cultural resource that became enmeshed with other binary ways of seeing the world – us/them, with us/against us, good/evil, civilized/uncivilized, right/wrong and so on – and restrained the ability to construct alternative positions in the debate. Articles using gendered categories and images, such as references to George W. Bush as a 'cowboy' and Europe as a 'wimp', consistently scored lower in terms of quality of public debate: they were more likely to present primarily one side of the argument, included on average more assertions and fewer reasons, levelled more *ad hominem* attacks, and were more likely to contain other binary ways of thinking.

Interestingly, the analysis also showed that gendered language was commonly used by both anti-war and pro-war actors, and had a similarly detrimental effect in both cases. The contrasting uses of the term 'cowboy' – usually mobilized to describe the behaviour of George W. Bush – are a case in point. While pro-war actors used the cowboy image as a positive symbol of US civilization and masculinity, eager to confront the 'outlaws', anti-war actors framed the cowboy as a reckless, unsophisticated and dangerous figure, and contrasted it with a more modern, sophisticated and diplomatic type of masculinity. Yet regardless of whether 'cowboy' masculinity was framed in positive or negative terms – and thus regardless of the gendered regime invoked – articles using the cowboy image shared the tendency to present the opposite position in the debate as 'feminine', and were more likely to score lower in terms of the quality of public debate.

The swift reversal to traditional gendered forms of nationalism in post-9/11 North America demonstrates that the transformation and contestation of preferred models of femininity and masculinity in contemporary societies and the media are not a matter of linear progression from traditional to liberal forms. In the context of heightened conflict or crisis, perceived threats to the nation – be it threats embodied in foreign influence, globalization or terrorist attackers – often assume the form of a masculine, penetrative force threatening the feminine nation, and prompt calls for a return to traditional gender roles. This is likely to happen in any nation, regardless of the political context and levels of gender equality, although we should of course acknowledge that these contextual factors will determine the extent and shape of such reversals to patriarchal ideals.

7
Times of the Media, Times of Nations

At first sight, nationhood and mass communication relate to the passage of time in fundamentally different ways. The media are obsessed with the present, with the passage of time here and now – not with the weeks, months and years measured by calendars, but with the hours, minutes and seconds measured by clocks. News production in particular is driven by the ideal of immediacy, and by the notion that news stories are, by definition, perishable: for journalists and editors, the most valuable stories are those of the immediate present, the 'breaking news', that get passed on to the audience virtually as they happen (Schlesinger 1978: 87–98). In the context of 24-hour news channels, a news story can lose its currency in a matter of hours: a piece of information that merited a programme interruption at 9 a.m. will become part of a regular news item by 9 p.m., and may easily slip into oblivion by the next morning.

Nations, on the other hand, are more oriented to the past and the future. If the media live by the clock, nations live by the calendar. This particular relation to time is inscribed into the very basis of national imagination: nations are conceived as imagined communities rooted in history, as solid organisms moving steadily onward through abstract, empty historical time (cf. Anderson 1991: 26). As a consequence, a nation's present is always seen as a product of its past, shaped by the legacy of particular historical events and experiences. The French nation is unimaginable without the French revolution and the storming of the Bastille in 1789; the Chinese nation inconceivable without the establishment of the People's Republic of China in 1949; and the American nation virtually unthinkable without the Declaration of Independence in 1776. The memory of these defining historical moments is enshrined in national calendars, which ensure a periodic reconnection of the nation's present with the sacred moments from its past.

Yet despite these differences, the time of the media and the time of nations are closely intertwined – and, in fact, interdependent. To start with, the 'timeliness' of events that dominate the cover pages and news bulletins often rests on tacit assumptions about long-term developments, historical watersheds and other temporal contexts that help journalists decide which of the many recent events are truly newsworthy, and what they actually mean (Schudson 1986: 82–88). For instance, the attacks on the World Trade Center and the Pentagon in 2001 would not have acquired such a prominent position in American and global collective imagination had they not been interpreted in the context of the major historical watersheds of the twentieth century. In the days following the attacks, the USA media were regularly comparing the events of the 9/11 to the assault on Pearl Harbor, implicitly suggesting that the terrorist attacks demand a response comparable in its magnitude and importance to that of the USA's entry into World War II (C. Weber 2003). Similarly, the recent economic downturn would probably not have provoked such anxiety if the media had not drawn a parallel with the Great Depression of the 1930s and its devastating effects on countries worldwide. The clock time that governs the routines of media production is therefore ultimately an extension of calendar time, and the news stories of today derive their meaning and newsworthiness from the historical narratives stretching back into the depths of calendar time.

Furthermore, both clock time and calendar time – and therefore both the time of the media and the time of nations – form part and parcel of the same standardized time reckoning that has its origins in Western Europe and was gradually adopted worldwide over the course of the nineteenth and twentieth centuries. The adoption of this standardized system went hand in hand with the growing interdependence of local places and societies, and was driven by the interrelated processes of industrialization and the speeding up of transport and communication networks, all of which demanded an increased ability to coordinate activities in different localities (Zerubavel 1982; Glennie and Thrift 2009: 22–64). To allow for the effective management of the coming and going of trains and postal carriages, and for the smooth operation of factories and schools, the infinite variety of local timekeeping had to give way to abstract measurements of hours and days shared everywhere (Vincent 2000: 105–6). At the same time, calendar time was becoming standardized as well. One by one, societies in Europe and beyond agreed to adopt the Gregorian calendar – initially perceived as a Catholic institution and used only within the boundaries of the Catholic world – and started measuring the passing of years and months in a uniform manner (Zerubavel 1985: 94–100).

New communication technologies played a vital role in the development and institutionalization of this modern, standardized temporal coordination. In fact, the shift to the abstract, universally observed sense of time and the spreading of modern means of communication were mutually interdependent: one could not have occurred without the other. Being able to catch the right train at the right time or turning up for factory work or school required at least basic literacy and numeracy skills, while newspapers and almanacs helped tie the local sense of time to the national calendar (Vincent 2000: 105–10). The British Post Office also played a key role in the standardization of time, and constituted the driving force behind the first recorded attempt to synchronize different local communities with the same national time. In 1857, the British postal authorities adopted the Greenwich Mean Time, and required its mail coaches and various post offices across the country to time their work in accordance with a uniform standard of time (Zerubavel 1982: 5–6). The telegraph and telephone brought another challenge. With their arrival, human communication was freed from the requirement of physical co-presence in the same location, and its pace was no longer dependent on the speed of the mail coach or the ship (Thompson 1995: 32–33). Yet in order for electronic communication to function at all, it was vital for all parties involved to follow the same standard of time-keeping and to be available at the exact same time, regardless of their spatial location.

The tight link between the modern media and the standardization of timekeeping is often discussed in connection with globalization and postmodernity rather than the rise of nations. The advent of electronic means of communication is thought to have contributed to the 'shrinking' of distances and the 'space-time compression' that we typically associate with life in a globalized world (Meyrowitz 1985; Harvey 1990; Rantanen 2005). Such assertions are rather simplistic and fail to acknowledge that the compression of time and space was usually accompanied by the introduction of new forms of distance. For instance, both telegraph and photography were involved in forging relationships of domination and exploitation, and helped establish hierarchical distinctions between the civilized 'now' and 'here' of the urban West and the barbaric 'then' and 'there' of working-class slums and colonial peripheries (Murdock and Pickering 2009). As the remainder of this chapter demonstrates, the shrinking of time and space and the world-wide adoption of the same standards of clock and calendar time also left plenty of room for national variation. In the next section, we start by taking a closer look at how the universal system of timekeeping became implicated in the mediated construction of a national sense of the passage of time. Following that, we explore how the divergent patterns of national calendars relate to the different grammars of nationhood and routes to modernity. The last part of this chapter turns to the mediation of national perceptions of time in the context of war, and examines how journalistic uses of the past relate to the patterns of wartime national imagination.

Media Nations and Time: Between the National and the Global

The worldwide standardization of clock and calendar time was undeniably an integral prerequisite for the speeding up and intensification of globalization. Indeed, case studies of calendrical reforms around the world suggest that the need to engage in transnational trade and foreign policy relations were among the key motivations driving the adoption of Greenwich Mean Time and the Gregorian calendar (see e.g. M. M. Smith 1998; Harris 2008). Yet this standardization of clock and calendar time did not erase all diversity. Rather, it provided a universal system that allowed different individual, local – and, increasingly, national – times to be mutually intelligible and comparable. Indeed, we could argue that the appeal of clock and calendar time came precisely from the manifold possible times it gave rise to, and from its ability to mean different things to different people (cf. Glennie and Thrift 2009: 97). The standardized system of measuring time thus became part and parcel of the globally intelligible grammar of nationhood – discussed in Chapter 2 – and contributed to *both* global standardization *and* worldwide nationalization of timekeeping. Within the constraints of the universal system of time-units, the emerging nation-states were busy carving out their own, distinct sense of the passing of time.

In some cases, a national sense of time was achieved by adhering to a slightly different version of clock time. In the 1970s, for instance, Afghanistan still followed a standard of time that was over 4 hours ahead of Greenwich Mean Time, while Liberia's standard time was running 44 minutes behind (Zerubavel 1982: 18). In other countries, a similar effect was achieved by combining the standard Gregorian calendar with elements of a parallel, traditional calendar. The Chinese national calendar provides a case in point; while based on the Gregorian calendar, it also retains elements of the traditional, lunar calendar. Even more common than this is the practice of national holidays, which serve to commemorate significant events from the national past – for instance, the commemoration of Bastille Day on 14 July in France, the observance of Independence Day on 4 July in the USA, or the celebration of the establishment of the People's Republic in China on 1 October. While all national calendars measure the passage of time in compatible ways, the patterns of national holidays differ, thus giving a distinct national rhythm to the universally adopted succession of days, months and years.

The modern media, from the early almanacs and newspapers to radio, television and the Internet, were closely involved in establishing a national sense of time, and continue to play a central role in imbuing the passage of time with distinct national patterns to this day. Our sense of clock and calendar time is interwoven with our use of the media, be it listening to the radio, checking our Facebook site, tuning in for TV news, reading a newspaper or watching the latest episode of our favourite TV series. Media producers, especially broadcasters, are well aware of that, and are trying to structure the contents they offer to fit with the daily and weekly routines of our lives – waking up, taking a bus to work, having a lunch break, enjoying a night out with friends, going on a family trip over the weekend and so on – offering us pieces of information, useful advice or light entertainment appropriate for the time of the day and week (cf. Scannell 1996: 149–51). The media are also implicated in marking major national holidays and are among the key agents contributing to the reproduction and negotiation of national narratives, traditions and ideas on such occasions (cf. Rodell 2009: 122–24). On public holidays, the media abandon the regular rhythms of broadcast schedules and publishing and instead provide their audiences with celebratory programming and content that often involves live coverage of major commemorative events and one-off entertainment programmes designed specially for the occasion. Together, these programmes are geared to promoting national solidarity and provide opportunities for the audience to confirm their commitment to the national imagined community (Skey 2006: 151).

The binding of local communities to a common national time can of course proceed in different ways for different segments of the society, and draw on a variety of different activities and media forms. In Malaysia, for instance, adult men and children mostly coordinate their time in accordance with the requirements of the workplace and school, while women and the elderly become attuned to national temporal structures primarily through the radio (Postill 2006: 159–66). While the daily and weekly routines follow broadly similar patterns in several different nations – at the very least those in the same time zone – the array of sounds and images, pieces of information or entertainment made available by the media inevitably differs. True, we do not usually perceive these differences as something that has to do with nationhood, yet the simple availability of a range of familiar media forms and programming at particular points in the day or week – a familiar face reading the evening TV news, a recognizable voice or song on the morning radio programme – contributes to that suffused, banal sense of being at home that sustains the national order of things.

Of course, the links between the media and the structuring of a national sense of time have changed dramatically over the past two decades. Back in the day of public broadcasting monopoly, before the proliferation of commercial stations and the rise of satellite television and the Internet, the involvement of the media in the national synchronization of clock time was hard to miss. Every day, families up and down the country would wake up to the same radio programmes, tune in to the same evening news bulletin, and watch the same TV series. On the occasion of national holidays and major sports contests, most of the population would sit in front of a TV or radio receiver and take part in the same media event, enacting an 'extraordinary mass ceremony' akin to the one engendered by the daily routines of newspaper reading described by Anderson (cf. Dayan and Katz 1992). In the context of contemporary media landscapes, the national patterning of media routines and events is far less clear-cut, and the extraordinary occasions that gather the whole nation together are few and far between (Katz 1996). The multitude of channels and various viewing and listening platforms allows individuals to consume media programmes at their own leisure, without much regard for the constraints of standardized clock and calendar time. The availability of satellite and cable television makes it possible for audiences in one country to tune into programmes offered by other national broadcasters and by transnational channels, all of which diverge from the national patterns of clock and calendar time observed by domestic programming. Even in the world's poorest economies, mobile phone use has been growing rapidly over the past decade, allowing inhabitants in hitherto isolated rural areas to keep in touch with friends and family living elsewhere in the country as well as abroad (Donner 2008).

Yet, as always, we should beware of confusing availability and access with actual choice and use. Empirical data on the changing patterns of media use prompted by the availability of podcasts and digital TV recorders remains very limited, yet it is reasonable to expect that the demands of work and family life will make radical departures from national patterns of clock and calendar time rather improbable. On a regular working day, one is unlikely to spend hours in the middle of the day chatting with friends over the Internet or watching pre-recorded episodes of one's favourite soap. Most likely, these activities will be restricted to evening hours and thus follow the broad contours of national patterns of daily routines, and will entail forms of communication or media content popular across large sections of the population in a particular nation-state. Furthermore, empirical research into media consumption patterns in different parts of the world suggests that despite the proliferation of transnational channels, audiences tend to prefer national media (Tunstall 2008). This indicates that, for the majority, the main patterns of media use will remain attuned to national rhythms.

We should also keep in mind that a significant proportion of the world remains peripheral to transnational media flows and in fact lacks even the basic domestic communication infrastructure. In sub-Saharan Africa, for instance, only 14 out of every 100 households had a television set in 2005, in contrast to 96 out of 100 in the European Union (World Bank 2007: 304–6). Similarly, Internet access in countries classified by the World Bank as 'developing economies' is still lagging well behind average figures for developed economies, with fewer than 20 per cent of the population using the Internet in 2007 (World Bank 2009: 266). While mobile phone use in the world's poorest economies has indeed been growing rapidly over the past decade, access to mobile telephony still remains low in several countries, particularly those in sub-Saharan Africa, where only 1 in 20 inhabitants holds a mobile phone subscription (ibid.). This suggests that for many of the inhabitants of the world's poorest nations, the temporal patterns of daily, weekly and monthly life remain rather localized, and largely disconnected from the mediated, standardized structures of timekeeping that have by now become so taken for granted in media-rich societies. In such a context, opportunities for tuning in to transnational media flows and alternative temporalities remain limited.

This is not to say that every single media user will organize temporal media practices solely within the confines of a single national media landscape. At the very least, many of us will surf the Internet and routinely venture beyond the confines of our respective 'national' Internet bubbles ending with .uk, .si or .cn – usually to surf through those ending with .com – or occasionally tune into one of the major transnational TV channels. Although these ventures into transnational media spaces will most often be timed in ways that conform to our domestic, national rhythms, we may at least sometimes decide to depart from those, stay up late to hear the preliminary results of the latest elections in the USA, or watch the live transmission of a football mach taking place on the other side of the globe. Members of immigrant families are likely to be particularly accustomed to simultaneous engagements with disparate mediated temporal orders, tied to different countries and different national communities (cf. Levitt and Glick

Schiller 2004). On a regular basis, they will navigate between the rhythms of their own daily lives and the daily and weekly routines of their friends and family members in the country of origin, with the aim of finding an appropriate time for a phone call or an Internet chat, or to tune in at the right moment for a major national media event. By engaging in these negotiations with disparate temporal orders, members of immigrant families will be contributing to the construction of a 'hybrid imagined community' characterized by multiple ties of belonging, spanning a 'network of homes' in different national contexts (Georgiou 2006: 20–24, 99–101).

Having clarified the broad contours of relationships between nations, the media and time, it is now time to return to some of the central arguments developed over the course of the previous chapters. If, as we have noted above, each nation-state appropriates the standard measures of timekeeping and develops its own distinct patterns of daily, weekly and yearly rhythms, (as well as its own distinct national memories and narratives of the past), how do these national patterns relate to the divergent grammars of nationhood and the different routes to modernity?

Media Nations, Temporal Orders and Visions of Modernity

Interest in different temporal orientations of entire societies has by now generated a sizeable literature, with contributions from cultural psychologists, sociologists and anthropologists (cf. Bergmann 1992) as well as, more recently, management and marketing experts (e.g. Hofstede 2001; Lin 2001). At the centre of these debates has been the threefold distinction between past-oriented, present-oriented and future-oriented societies. While past-oriented societies are believed to be bound by tradition and hold a sceptical attitude to change, present-oriented societies are generally regarded as hedonistic and oriented to immediate gratification, and future-oriented societies are seen as more open to change and accustomed to deferred gratification. Yet, as Bergmann (1992: 92–66) pointed out, scholarly debates about cultural differences in temporal perspectives have typically provided insufficient empirical support for their generalizations, and have underplayed the internal diversity of time orientations in modern societies. Authors also often relied on stereotypical contrasts between 'modern' and 'traditional' or 'industrial' and 'agrarian' societies, and adopted an ethnocentric and teleological understanding of modernity. For instance, an often quoted study of time orientations among ethnic groups in the USA established that Hispanic Americans were mostly present-oriented,

Chinese Americans past-oriented, and white North Americans future-oriented (Kluckhohn and Strodtbeck 1963). Such approaches evidently leave little room for appreciating the links between different temporal orders and competing visions of modernity and nationhood. This is true also of much of the research that examines cross-national differences in time orientations apparent in contemporary advertising, which often draws sharp contrasts between Western, future-oriented societies and Eastern, past-oriented societies (e.g. Lin 2001).

Instead of following this route of enquiry, we will explore differences between mediated national orders and their links with alternative modernities by focusing on national calendars and the mediation of national holidays. Around the world, calendars are typically structured in accordance with the mainstream national narrative, and include holidays that commemorate key 'sacred' events and periods from a nation's past (Zerubavel 2003). The historical narratives encapsulated in calendars are central to the engendering, reproduction and transformation of national imagination. As with other historical narratives, they provide nations with particular trajectories that not only tell a story about where they come from, but also serve to define their present identity and help choose a direction for the future (cf. Liu and Hilton 2005). Given that national calendars are so closely related to national imagination, it is reasonable to expect that they will also reflect divergent understandings of modernity and bear the marks of different grammars of nationhood as discussed in Chapter 4. The divergent national narratives, tied to competing visions of modernity, should also be apparent in the media events accompanying the key national holidays. To explore this proposition, we will examine the evolution of the Chinese national calendar, starting with the calendrical reforms in late imperial and early republican China, moving on to the Communist national calendar and its changes in the post-Mao era, and concluding with the recent reinstatement and official endorsement of traditional lunar holidays.

From the very start of Chinese calendrical reforms in the late nineteenth century, the national calendar constituted a battleground for competing visions of China's modernization and national identity (Harris 2008). Following China's defeat in the Sino-Japanese War (1894–95), which forced the Chinese to cede the island of Taiwan, leading Chinese intellectuals and political leaders agreed that the roots of China's military weakness lay in its failure to modernize state institutions and in the lack of a strong national identity (Zheng 1999: 24–26). Both those advocating reforms within the existing Qing state and those arguing for the overthrow of the Qing Dynasty identified the traditional lunar calendar and dating system as one of the symptoms – as well as causes – of failed modernization. Yet while reformers such as Kang Yuwei suggested adopting Confucianism as state religion and starting the new dating system with Confucius' birth, the revolutionaries argued that the new calendar should be based on the birth of the Yellow Emperor, the ancestor of the majority Han population (Harris 2008: 20). The two proposals were embedded in very different visions of Chinese modernization: the former saw modern China as a multiethnic empire based on a common religion while the latter conceived Chinese modernity in terms of a nation-state dominated by the Han.

The establishment of the Chinese Republic in 1911 was followed by the first attempt to replace the traditional lunar calendar with the Gregorian solar calendar used in the West (Harrison 2000: 65–69). Both the Provisional Government in the early days of the Chinese Republic and the Nationalist Party Government in the late 1920s and early 1930s have promoted the Gregorian calendar as a tool of China's modernization. The new system of time-reckoning, they believed, would help eradicate superstitious beliefs and practices associated with the lunar calendar, facilitate China's participation in overseas trade, and allow the country to catch up with Western modernity (Harris 2008). Yet, more often than not, the repeated proclamations, new policies and bans fell on deaf ears. The new Chinese republic lacked strong state institutions and adequate financial resources that would help defeat local warlords, fend off the imperial appetites of the West and Japan, and rebuild and integrate the battered country (Grasso et al. 2004: 71–122). In their urge to maintain control over the population and keep political competitors at bay, some of the governing parties also resorted to rather harsh measures, which exacerbated popular discontent. When combined, these contextual factors presented significant obstacles to the popularization of the new calendar. While banks, state institutions and mainstream newspapers did gradually shift to the new standard of time-reckoning, much of the population continued to follow the rhythms set by the lunar calendar (Harrison 2000: 66–67, 199–201).

A more concerted and successful effort to institute the Gregorian calendar came with the founding of the People's Republic of China in 1949. In line with the communist modernizing project and the historical-materialist interpretation of history, the stated intent of the Red Army and the new communist authorities was to free China from the oppressive forces of its past – above all, imperialism and feudalism (Hung 2007: 412). Yet while sharing the fundamental premise of modern identity construction – namely the opposition between the modern, civilized Self and the underdeveloped, backward and primitive Other (Pickering 2001: 51ff) – the communist vision of modernity rejected the assumption that modernization went hand in hand with the advancement of market economy and liberal democracy. Instead, progressiveness, civilization and modernity were associated with political and economic doctrines and practices adopted in the Soviet Union – internationalism, anti-imperialism, a centrally planned economy, and working-class rule – which were seen as more advanced than those of the capitalist West (Mihelj 2010).

This new Chinese national narrative, premised on a radical break with the past and the expectation of a bright communist future, was encapsulated in the new national calendar. The eponymous dating based on the 1911 founding of the Republic was eliminated, and traditional festivities associated with the lunar calendar such as the Tomb Sweeping Festival and the Dragon Boat Festival abolished (Harris 2008). The major national holidays included in the new calendar were all attuned to the new narrative of the past and the future, and were meant to mark the eradication of the feudal, imperial past and the commencement of a new, Communist-led modernity (Hung 2007: 414). In accordance with these intentions, May Day (1 May) was aimed at celebrating the achievements of the working classes worldwide, the Youth Festival (4 May) was centred on the Chinese youth as the symbol of the country's Communist future, the Army's Day (1 August) was designed to commemorate the founding of the first armed uprising to the Nationalist Party government in 1927, and National Day (1 October) was dedicated to the founding of the People's Republic in 1949.

The parades held on national holidays, all meticulously planned by the Chinese Communist Party, were underpinned by the same historical narrative. They were designed to symbolically demolish the old order and usher in a new era, as well as help legitimate the new authorities and display their achievements. In terms of their main social and political functions, these festive occasions had much in common with other mass events characteristic of modern, industrial societies. From revolutionary France to the Soviet Union, from the post-independence American Republic to Nazi Germany, festivals, parades, processions and other popular political rituals have served as key instruments of exercising and displaying sovereignty (Mosse 1975; Lane 1981; Ozouf 1988; Newman 1997). The modern media – first newspapers and films; later radio and television – played an important role in such events everywhere, helping eclipse distances between the physical location of public celebrations and the widely dispersed locations of addressees. Communist China was no exception. During the parades in the 1950s, patriotic films were shown in open-air cinemas, and the news media joined in the celebrations, echoing the self-congratulatory speeches of the Communist authorities and providing exalted portrayals of mass celebrations.

According to a newspaper story published following the mass spectacle held in Beijing on the National Day in 1950, the people were all 'warmly applauding the new China' (quoted in Hung 2007: 413).

National festivities in Mao's China were not intended to be explicitly nationalist. To start with, the dominant national narrative underpinning the celebrations paid little attention to China's traditional national Other – Japan. The Second Sino-Japanese War (1937–45), which took tens of millions of Chinese lives, virtually disappeared from public view and official commemorations instead focused on the heroic achievements of Chairman Mao and the Communist Party (Coble 2007: 395–96). The festivities also had strong internationalist overtones and, in particular, the May Day parade was characterized by large-scale portraits of foreign communist leaders, slogans expressing China's gratitude to the Soviet Union and the ubiquitous use of the hammer and sickle icon (Hung 2007: 422). Yet, even in this context, nationalism far from disappeared. The parades regularly incorporated symbols and dances derived from Chinese folk culture, which resonated with the wider population and helped boost patriotic feelings and support for the regime (ibid.).

From the early 1980s onward, however, nationalist narratives and symbols started to become more apparent. In the context of rising unemployment and inflation, Communist ideology was loosing its appeal, and in order to fill the legitimacy vacuum, the authorities resorted to nationalism. The first Japanese history textbook controversy in 1982 marked the beginning of a revival of anti-Japanese sentiments, which have been central to Chinese nationhood and memory ever since. This episode also signalled the gradual rise of a new national narrative, one centred on China as a victim and Japan as its major enemy (He 2007: 6–7). Over the course of the following years and decades, the heroic narrative of Mao's China was gradually giving way to the pre-1949 victimization narrative, oriented to the historical acts of 'humiliation' inflicted on the Chinese by the West and above all by Japan (Gries 2004). The new narrative was soon inculcated into primary and secondary school history education, and the mass media followed suit – several films and popular books released during the 1980s were centred on the Nanjing massacre (He 2007: 7–8).

Attempts to promote Chinese nationalism and propagate a new sense of China's history and its position in the modern world, received a new boost in the aftermath of the 1989 Tiananmen Square events. In the early 1990s, the Communist government launched an ambitious patriotic education campaign, which was designed to stem domestic discontent and channel it into patriotic pride (Wang 2008: 788–89). The main objectives of the campaign remained embedded in the Communist narrative of modernity and called for the formation of a united patriotic front capable of building 'socialism with Chinese characteristics'. Nonetheless, far more emphasis was now put on the historical position of China as a victim, as well as on Chinese traditional culture, including Confucianism and even practices such as ancestor worship that had hitherto remained taboo for the Communist authorities (Zhao 1998). Chinese Communist modernity was no longer premised on the destruction of tradition as it was in the early decades of the People's Republic. Instead, tradition was now believed to constitute its spiritual core and made modern China inherently incompatible with 'Western' values and practices. The basis of legitimacy for Communist Party rule shifted accordingly. Instead of being dependent on Communist ideology and the ideals of workers' rule, it was now rooted in the Party's commitment to national interests and the preservation of Chinese cultural traditions (Wang 2008: 790).

The campaign reached its peak in 1994, when the Communist Party released a document outlining the guidelines for patriotic education and specifically called for their incorporation into teaching at all levels, from kindergartens to universities (Yanru 2004: 292–93). A wide variety of media and cultural forms, activities and institutions were drawn into the effort, including singing contests, patriotic films, mass rallies and festivals, national music clubs, as well as magazines, newspapers, television and radio programmes (Zhao 1998: 293–96). In addition, a number of museums, monuments and sites of important battles received financial support for renovation, and began to be used for organized visits involving school children, army personnel and government officials (Wang 2008: 794–96). The contribution of the media to patriotic education was particularly clearly evident during major national holidays. In 1994, on the occasion of the 45th anniversary of the establishment of People's Republic, the China Central Television actively contributed to the building-up of expectations in the days preceding the event, and then joined the government in promoting the image of China's strength and unity, symbolically enacting a sense of togetherness and devotion to a common mission – the building of 'socialism with Chinese characteristics' (Yanru 2004).

By all accounts, the state-orchestrated patriotic education campaign was hugely successful. Over the course of the 1990s and the 2000s, China has witnessed a surge in mass demonstrations fuelled by nationalist sentiments, typically directed either at the Japanese enemy – as was the case with the recent Japanese history textbooks controversy in 2005 – or at the West – as exemplified in the demonstrations following the disruption of the Olympic Torch relay in the French capital in 2008 (cf.

Wang 2008: 799). Yet it is unlikely that the campaign would have ignited such widespread popular support for nationalism without a simultaneous transformation of the Chinese media and their relationships with the state. The commercialization and diversification of the media market, along with the growth of Internet use, put an end to Communist Party monopoly on information exchange and helped establish the media as a semi-independent actor influencing the public opinion (He 2007: 17). Driven by commercial interests and competition for audiences, the media started exploiting the popular appeal of nationalism and anti-Japanese sentiments not simply for the sake of state-driven patriotic education, but also for their own benefit (cf. Shirk 2007).

Another factor to note is the fact that the recourse to nationalism offered a relatively safe route for expressing criticism of the government (He 2007: 18). For a state that prided itself on being the guardian of national interests, public grievances couched in national terms were difficult to brush aside. While nationalism certainly proved to be a powerful tool of legitimation for the governing elites, its popular varieties were becoming increasingly difficult to control and presented a threat to the country's stability (cf. Zheng 1999: 87–110). The media, no longer dependent solely on the state for their sources of funding, quickly learned how to use nationalist discourse to foster their own agendas – or those of their owners – and boost their sales. Increasingly, media coverage was no longer attuned solely to the interests of the Communist old guard, but was instead shaped also by the interests of the rising economic elites that have profited from the reintroduction of open-door policies after 1978. The mediated national imagination shifted accordingly. For instance, when covering China's entry into the WTO in 2001, market-oriented newspapers were framing the event from the perspective of the business elites, and constructed 'China's ordinary folk' as an imagined community centred on the figures of investors, stock owners and affluent urban consumers (Zhao 2003).

Another expression of this change is the proliferation of popular consumer nationalism. This form of nationalism ties Chinese national interests to the process of consumption and turns the act of buying or rejecting specific goods into a patriotic act. Typically, Chinese consumer nationalism targets Japanese goods and companies as well as ads for Japanese products. For instance, in 1999, Toshiba agreed to pay compensation to US customers who bought its notebook with a faulty floppy-disk drive, yet refrained from offering a similar settlement to Chinese customers. The news of this differential treatment provoked anger in China. The media framed the story in unmistakably nationalist terms and often presented the incident as evidence of Japan's discrimination against

Chinese customers (Wang 2006), thus reinforcing the victim narrative. The same narrative was apparent in the media outrages sparked by the adverts for Toyota cars and Nippon paint in 2003 and 2004. The controversial adverts featured objects that functioned as symbolic depictions of China, and displayed them in ways that Chinese audiences found unacceptable and downright humiliating (Li 2009). One of the Toyota adverts featured a Chinese-looking military car being towed by a Japanese land rover, while the other showed two stone lions – traditional symbols of Chinese culture – bowing to and saluting Toyota Prado. Dismayed at the ad, some of the outraged Internet posters interpreted the ad in the context of the historical victim narrative, and compared it to past Japanese invasions of China (ibid: 444–45). An anonymous Internet user even posted an alternative 'advert' featuring two giant stone lions toying with a Toyota car (Li 2009; see Figure 7.1).

The most recent reforms of the Chinese national calendar are fully in line with the shifts in perceptions of the country's past and future that we have just traced. In 2007, following a long and rather heated debate, China's central government abolished the Labour Day Golden Week and reinstated the three traditional holidays that were eliminated by the Communist authorities in 1949: the Tomb Sweeping Festival, the Dragon Boat Festival and the Mid-Autumn festival (York and Zhang 2010). A circular issued by the CCP and the central government in 2005

Figure 7.1   Alternative 'advert' for the Toyota Land Cruiser. © Anonymous

explained that these traditional holidays 'embody the unique spirit and affections and feelings of the Chinese nation and reflect Chinese civilization' and play an important role in promoting social harmony and national reunification with Hong Kong and Taiwan (quoted in Xinhua 2005). The reintroduction of traditional holidays was also presented as a response to public concerns over the corrupting impact of cultural globalization and, in particular, the tendency among younger Chinese to celebrate 'Western' holidays. The pattern of change is clear: in line with the transformations that have been gaining ground ever since the end of the Mao era, the importance of the Communist narrative of modernity – embodied in the May Day celebrations – was reduced to make room for the ethno-nationalist narrative – encapsulated in the traditional holidays.

As one can infer from the trajectory of calendrical reforms in China, changes in national perceptions of time form part of broader processes of transformation occurring in the realms of politics, economy and culture, as well as in the media. The rise of the ethno-national narrative, anchored in China's millennial cultural traditions, would never have encountered such widespread popular endorsement without simultaneous economic liberalization, growth of commercial media, and the changing relationships between the media and politics. As with the altering visions of modernity and nationhood, the changing perceptions of a nation's past, present and future are closely intertwined with shifts in the relative balance of political, economic and cultural forces in a particular society.

Mediating National Memories in Times of War

Much of our discussion in the previous section focused on the construction of national memories and perceptions of time in the context of major national holidays. Such occasions are purposefully designed to provide an opportunity for members of the nation to temporarily suspend concerns about the present, reconnect with the sacred moments from the nation's past and confirm their commitment to a common future. The major media events accompanying these commemorative events follow the same logic: they are aimed at reminding the audience of the shared past and at facilitating the symbolic fusion between the nation's past, present and future. While reporting on public celebrations, wreath laying or ceremonial speeches – or commenting on their live coverage – journalists re-tell the story of the historical event that is being commemorated and recall its significance for the nation (Edy 1999: 74–77). They may show the historical video footage of the event, ask survivors to recall their memories, talk to the relatives of the deceased, or make room for re-tellings provided by historians – all the while re-confirming their own role as custodians of memory (Zelizer 1992). Similar forms of journalistic remembering also appear sporadically outside of the designated festive periods, for instance on important anniversaries or in response to deaths of notable politicians, writers, artists or sport stars (see e.g. Kitch 2005; Fowler 2007).

Nevertheless, although symbolically anchoring the nation's present in its sacred past, these commemorative practices do rather little to make historical events meaningful for the present. Often, the events of the past are simply too far removed from contemporary concerns to have much direct bearing on the here and now (Edy 1999: 76–77). For history to erupt into the present in more significant ways, a more radical disruption of everyday routines is needed – not one that is pre-planned and managed according to a well-rehearsed script, but one that takes the authorities, the media and the audience by surprise. Such disruption is typically provoked by unexpected and dramatic changes, such as those brought by a natural disaster, a momentous political transformation or a rapidly evolving conflict. On such extraordinary occasions, media producers are suddenly thrown out of their temporal routines and left without a script to cling to. At the same time, their actions acquire unprecedented importance: with traditional political institutions and authorities in disarray, the media are often expected to 'run the show' and provide the nation with reassurance, guidance and interpretation (Liebes 1998). Under such pressures, and in the absence of other author-itative sources, journalists are likely to resort to national memories and narratives, and use explicit historical analogies to help interpret present developments, predict their outcome or provide guidelines on how to react. In contrast to re-tellings of past events during pre-planned commemorative events, such ad hoc analogies establish a meaningful and substantive connection between the past and the present. No matter how historically removed, events and personalities of the past are no longer merely distant moments and figures of a bygone era, but provide powerful models and lessons for the present.

Examples of such journalistic uses of historical analogies abound. In response to the assassination of Israel's Prime Minister Yitzhak Rabin in 1995, the Israeli media incorporated the event into the 'nation-constitu-tive myth' originating in the 1948 Arab–Israeli conflict, and presented Rabin's death as an act of heroic sacrifice comparable to the deaths of courageous soldiers during the 1948 war (Peri 1999: 108–9). Similarly, the Israeli television coverage of a fire in the Carmel Forest in 1989 linked the incident to the Biblical past and presented it as a parable of

Jewish martyrdom (Ha-Ilan 2001: 210–11). The crash of the space shuttle Columbia in 2003 prompted American journalists to establish an analogy with a comparable accident from 1990 involving the Challenger shuttle and use it to draw lessons for the present (Edy and Daradanova 2006). Likewise, in the aftermath of 9/11, both British and US newspapers frequently established a link with the World Trade Center bombing in 1993 and compared the impact and scale of the attacks to that of the 1941 Pearl Harbor raid and the 1995 Oklahoma City bombing, each time using the historical event to interpret current developments, look for their causes, or anticipate their long-term impact (Winfield et al. 2002). One of the *New York Times*'s commentators, for instance, likened the 9/11 attacks to Pearl Harbor, suggested that the world has just witnessed the beginning of World War III and concluded that Americans should brace themselves for a 'long war against a brilliant and motivated foe' (Friedman, *New York Times*, 13 September 2001, p. 27).

The proliferation of historical analogies in moments of crisis is rooted in their appearance of objectivity – after all, the past event *really* happened, the current event is equally *real*, and drawing comparisons between the two seems to satisfy the standards of the journalistic profession (Edy 1999: 77). Yet, as with every other narrative device, historical analogies do not merely provide a neutral frame for telling a meaningful story about the present, but impose tacit assumptions about its nature, about the identity of its key actors, victims and perpetrators, about the likely outcome, as well as about the preferred response (cf. Peri 1999; Winfield et al. 2002; Edy and Daradanova 2006). If the shocking events of the present have their precedents, there is hope that the damage will ultimately be repaired and future disasters avoided – as long as we follow the lessons of the past. Likewise, rapid changes, even if pre-planned, may seem less disruptive if they are presented as logical consequences of long-term developments. Interpreting the present in the light of the past can therefore provide audiences with a cognitive reassurance of understanding what happened, help re-establish social bonds and offer a sense of direction. This renewal of bonds of belonging, however, can be mobilized to serve strikingly different ends. On the one hand, recalling instances of past solidarity can help drum up voluntary support for rescue activities and muster financial injections for post-war rebuilding. On the other hand, memories of past military victories or defeats can also be used as a pretext for confidence-boosting and calls for revenge. The seemingly innocuous and objective references to past events therefore allow the media – along with other opinion-makers – to steer the course of events in very different directions, while presenting their choices as stemming from incontrovertible facts and historical truths.

To demonstrate these diverse journalistic uses of historical analogies and their involvement in the mediation of national memories in times of crisis, I will now briefly examine selected excerpts drawn from the TV news coverage of the armed conflict that took place in the Yugoslav republic of Slovenia in 1991. As explained in Chapter 5, this conflict marked the beginning of the Yugoslav Wars and formed an integral part of a wider process of social, economic, political and cultural transformations in the federation, which were accompanied by a reconfiguration of national imagination. The socialist Yugoslav identity matrix entailed a two-layered pattern: the common Yugoslav identity coexisted with distinct, institutionally supported national identities – Slovenian, Serbian, Croatian and so on. Over the course of the 1970s and the 1980s, the institutional and political infrastructure underpinning Yugoslav unity was slowly weakening. The series of reforms that culminated in the adoption of a new constitution in 1974 effectively strengthened sub-state national loyalties at the expense of pan-Yugoslav ones. The death of Yugoslavia's life-long president Josip Broz Tito in 1981 dealt another blow to the already fragile infrastructure of Yugoslavism. In the years that followed, these problems were compounded by rising foreign debt, spiralling inflation rates, growing unemployment and marked regional and ethnic disparities (Lampe 2000: 321–34).

The reconfiguration of the Yugoslav identity matrix went hand in hand with the reshuffling of national memories and perceptions of the past and the future. According to the socialist Yugoslav national narrative, the 'brotherhood and unity' of Yugoslav nations was forged during World War II and found its expression in the Anti-Fascist People's Liberation Struggle, led by the Yugoslav Partisans (Perica 2002: 95–98). This idealistic vision of the Yugoslav past left little room for the parallel history of hatred and violence among Yugoslav nations; these parallel memories were either suppressed altogether or subsumed under a set of simplistic dichotomies that pitted 'revolutionaries' and 'liberators' against 'foreign occupiers' and 'domestic traitors' (Höpken 1997). Over the course of the 1980s, however, several key socialist Yugoslav myths lost their taken-for-granted status, and the official historiography was being openly questioned. Memories of the heroic partisan struggle were increasingly challenged by narratives emphasizing fratricidal wars, in particular those involving the Independent State of Croatia, the associated Croatian nationalist Ustashe movement, and the Serbian nationalist Chetnik movement (Denich 1994; Dragović-Soso 2002). As Dejan Djokić (2002) argues, the rise of these alternative narratives about World War II simultaneously contributed to the internal, intra-ethnic reconciliation of individual Yugoslav nations, as well as to their inter-ethnic 'irreconciliation'. By the start of the Yugoslav Wars, the media therefore had a variety of potentially useful historical narratives at their disposal, ranging from those emphasizing the common Yugoslav partisan struggle to those underscoring fratricidal wars between Yugoslav nations. By making a choice between these, Yugoslav journalists and editors became engaged not only in shaping collective perceptions of the past, but also in determining the course of future developments.

To demonstrate this, we will now briefly examine the uses of history in prime-time television news bulletins broadcast by two TV stations, located in two different Yugoslav republics: TV Belgrade in the Republic of Serbia and TV Ljubljana in the Republic of Slovenia. Given that the mainstream political elites in each of the republics defended contrasting visions for the future of the country – with those in Slovenia pushing for independence and those in Serbia trying to keep the federation together – it is reasonable to expect that the uses of history in the media will differ accordingly.

Prior to the beginning of armed confrontations, mentions of historical events and experiences were already relatively frequent, yet were largely limited to reported speech and direct quotes, and hardly ever appeared in journalists' own interpretations and commentaries. For instance, a news bulletin broadcast by TV Ljubljana a week before the beginning of the war included a report summarizing the political disputes over Slovenia's new flag, which revolved around the interpretation of Slovenia's recent history, and specifically around the question of whether or not the new flag should retain the red star (TV Ljubljana, 20 June 1991). Although this indicates that, at the time, interpretations of history were a rather important public issue, the journalists, for the most part, maintained their professional distance and gave voice to different opinions within Slovenia.

With the start of the armed conflict, the tone of reporting changed dramatically. History became much more prominently present and historical analogies were now regularly used also by the journalists themselves. By far the greatest share of historical references used was tied to World War II and in all cases the selected historical events were incorporated into an unfolding national narrative culminating in present events. The following excerpt provides a particularly clear example:

> We have faced several challenges; we have been tormented by prob-
> lems, natural and other catastrophes. Yet we have always stayed firm,
> and we remain so, since we always relied primarily on ourselves,
> although friendly neighbours eased our pain and wounds. This time,
> solidarity will emerge once again, since the locations where the army

hordes raged are the same as 46 years ago. Gornja Radgona, one of the worst stricken municipalities, was visited today by the Slovenian parliamentary delegation. (TV Ljubljana, 6 July 1991)

In line with conventions of wartime reporting identified in Chapter 5, the news presenter adopts the position of a collective 'we' – the Slovenian nation – and begins by recalling past experiences of anguish, resilience and neighbourly support, going almost half a century back in time to establish a continuity with the suffering and solidarity in the aftermath of World War II. In the second step, he turns to the subject of the report, namely the visit of a parliamentary delegation to one of the Slovenian towns damaged during the conflict, and introduces it as an integral part of this long historical chain of collective experiences.

The exact functions of such historical analogies with World War II varied. The above-quoted excerpt is a typical example of a historical analogy established with the aim of boosting the feelings of unity, as well as conveying the hope of recovery from the trauma of war. The past is used simultaneously as a model of unity and a guarantee that feelings of solidarity will emerge again in response to present suffering. In addition, this analogy also serves to dramatize the present situation, and thereby instigates fear and hatred. Arguably, the comparison with World War II in this context functions as a hyperbole: given that the scale of devastation caused by the 1991 conflict was incomparably smaller than that left behind by World War II, such analogies clearly exaggerated its impact and consequences for purposes of rhetorical effect. Such hyperbolic analogies were used on a regular basis by both TV Belgrade and TV Ljubljana. One of the wartime news bulletins broadcast by TV Belgrade, for example, started with the following dramatic opening: 'Dear viewers! Yugoslavia is experiencing its most dramatic moments since World War II,' (TV Belgrade, 2 July 1991), succeeded by a lengthy direct address by the Yugoslav People's Army's Chief of the General Staff.

Apart from dramatizing current events and inciting fear and hatred, historical analogies also helped identify the key agents of present events and distinguish victims from perpetrators. Predictably, the two broadcasters, although using the same historical analogies, identified the agents in different ways. From the point of view of TV Ljubljana, the role of the Nazis was played by the Yugoslav People's Army. On one occasion, a journalist – distraught after having just witnessed the damage caused by the Yugoslav Army's attack on a Slovenian border town – concluded: 'Only Nazis were capable of such barbarity. Yet these are Nazis with a five-pointed red star' (TV Ljubljana, 2 July 1991). In contrast, from the perspective of TV Belgrade, the roles were reversed, and the modern Nazis were to be found in Slovenia and Croatia. A particularly interesting example appeared in a news bulletin broadcast towards the end of the conflict, which included two archival newsreel stories from 1941. The first one was a report about Adolph Hitler's visit to the Slovenian town of Maribor, which was annexed to the Third Reich in April of that year. This item contained several images of cheering crowds greeting Hitler upon his arrival, as well as images of Nazi flags all around the city. The second news story focused on the declaration of war against the UK and the USA, announced by the Independent State of Croatia in December 1941. The anchor's introduction suggested that current events in Slovenia and in neighbouring Croatia, which announced its independence at the same time as Slovenia, were effectively a repetition of these historical events, and hence of the Nazi occupation:

> In the following part of the programme, dear viewers, the news bulletin is going 50 years back in time. With the help of archival films [...] you will be able to see the images of events that in many ways resemble what is going on these days. Memory as a warning. (TV Belgrade, 5 July 1991)

It is important to note that, at the same time, intra-republican struggles over the correct interpretation of recent history disappeared from view. History was no longer presented as a matter of public dispute within each of the two republics, but as an eternal, reliable reservoir of truths to which all Slovenians on the one hand, and all Serbs on the other, stood in equal relation. The only significant differences in interpretation appeared between, and not within, each nation. Arguably, the two broadcasters participated in the parallel processes of intra-national ideological reconciliation, and the cross-national 'irreconciliation' briefly mentioned earlier. When choosing from the available range of possible historical analogies, both televisions privileged those narratives that emphasized the history of conflicts between Yugoslav nations over the history of either cross-national cooperation or intra-national ideological divisions. Although a powerful narrative of successful pan-Yugoslav cooperation was available, and was occasionally invoked by some of the interviewees and sources quoted in the bulletins, it was virtually never adopted by the journalists themselves.

We can therefore conclude that in times of crisis, the mediated perceptions of national time tend to follow the broad contours of narrative conventions discussed earlier in the book. Routine, fairly inconsequential commemorations of historic events are replaced by historical analogies that bring the past to bear directly on the present. Open-ended accounts that allow for the coexistence of several competing interpretations of the past and the future are marginalized to make room for a single, unifying account of the nation's past, present and future.

8

Media Nations, Cultural Diversity and Cosmopolitanism

As the preceding chapters have demonstrated, nations and nationalisms show little signs of fading in significance. Nation-states are still capable of regulating the public forms of collective identification, although the forms and extent of this regulation have been transformed. Apart from that, neither market forces nor other non-state actors seem to be willing to forsake the appeal of nationalism. Instead, they continue to use it to their own ends and draw on nationalist ideas and outlooks to attract customers or to mobilize populations for a particular cause. Rather than leading to a demise of nationalism, the decoupling of states and nations has therefore led to a proliferation and diversification of national imagination, often aligned with the rise of national imagery centred on the figure of the consumer. Media nations have undergone a similar transformation. In spite of the intensification of transnational communication and exchanges, nationalism continues to shape the processes of media production, representation and consumption, particularly in periods of crisis. Regardless of the flexibility of media use afforded by new communication technologies, our patterns of media consumption remain wedded to national perceptions and structures of time, often in hardly visible ways. At the same time, the dominant modes of mediated national imagination are changing. Cultural and political markers of national identification are being recoded to suit the language of market exchange and consumerist lifestyles, attuned to the exigencies of commercial media and transnational corporations.

To many, the persistence of nationalism and media nations is a cause for concern. In both everyday talk and academic discourse, nationalism often appears in a negative light, and is associated with narrow-mindedness and prejudice if not outright aggression and bloodshed. Nationalist attachments are seen as vestiges of the past that make little sense in today's interconnected and interdependent world, and should soon give way to cosmopolitan forms of belonging. There is of course no doubt that nationalism was implicated in numerous atrocities, and continues to underpin a dishearteningly wide range of discriminatory and prejudicial practices. Appeals to national interests present a powerful resource for mobilizing fear and hatred directed at outsiders, as well as for justifying internal suppression of dissenting voices. Those who have experienced the devastating consequences of nationalist excesses at first hand may find it rather difficult to imagine that nationalism can ever be mobilized as a force for good.

Yet we should not forget that nationalism also provides the basis for social inclusion and solidarity. Both its historical rise and contemporary transmutations are closely intertwined with processes of democratization as well as struggles against discrimination and oppression. The nationalist idiom provided the discursive basis for the extension of citizenship rights beyond the propertied classes, and demands for equal political, social and economic rights for both sexes were also often couched in nationalist terms. From eighteenth- and nineteenth-century Europe to twentieth-century India, from post-Communist Central and Eastern Europe to contemporary China, the extension of voting rights went hand in hand with the proliferation of nationalist rhetoric and popular nationalism (Hroch 1985; Tismaneanu 1998; Liew and Wang 2004; Hansen 1999; Snyder 2000; Mansfield and Snyder 2005). To this day, nationalism continues to serve as the language capable of articulating and mobilizing the collective will of disenfranchised populations in the global South, and is used as a shield against exploitative and unequal globalization (e.g. Yeğenoğlu 2005). The reason for this is plain: as a principle of legitimacy that requires power to be exercised in the name of the people, nationalism is clearly compatible with democracy. No matter how much we may want to disentangle the democratizing, inclusive thrust of nationalism from its exclusivist, illiberal potential, we should first acknowledge that, in practical terms, the two often go hand in hand. To put it differently, not only is nationalism unlikely to disappear, it may in fact be wiser not to wish it away without having first found an adequate substitute.

This fundamental tension between inclusion and exclusion, equality and discrimination, is inscribed in the very fabric of national imagination. On the one hand, nations are imagined as communities of equals, tied together by 'horizontal comradeship' that is meant to overcome social, geographic and cultural divisions (Anderson 1991). On the other hand, nations are also held together by bonds of dependence and hierarchy, coupled with a feeling of obligation that drives individuals to commit sacrifices not only out of a sense of loyalty to their co-nationals, but also in order to protect one's dependants – those members of the nation who are seen as too weak to protect themselves on their own (Lomnitz 2001). A similar tension runs through attempts to create a common, national public sphere. The expansion of broadcasting brought into being a shared public culture – complete with sporting events, opera and theatre productions, music concerts and public speeches and celebrations – and made it available to every member of the nation regardless of class, gender, age or ethnicity (cf. Scannell and Cardiff 1991: 277–78). At the same time, broadcasting was also marked by existing hierarchies of power, and inevitably used images of national unity to obscure and naturalize enduring forms of control, exploitation and exclusion within the putative national fraternity (cf. Morley 2000: 110–12).

One may be tempted to resolve these tensions by devising typologies of 'good' and 'bad' nationalisms, or by reserving the term nationalism solely for chauvinist and xenophobic attitudes, while associating feelings of solidarity and inclusiveness with 'good' forms of belonging such as patriotism and cosmopolitanism. Yet, as I suggest in the next section, these divergent dimensions of nationalism are not that easily disentangled from one another. While it may be possible and even desirable to distinguish between them for analytical purposes, they are usually found to be inextricably interwoven in practice. Most importantly, the normative hierarchies typically associated with such typologies can be questioned, leaving one to wonder whether 'civic' nationalism or 'patriotism' are really as unquestionably good as is often assumed. Similar questions arise in relation to the competing approaches to managing cultural diversity, both in societies at large and specifically within the media sector.

Between Equality and Unity: Types of Nationalism, Forms of Belonging and Approaches to Cultural Diversity

One of the earliest and most influential formulations of the normative opposition between 'good' and 'bad' nationalism can be found in Hans Kohn's *Idea of Nationalism* (1944). Kohn traced the evolution of the idea of nationalism back to ancient Greece and Israel, and argued that the rise of modern nationalism in the late eighteenth century was tied to the proliferation of Enlightenment ideals, processes of democratization and liberal universalism. Yet by the time nationalist ideals spread to Central and Eastern Europe, their liberal kernel was lost, and aspirations to universalism were replaced by ethnocentrism and cultural protectionism. To this day, literature on nationalism remains replete with references to two types of nationalism: one civic, liberal, inclusive and compatible with democratic values and norms; the other ethnocentric, illiberal, collectivist and inimical to democracy (e.g. Plamenatz 1976; Ignatieff 1993). While authors may disagree with Kohn's attempt to associate 'good' nationalism with the West and 'bad' nationalism with the East, they often share the same urge to isolate the positive, inclusive and democratic traits of nationalism from their dark, illiberal, ethnocentric counterparts.

Attempts to distinguish between patriotism and nationalism form part of the same intellectual drive. The beneficial aspects of social bonds, such as the feelings of loyalty and solidarity among the in-group, are divorced from negative ones, in particular the irrational hatred of others. Jürgen Habermas' (1998) discussion of 'constitutional patriotism' and its relationship with 'pre-political', ethnic nationalism is a case in point. Habermas acknowledges that, historically, national consciousness facilitated the democratic extension of citizenship rights to all members of the population by providing the cultural framework that helped legitimate claims for equal rights and duties. Yet, in the context of culturally diverse societies, nationalism is no longer able to serve as the basis of solidarity. Instead, argues Habermas, social bonds should now be anchored in 'constitutional patriotism', namely the allegiance to a shared public culture centred on democratic values and human rights, which is strictly divorced from 'pre-political' identities, including those tied to majority culture.

While not without their merits, such distinctions between 'good' and 'bad' forms of social solidarity, or 'good' and 'bad' nationalisms, are fraught with difficulties. To start with, it is unclear whether a shared, civic public culture can ever constitute a viable substitute for the bonds of solidarity rooted in notions of common descent (e.g. see Müller 2007; Calhoun 2007). While acknowledging this dilemma, Habermas and those inspired by the promise of constitutional patriotism provide little by way of persuasive answers. Advocates of patriotism and civic nationalism fare no better. More often than not, the efficacy of civic, liberal forms of solidarity is simply assumed rather than proven empirically. If the dilemma is addressed at all, answers tend to remain vague and lack empirical support. To some, the required level of affect and loyalty can be generated though political involvement in the process of creating, criticizing and revising a shared set of civic values, duties and rights; to others, feelings of solidarity emerge from experiencing the benefits of equal opportunities and welfare state provisions. All of the answers, however, sound far less compelling once we test them against historical and contemporary realities of social solidarity and political action. Even if we accept the desirability of purely liberal, civic forms of collective attachment, we still need to explain why such 'good' forms of collective attachment are proving so difficult to disentangle from their 'bad' counterparts. We also need to acknowledge that, in practical terms, civic forms of social integration are not entirely immune to exclusionary tactics and ideological witch-hunts, usually directed against those who are found lacking in the desired civic or cosmopolitan virtues.

Empirically grounded studies of popular conceptions of nationhood and symbolic boundaries raise serious doubts over the normative distinctions between types of nationalism and social solidarity outlined above. To start with, binary distinctions are often criticized for being too crude to capture the variety of actual forms of collective identification and exclusion. In particular, language and culture, but also religion, have proved difficult to map onto the ethnic–civic distinction, and several authors have instead suggested using more complex typologies (e.g. Zimmer 2003; Janmaat 2006; Bail 2008). Also telling is the fact that among the general population, 'ethnic' and 'civic' markers are not necessarily perceived as mutually exclusive (Jones and Smith 2001; Janmaat 2006, Pehrson et al. 2009). This fact alone suggests that the value-laden, normative distinctions drawn by political theorists find little echo in popular conceptions of belonging. Most importantly, results of empirical studies examining the relationship between types of nationalism and levels of xenophobia are contradictory and inconclusive. While some studies suggest that a civic national identity is indeed more likely to go hand in hand with high levels of tolerance or with preference for less restrictive immigration and citizenship policies (Hjerm 1998; Kunovich 2009), others conclude that attitudes to foreigners and immigrants are not dependent on the *type* of nationalism, but rather on the *intensity* of national feelings (Shulman 2002; Janmaat 2006), and yet others argue that it is conceptions of nationhood based on language rather than ancestry that appear to be most strongly correlated with anti-immigrant prejudice (Pehrson et al. 2009).

Comparative studies of citizenship and immigration regimes yield similarly diverse answers, and lend little support to any hard-and-fast distinctions between intrinsically liberal and inherently exclusive policies. Historically, states have responded to the challenge of diversity in a variety of ways, and it is worth pausing for a moment to consider the full range of these different strategies before looking specifically at those that are most common in the contemporary world. John McGarry and Brendan O'Leary (1993) proposed to distinguish between two broad categories of ethnic conflict regulation. The first includes policy options aimed at eradicating or at least minimizing difference, ranging from genocide and mass population transfers to different forms of assimilation or integration. The other comprises strategies for 'managing' difference, such as various forms of territorial autonomy including federalism, different types of non-territorial (or cultural) autonomy, including consociationalism, and the establishment of hegemonic control or 'majority rule', whereby one ethno-cultural group assumes control over others and makes any challenge to its authority unthinkable. It should be clear from this list alone that a simple binary dichotomy will not get us far in describing the variety of approaches to cultural diversity.

Today, many of these strategies are of course considered illegitimate and indefensible, and contemporary observers and policymakers tend to advocate one of the following three options: federalism or territorial autonomy; consociationalism or cultural autonomy; or one of the options along the continuum between integration and assimilation (e.g. Liebich 2007: 36). Much of the literature on citizenship and integration policies in the West focuses on the latter category and emphasizes the distinction between the difference-friendly multicultural model aimed at integration, usually exemplified as in the UK, and the assimilation-oriented republican model, typically associated with France (e.g. Favell 1998; Kymlicka and Norman 2000; Koopmans et al. 2005). While both are broadly compatible with the 'civic' model of nationhood, and thus differ from the more segregationist approach associated with ethnic models of nationhood, a more nuanced conceptual instrument is needed to describe their similarities and differences. To complicate matters further, states often discriminate between different types of cultural minorities, and are typically far more generous when dealing with long-established, 'historic' or 'autochthonous' groups, such as the Welsh and Scottish in the UK or Catalans in Spain. For instance, Poland's Minority Law, adopted in 2005, recognizes thirteen minorities, and distinguishes between those who have an external homeland – Germans, Belarussians, Ukrainians, Russians, Lithuanians, Slovaks, Jews, Armenians, Czechs, Tatars – and those who do not – Roma, Karaites, Lemkos (Vermeersch 2009: 442). While the latter are granted linguistic and cultural rights, the former also enjoy special electoral rights, including a lower electoral threshold (Dembinska 2008: 921). Most importantly, the law leaves several groups – including the more recently established immigrant minorities and the country's largest minority, the Silesians – without any recognition whatsoever.

Apart from providing an inadequate tool for describing the actual variety of citizenship policies and immigration regimes in different countries, the binary distinctions between types of nationalism and forms of social solidarity also provide a rather poor guide for normative assessments. This becomes evident once we have a look at recent changes to integration policies within the EU. The agreement to harmonize immigrant integration policies across the EU has led member states to adopt increasingly similar policies, all of them broadly attuned with liberal, civic notions of nationhood and aimed at attaining integration and equal treatment without cultural assimilation. Even Germany's policies, which are regularly singled out as 'segregationist' and rooted in an ethnic model of nationhood, have been liberalized considerably and made to comply with more civic notions of citizenship (Joppke 2007: 12). Yet this convergence towards a civic integration model is sometimes conducive to somewhat exclusionary, if not illiberal, practices (Guild et al. 2009). Examples include the imposition of liberal values and lifestyles in traditionally multicultural Netherlands, and the infamous requirement to scrutinize the candidate's 'inner disposition' to liberal values as part of the naturalization procedure in the German federal *Land* of Baden-Württemberg (Michalowski 2009; Joppke 2008). To be sure, these discriminatory practices are not an inherent or unavoidable part of all citizenship and integration policies founded on liberal values. Many of the current practices are consistent with a purely procedural understanding of liberalism, which allows for the coexistence of multiple ways of life and value systems in the same society and is directed at regulating citizens' external behaviour while remaining indifferent to their inner, private dispositions. Still, as Joppke (2008: 543–44) notes, liberalism also appears in a different form and can function as an identity that requires newcomers to share particular norms and lifestyles that go well beyond the values of justice and equal treatment. The existence of this substantive, potentially exclusionary type of liberalism reminds us that even the most resolutely civic approach to cultural diversity and integration is not immune to discrimination and prejudice.

Also worth noting is the fact that recent shifts in citizenship and immigration policies in the EU are moving hand in hand with the shrinking of welfare provisions and the growing prominence of economic liberalism. While putting far more emphasis on immigrant integration and compliance with liberal values, EU member states are offering a considerably more restricted range of welfare provisions, and are even shifting much of the economic and social burden of immigration onto immigrants themselves (cf. Schierup et al. 2006). The common principles underlying the 2004 European Council agreement on European immigrant integration policies, which emphasize the importance of inclusion and equal opportunity, are grounded in market liberalism and premised on the retreat of the state as the agent responsible for the well-being and integration of immigrant populations. Perhaps most telling is the fact that EU policy documents do not envisage social inclusion as a good in itself, but as a means of furthering the EU's capacity to compete in the global market (Joppke 2007: 17–18). As some commentators note, the recent signs of disaffection among immigrant youth in France and the US, along with attacks on minority members in other immigrant societies, result precisely from this confluence of the global spread of economic liberalism and the parallel retrenchment of welfare state provisions (Castles and Miller 2009). Taken together, these developments left immigrant societies facing demands for greater integration while at the same time lacking the necessary social and economic basis for solidarity among strangers.

Both the sheer diversity of existing forms of collective attachment and institutional approaches to cultural diversity, as well as the rather mixed record of their social consequences, should make us proceed cautiously when speculating about the relative advantages and disadvantages of different types of nationhood and different modes of citizenship and integration. This is not to say that we should abandon the efforts to create and foster a truly liberal, inclusive form of social solidarity, but merely that we should be wary of assuming that only some types of nationhood and some forms of social bonds are amenable to democratic and civic values or to social integration, or that some citizenship and immigration regimes are inherently immune from illiberal practices. The same applies to approaches to cultural diversity within the media, and to normative discussions about the benefits and drawbacks of minority media. It is to these issues that we now turn.

Mediating Cultural Diversity: The Ills and Gains of Public Sphericules

How should we accommodate the divergent media and cultural preferences of contemporary societies? Should we stimulate the formation of designated outlets serving the needs of different niche audiences, or instead channel public funding into overarching media and make sure they are capable of appealing to diverse cultural tastes? To many observers, the contemporary fragmentation of national media landscapes, driven by technological changes, cultural diversity and the intensification of transnational communication, poses a threat to the quality of public deliberation. In their view, the centrifugal forces of 'public sphericules' prevent us from engaging in a sustained discussion of shared interests beyond cultural, social and ideological differences, and from debating competing solutions to common problems (Gitlin 1998). Rather than addressing the communicative needs and interests of culturally diverse audiences via segmented spaces of communication, we therefore ought to seek ways to integrate these audiences into the same, nation- and state-wide communicative sphere. Apart from that, critics also raise doubts over the quality and popularity of special minority programming and outlets, and point out that the existence of dedicated time slots and media can sometimes be used as an excuse for neglecting minority issues in mainstream programming (for an overview, see Leurdijk 2006: 27–28). Culturally segmented communication is seen as particularly harmful in the context of societies already riven by deep-seated suspicions and hostilities between culturally distinct groups. In such cases, separate minority outlets are believed to exacerbate rather than alleviate existing fissures, and threaten civic bonds and solidarities. Due to that, argues one commentator, 'ethnically segmented media markets should be counter-acted by the promotion of civic-territorial conceptions of national iden-tity', promoted through an 'integrative press' (Snyder 2000: 180).

The proliferation of commercial ethnic media and the accessibility of television programming from kin-states – brought by satellite links and the Internet – gave rise to similar fears in virtually all media-rich and culturally diverse countries. In Macedonia, alarms were raised over the potentially harmful effects of commercial ethnic television channels, which have proliferated in the country during the 1990s. According to one commentator, these media allowed minority ethnic audiences to link with what they perceived as their co-nationals worldwide and thereby led to a fragmentation of Macedonian audiences along ethnic and lifestyle lines (Kolar-Panov 2004). Instead of promoting integration into the Macedonian mainstream, these media outlets allegedly saw their audiences as 'fragments of a neighbouring homeland' and encouraged them to identify with neighbouring Kosovo, Albania and Serbia instead of Macedonia (Kolar-Panov 1997: 80). Media analysts in Estonia were likewise concerned that the availability of Russian satellite channels was deepening existing social divisions and hampering the integration of the large Russian-speaking minority into Estonian society (Vihalemm 1999). These fears are not limited only to European states. In Chapter 4, we have seen how the rise of commercial satellite channels targeting distinct linguistic, cultural and religious communities in India has been implicated in the demise of India's 'unity in diversity' ideal and in the proliferation of sectarian forms of political identity.

Yet the social impact of a culturally segmented mass communication is not necessarily so grim. Although public sphericules are expected to be particularizing, their particularism does not automatically involve a rejection of universalism or a retreat from the wider public sphere (Dayan 1998; Siapera 2010: 106–10). In some cases, minority outlets can in fact expose values that are far more inclusive and universal than those endorsed by the mainstream public sphere. The history of Chicago's foremost African-American newspaper, *The Chicago Defender*, provides a good example. Although the newspaper's key function was community building, its creators also endeavoured to create a parallel public and electoral sphere for Chicago's black citizens, who at the time faced tremendous obstacles to political and public participation (Herbst 1994: 71–79). *The Defender*'s parallel public sphere was not created with an isolationist goal in mind, but, quite the opposite, with the aim of helping Chicago's black citizens penetrate into mainstream public discourse as well as into mainstream city politics. Most significantly, the parallel, marginal status was not a matter of choice but a direct outcome of exclusionary practices in the mainstream, which prevented blacks from finding employment with already existing Chicago newspapers. This case reminds us that minority media can often provide a safe space inside which a marginalized minority can search for ways to improve its present situation. Rather than being an obstacle to public deliberation and civic identification, minority media can in fact themselves contribute to the formation of more integrative and inclusive public spheres and identities.

It is also important to note that even when minority media do fall prey to exclusionary practices and isolate themselves from mainstream concerns, their audiences may not necessarily accept their messages at face value. As Asu Aksoy and Kevin Robins (2000) show, Turks in Germany use transnational television from Turkey 'to think across cultural spaces' and counter the homogenizing national discourse offered by the Turkish-made programmes. While the producers may have believed that Turkish satellite television keeps Turks in Germany 'in touch with their homeland', the viewers were not always eager to accept the claim that Turkey is their true 'homeland', and instead situated themselves in relation to, as well as at a distance from, two cultural spaces: the German and the Turkish one. These patterns are not an exception. The results of quantitative studies of media use preferences among the Turkish diaspora in Belgium and Germany (Gezduci and D'Haenens 2007; Trebbe 2007) point to a roughly similar conclusion. Participants who expressed a strong attachment to Turkey were likely to be avid consumers of *both* Turkish language news *and* local news in

German, Dutch or French. These results suggest that even the particularlistic, essentializing minority media discourses can serve as a pretext for civic and perhaps even cosmopolitan attachments.

How about the alternative approach to dealing with cultural diversity within the media, namely the creation of 'integrative' media that cater for all cultural groups at once, or even explicitly encourage cross-cultural exchanges and dialogues? To start with, it is worth noting that over the past decades, integrative, cross-cultural programming has been embraced as the preferred option by an increasing number of media professionals, at least in Western Europe and in immigration countries such as Canada, the USA and Australia. Earlier forms of programming and publishing, targeted specifically at minority groups, have been giving way to cross-cultural formats that seek to appeal to both mainstream and minority audiences (Leurdijk 2006; Podkalicka 2008, Brook 2009, Malik 2010). The reasons for this shift are multiple and vary from country to country, but typically involve a combination of market pressures, technological changes, audience demand and changing philosophies of integration. The latter cannot be disentangled from changes in the broader socio-political environment since the 9/11 attacks.

The history of US films and TV shows with ethno-racially diverse characters stretches back to the early World War II combat films of the 1940s, yet it is only recently that similarly diverse casts have started appearing in entertainment genres that focus on private relationships and everyday life. Unlike their predecessors, successful multiracial soaps such as *Lost* (2004–), *Grey's Anatomy* (2005–) and *Ugly Betty* (2006–) all feature racially diverse characters who are mutually supporting, put on an equal footing, and often involved in romantic relationships (Brook 2009). The fact that these shows were designed with a global distribution in mind certainly played a role in stimulating the adoption of such a format, as did the growth of non-white audiences and the increasing acceptance of ethno-cultural diversity in the USA (ibid.). In Europe, popular cross-cultural programmes such as the British satirical TV series *Goodness, Gracious Me* (1998–2001) and the Dutch late-night comedy talk show *Raymann Is Late* (2001–) were produced by public rather than commercial broadcasters, yet the motivations were often similar to those in the USA, namely commercial competition (Leurdijk 2006: 29). Changing citizenship and immigration policies at European level, particularly the convergence towards the civic integration model charted earlier in this chapter, have played a role as well. Prompted by these wider policy debates, several European broadcasters issued policy documents aimed at securing a greater involvement of broadcast media in aiding social integration (Horsti 2009: 340). The contribution of mass communication to cross-cultural cohesion has come under renewed scrutiny also in traditionally divided societies with long-established segmented media systems, such as Switzerland and Belgium, as well as in the newly independent and ethnically diverse states of Eastern Europe, such as Estonia, Macedonia and Bosnia and Herzegovina (cf. Salovaara-Moring and Kallas 2007: 69–71; Bašić-Hrvatin et al. 2008).

Yet, is the integrative, cross-cultural content necessarily better than the provision of special programme slots or media outlets for minority audiences? Again, much as with the segmented media system and minority media, there are no universally applicable answers to this question either. Studies that explicitly examine the audience reception of these newest cross-cultural genres are too few and far between to allow firm conclusions to be drawn. Some results are encouraging and suggest that programming that explicitly seeks to subvert dominant discourse, present minority characters in a non-stereotypical and positive way, and invite viewers to identify with characters from a different ethnic background, does have the potential to lower perceptions of ethnic threat (Müller 2009; cf. also Coover 2001). However, it is doubtful to what extent the multicultural shows that have proved to be most appealing to mainstream audiences actually correspond to the cross-cultural depictions used in the studies. In one case, the stimulus materials involved news segments created specifically for the purpose of the study, which may not have adequate counterparts in actual news coverage. In the other study, episodes of an actually broadcast multicultural drama were used, yet it was a programme that attracted relatively low audience numbers and, unlike similar but more popular programmes, explicitly sought to subvert dominant stereotypes.

As noted earlier, the recent growth in cross-cultural content is often stimulated by commercial imperatives. Given that the market logic inevitably imposes limitations on the forms of collective imagination fostered in such programmes, one is left wondering whether these shows are indeed able to contribute to the subversion of stereotypes and identification with out-groups. American multiracial soaps may well have put ethnically and culturally diverse characters on an equal footing and helped normalize interracial romance, yet they often did so at the price of neglecting the historical legacies of oppression and persistent ethnoracial inequalities (Brook 2009). Many popular cross-cultural programmes have of course avoided such flattening out of differences and derived their popularity from mocking – rather than ignoring – the prejudices of both mainstream and minority populations, as for instance in the TV show *Goodness Gracious Me*. Yet ethnic humour is not necessarily as benign as we are often led to believe, and it is difficult to draw a clear line between innocuous and offensive jokes without taking into account the broader context of joke-telling, including both the teller and the audience as well as the political and ideological environment in which they are situated (cf. Billig 2005; Kuipers 2006; Lockyer and Pickering 2008).

It is also worth highlighting that commercially driven multicultural programmes typically avoid dealing with the less entertaining, and hence less easily 'consumable', aspects of inter-ethnic relations. In the search for universally appealing angles and topics, cross-cultural media producers are often compelled to downplay cultural differences and controversial issues and focus instead on lifestyle choices and individual experiences (cf. Leurdijk 2006). As a consequence, the programmes they produce will probably make only a limited contribution to the development of civic virtues and sensibilities that are essential to the functioning of a multicultural democracy, namely multicultural literacy, moral deference, and openness to emotional realignment (Jaggar 1999: 323–26). The awards for the best multicultural programme in Europe, Prix Europa Iris, do little to counter these trends. Initially, the prizes were awarded to shows that were deemed to be best at highlighting discrimination, ethnocentrism and racial prejudice. In recent years, the main emphasis shifted and awards are now increasingly given to shows that portray instances of 'harmonious multiculturalism' and focus on experiences of individual minority members eager to integrate into host societies (Horsti 2009). These trends are evidently in tune with the tendency of current integration policies to shift the burden of integration onto immigrants themselves, and absolve the host population from acknowledging their own role in overcoming social exclusion. Furthermore, we should also note that successful, award-winning, cross-cultural programming – being driven by market demand – typically speaks to the tastes of young, multicultural and relatively well-off urban audiences, usually at the cost of older, first-generation immigrants (Leurdijk 2006). It is also difficult to see how such programming might contribute to tackling the exploitation of the growing numbers of low-wage immigrant workers in the Western metropolises.

These recent changes in multicultural programming are clearly in line with the transformation of media systems and mediated grammars of nationhood that we have traced in Chapters 3 and 4, in particular with the proliferation of commercial media and the growing prominence of consumerist imagination. The forces of economic liberalization and media commercialization have doubtlessly helped diminish the ethno-cultural segmentation of media markets, pulling minority characters and experiences away from the 'ghetto' of special minority programming and transforming them into integral elements of national media culture. Yet, while pulling mediated national imagination away from the homogenizing pressures of the nation-state, commercially driven multicultural programming has simultaneously subjected it to the logic of the market and economies of scale. As a result, this type of cross-cultural media content is not particularly well placed to address the needs of the poor and the elderly, regardless of ethno-cultural background. Much as with the media output in post-Apartheid South Africa and post-1980s India, these multicultural programmes have widened the scope of national imagination beyond ethno-cultural divides, but often did so at the price of neglecting persistent forms of racial and ethno-cultural discrimination, particularly those interlocked with socio-economic cleavages. Let us be clear: this does not suggest that the mainstreaming of cultural diversity via commercial media does not deserve our support – it most certainly does, not least for strategic reasons. Yet we should also make sure that this particular form of cross-cultural imagination does not become the only one available, or comes to be seen as a panacea for all the ills of contemporary multicultural societies.

What lessons can we derive from these conflicting messages about the promises and drawbacks of competing approaches to the mediation of cultural diversity, both those premised on the recognition and accommodation of difference within a segmented media system, as well as those dedicated to fostering individual equality and transcultural solidarity through integrative media outlets? Above all, these messages confirm that there are no universally applicable or enduring solutions to the challenges of cultural diversity. Intuitively it may seem that support for programming and publishing that transcends ethno-cultural boundaries within a society is the right way to go. Yet, in and of itself, the fact that a particular form of communication fosters modes of belonging beyond the confines of the local culture is neither a cause for celebration nor a reason for concern. To be able to asses cross-cultural communication from a normative standpoint, we have to first ask what kinds of inclusion and exclusion it engenders, and keep in mind that the mere transcendence of ethno-cultural divisions within a state does not necessarily bring about connections that are open to everyone, but can easily end up replacing one form of exclusion with another. Due to that, multicultural programming that proved effective in one political, cultural and historic context will not necessarily bring the same results in a different environment. When evaluating which approach to the mediation of cultural diversity may be best for a particular society at a particular moment, we need to be mindful of the broader political, economic, historical and demographic factors that are likely to influence the mediation of cultural difference and determine its social consequences. These are likely to include a range of domestic factors such as ethnic composition, historical legacies of nation-building, citizenship and integration policies, economic performance, advertising expenditure and strength of public service broadcasting, as well as international factors including the presence of kin-states and kin-state satellite channels, and various international political actors (Mihelj 2009). We will see that similar reservations are in order also when assessing the potential benefits of cosmopolitan communication.

National Public Spheres and Cosmopolitan Connections

In contemporary media and communication research, cosmopolitanism often functions in similar ways as 'good', civic or liberal nationalism did in the past, namely as a form of loyalty that is opposed to and incompatible with 'bad', intolerant and exclusivist modes of belonging. Transnational communicative exchanges, we are told, have given rise to attitudes and feelings that diverge significantly from those characteristic of the nation-state era, and present us with glimpses of a new, de-territorialized, cosmopolitan society in the making. Likewise, challenges posed by global migration and environmental problems are supposedly disrupting the traditional structures of national citizenship and calling for the establishment of global forms of citizenship, solidarity and action.

While an appreciation of cosmopolitan realities of modern communication is certainly necessary, it would be wrong to assume that the current disjunction between nation-states, loyalties and communicative spheres constitutes an entirely new phenomenon – or, for that matter, that old conceptual instruments are entirely unfit for describing the present condition. As pointed out in Chapter 3, the trajectories of nation-state building in modernity have been fraught with difficulties and had to compete with alternative forms of political sovereignty and collective identification, including in particular multinational empires and federations. For the peripheral states and former colonies, contemporary processes of transnationalization and fragmentation of state sovereignty do not constitute a radical change: the vulnerability to transnational intervention and dependence on foreign loans and technology transfer is a reality they have learned to reckon with long ago. Due to that, it makes sense to interpret these recent transformations of citizenship in relation to long-term historical processes, including colonial and postcolonial experiences of overlapping sovereignties, external interventions and multiple forms of belonging (cf. Randiera 2007).

This brings us to the next key point. Often, cosmopolitanism is conceived as a stable set of cognitive and emotional dispositions that pertain to some social groups but are entirely alien to others. Transnational elites and globally dispersed diasporas have often been identified as particularly prone to nurturing cosmopolitan modes of belonging, while rural inhabitants and low-waged national citizens were believed to be locked in parochial, xenophobic forms of solidarity. Yet empirical inquiries into the nature of ordinary, everyday expressions of cosmopolitanism reveal that these two forms of loyalty are not necessarily mutually exclusive. Hence, cosmopolitanism is better conceived as a set of resources, values and dispositions that are selectively mobilized and appropriated by diverse groups of people in everyday, ordinary situations (cf. Skrbis and Woodward 2007; Nowicka and Rovisco 2009). Understood in this way, cosmopolitanism is not incompatible with national or local outlooks but, rather, constitutes one of the potential, multiple forms of attachments that human beings enact, depending on the particular situation they find themselves in (cf. Robbins 1998), usually in the context of engagements with various transnational forms and representations (Woodward et al. 2008). Rather than presenting a radical departure from conditions of modernity and the world of nation-states, cosmopolitanism so understood is 'embedded in structural conditions defined by citizenship and the nation-state' (Vertovec 2004: 116). In other words, while cosmopolitanism is certainly linked to universalism, this does not automatically make it hostile to particularism. Instead, cosmopolitanism can and most often does adopt a form that embraces particular identities and 'seeks to suffuse [them] with a sense of moral accountability to other human beings' (Liklanter 2007: 36).

Apart from overstating the contrast between the past and the present, and assuming an incompatibility between cosmopolitan universalism and nationalist particularism, the 'strong' theories of cosmopolitanism outlined above also tend to miss the potential of cosmopolitanism to turn into an exclusivist identity. Once we start unpacking the notion of cosmopolitanism empirically, it becomes evident that attitudes and practices that usually pass as 'cosmopolitan' – such as the ability to recognize and appreciate cultural products (music, food, language and so on) – can easily function as a marker of moral superiority and higher social status, and hence as a tool of exclusion (cf. Skrbis et al. 2004: 130–31). Values and norms that typically motivate cosmopolitan practices, such as the belief in universal human rights, can also easily serve as an instrument of continuing domination and exploitation. It is enough to recall the intermingling of liberal feminist criticism and imperial arrogance in Katherine Mayo's *Mother India* (1927), discussed in Chapter 6, to understand that even the most noble cause can easily run astray if the actors do not take into account their own embeddedness in existing power relations. To Mayo, Britain had a duty to oppose India's independence out of compassion for Indian women, who allegedly had little hope of liberation if they were to be left at the mercy of tradition-bound, inherently patriarchal Indian men. Contemporary debates about human rights violations in China or oppression of women in the Middle East often bear more than just superficial resemblance to these old colonial discourses. This yet again reminds us of the necessity for historical contextualization of cosmopolitan practices and beliefs.

If it is the case that cosmopolitanism is not necessarily as inclusive as we are often led to believe, then how viable is it to automatically assume its normative superiority over nationhood? This is a question that much of the current literature on cosmopolitan communication, consumed by its urge to expose the drawbacks of national communicative spheres, fails to address. As Nancy Fraser (2007) notes, debates about transnational public spheres, focused as they are on issues of cultural identity, hybridity and glocalization, often neglect questions that are of key importance to critical theory, namely whether such a sphere is actually inclusive enough to provide access to all those affected, whether it allows communicators to participate as peers, and whether the collective will formed in such a sphere has any capacity to affect political decision making. In other words, cosmopolitan communication is not a universal remedy for all the ills of nationally bounded communication. While capable of transcending national boundaries, it can easily end up instituting new forms of exclusion – based, for instance, on race, religion or class – or engender public deliberation that is unable to translate collective will into administrative power or legally binding rules. Also questionable is the ability of cosmopolitan communication to engender communicative exchanges that are conducive to multicultural literacy or openness to emotional realignment (cf. Jaggar 1999). We may disagree over the relative importance of each of these principles, argue that they raise the bar too high, or even suggest that some of them remain too embedded in a liberal-capitalist vision of modernity to serve as universally applicable benchmarks (e.g. Conway and Singh 2009). Yet none of this detracts from the simple fact that the normative debate over cosmopolitanism and transnational communication is in dire need of empirically and historically situated analysis. However contestable the normative criteria may be, it is only by engaging in empirical research that we can hope to make them better.

With these observations in mind, let us now turn to some of the existing empirical studies that set out to examine whether and to what extent

cosmopolitan (and, more broadly, transnational) communication actually merits being seen as 'better' than national communication, and also
whether national and cosmopolitan communication are necessarily
incompatible. These include studies of the European public sphere,
transnational broadcasting and entertainment, and computer-mediated
communication. Within the European Union, transnational debates
clearly could, at least in principle, be capable of influencing decision-
making and turning collective will into binding laws. Given the paucity
of truly pan-European media, some commentators remain sceptical
about the possibility of cosmopolitan deliberation in Europe. Such a
view remains wedded to a false assumption that national communication
is necessarily incompatible with cosmopolitan exchanges. Several
authors have argued that we should look for traces of the European
public sphere in national media themselves, and examine the formation
of a cosmopolitan consciousness that is becoming visible in debates
about European topics, references to European actors and shared values
(e.g. Schlesinger 1999; Van de Steeg 2002). Numerous empirical studies have followed up on this approach, examining the extent of
Europeanization and its different inflections in various national public
spheres (e.g. Trenz 2004; Downey and Koenig 2006; Krzyzanowski
2009).

While certainly valuable, these contributions say little about whether
such 'Europeanized' national debates actually encourage readers to
engage with issues on an equal footing, and approach them as members
of an imagined community that is culturally diverse yet nonetheless
shares common political values. The few studies that explicitly address
these normative issues are not particularly optimistic in their assessments. For instance, a quantitative examination of newspaper debates
over Turkey's accession to the EU in five European states demonstrated
that only a minor proportion of coverage encouraged readers to see
themselves as equal partners in a critical-rational deliberation. Instead,
the majority of reports and commentaries fostered an identification with
distinct cultures or civilizations that had little if anything in common
(Koenig et al. 2006). A study of debates on the European Constitutional
Treaty in Estonian and Latvian print media equally showed that the mere
presence of transnationalization does not necessarily mean greater diversity or inclusiveness (Evas 2007). In both countries, the debate lacked
the usual divisions between left- and right-wing interpretations, between
opinions pro- and against EU integration, as well as between supporters
of the welfare state and market liberalism. The positions advocated were
largely uniform and the only significant polarization occurred at a
transnational level, in the sense that the uniformly positive attitude to the

Constitutional Treaty domestically was contrasted with the negative attitudes in France and the Netherlands. Apart from that, the newspapers in both countries also failed to give voice to the substantial Russian-speaking minorities. Given its exclusivity and uniformity, the coverage was not particularly conducive to deliberation and could not be justifiably labelled as 'public' in the strong sense of the word.

Studies of transnational news broadcasters such as the CNN, BBC World and Al Jazeera bring equally mixed results. A recent analysis of the CNN news coverage of the Tibetan uprising in 2008 (Moyo 2010) pointed out that although the reporting was motivated by unmistakably cosmopolitan ideals, it was far from disinterested. The coverage was rooted in a sense of moral obligation to inform viewers of injustices perpetrated in various parts of the globe, yet unwittingly promoted a relatively narrow set of values. Priority was given to civil and political liberties, while issues of economic inequality and distributive justice received little consideration. This particular omission was arguably self-serving; being a global corporate actor, the CNN can profit from a worldwide extension of civil and political liberties, but does not stand to gain much from global economic redistribution or the global extension of welfare state principles. This is not to say that all transnational broadcasters are equally biased in their appropriation of cosmopolitan attitudes, or biased in the same way. According to at least some commentators, Al Jazeera English presents a welcome alternative to other global news broadcasters, manages to avoid the stereotyping of cultural 'others', and is capable of encouraging cross-cultural empathy, dialogue and reconciliation (el-Nawawy and Powers 2010). However, other analysts point out that despite its claim to represent stories from the perspective of the underprivileged and disenfranchised, and provide a platform for oppositional and controversial voices, the sources of Al Jezeera English remain mostly elite and male (Figenschou 2010).

Arguably, digital technologies have the potential to overcome many of the limitations of transnational communication we have just outlined. Given their participatory potential and accessibility, online forums, discussion lists and platforms such as YouTube have the ability to bridge national divides, but also to expand deliberation to ordinary citizens, and thus open up spaces for truly inclusive cosmopolitan exchanges across a wide range of opinions. There is certainly much cause for excitement and optimism in the face of the new venues for participation and transnational networking enabled by the fast-changing digital culture. Yet, at the same time, we should keep in mind that these digitally enabled transnational bonds and exchanges may not necessarily live up to the ideals of civic solidarity and public deliberation, and that their capacity to affect political decision-making is limited. For instance, an analysis of online forums and discussion lists formed by three transnational civil society actors (Cammaerts and Van Audenhove 2005) demonstrated that, while stretching beyond the local–national setting and addressing a range of transnational issues, debates were often dominated by like-minded, mostly male participants who were already politically active off-line. Only in the case of one of the civil society organizations did the debate attract a wider range of opinions and participants. Also worth noting is that the participants remained firmly rooted in local and national contexts, thus confirming that national and cosmopolitan attachments are not necessarily in conflict.

Studies of participation and transnational communication on YouTube bring us to a similar conclusion. Through allowing users around the world to engage in uploading, viewing or commenting on various videos, YouTube is inviting creative participation and networking at a hitherto unprecedented scale (cf. Burgess and Green 2009). Given its accessibility and opportunities for participation, YouTube is clearly well equipped to provide a highly inclusive platform for deliberation on issues of transnational relevance. Indeed, an exploration of YouTube responses to the anti-Islam video *Fitna*, produced in 2008 by the controversial Dutch politician Geert Wilders, demonstrated that the exchange on YouTube was far more inclusive than that in the mainstream media (Van Zoonen et al. 2010). This study also uncovered exemplary cases of civic, cross-cultural engagement. In one such case, the poster – a young man – speaks to the camera, introduces himself as 'Dutch' and then goes on to express his dismay at his compatriot Wilder's ignorance of Islam and appeal to universal humanitarian values and cross-cultural understanding. In doing so, he simultaneously situates himself within the national as well as the transnational community, and counters *Fitna* using evidence-based claims. However, not all of the responses were so eager to adopt an inclusive stance or treat other participants as equals, and some appealed primarily to emotions without using much evidence to support their claims. For instance, some of the pro-*Fitna* videos perpetuated anti-Arab and anti-Muslim stereotypes, suggesting that Islam is an inherently violent and anti-democratic religion and hence Muslims had no right to be treated as equals. On the other hand, some of the critical, anti-*Fitna* videos attacked Wilders personally, mocked his appearance or described and visualized him in demeaning ways, without providing much explanation for their disagreement with Wilders or his video.

Finally, entertainment genres and commercially driven cultural production and consumption also deserve our attention here. Arguably, entertainment genres – particularly those relying on visual modes of expression and centred on universal experiences and emotions of birth, death, friendship and love – may be better tailored to engender cosmopolitan attitudes than mainstream news programming. In particular, it seems feasible to suggest that fiction genres may be capable of contributing to a 'banal cosmopolitanism', visible in casual references to humanity and in a diffuse sense of belonging to a global community (e.g. Beck 2002; cf. also Urry 2000). This is also the conclusion of a large-scale audience study examining the patterns of reception of the fantasy trilogy *Lord of the Rings* (Kuipers and de Kloet 2009), which revealed that audiences worldwide interpreted the films by drawing on largely similar repertoires of evaluation. As the authors point out, these shared readings do not necessarily signal a decline of national differences and interpretive frameworks. Rather, they result from a conscious effort of global media corporations to appeal to diverse audiences by developing multiple storylines and points of identification that are not culturally specific, and thereby feed into the shared 'wish of audiences to experience globality in their everyday lives' (ibid.: 18). Of course, all the reservations we have voiced when discussing multicultural entertainment programming at national level apply here as well. One cannot help but doubt whether such banal cosmopolitanism can help engender cross-cultural understanding and engagement with radically different views, or whether it merely sweeps differences and tensions under the carpet for the benefit of the market. Yet, for better or worse, we have little choice but to learn to make do with the opportunities that such market-driven, entertainment-induced forms of cosmopolitanism offer, not least because traditional political identities and sharp lines of demarcation between citizens and consumers are increasingly giving way to far less clear-cut forms of political engagement (cf. Bennett 2004).

These examples clearly suggest that we should proceed with caution when making blanket assessments about the relative advantages and disadvantages of cosmopolitan and national communications in general, or about their mutual incompatibility. Cosmopolitan communication is not inherently more valuable than national communication, nor does it necessarily stand in opposition to it. The forces we encountered back in Chapters 3 and 4, when examining the shaping of collective imagination and mass communication at national level – market pressures, state institutions, religious institutions, competing political ideologies and so on – are at work within cosmopolitan modes of belonging and communication as well. Much as in the case of national imagination and the national media, they are clearly capable of inflecting cosmopolitan communication in ways that best serve their own interests, be they economic, political, cultural, or all of those together. Cosmopolitan communication, then, does not automatically equal 'limitless communication', in the sense of a communication that would embrace 'diverse global communities of discourse which reflect the heterogeneous quality of international society' (Liklanter 1998: 36). If it is such 'limitless communication' that we are after, we should therefore avoid the assumption that any form of cross-national communication will automatically be able to engender it. This is not to say that we should abandon our search for forms of communication and solidarity that are capable of overcoming the drawbacks of national communicative spheres and identities, but merely that it may be wiser to look for solutions that harness the potential of existing national frameworks, and help open them up to transnational loyalties and mediated bonds.

It is only by keeping such cosmopolitan and civic connections embedded in local and national frameworks that we will be able to ensure that the deliberations taking place within such spaces actually have the capacity to influence political decision-making. Until we see the establishment of effective transnational political institutions capable of operating on their own, without deferring in part to the sovereignties of individual nation-states, cosmopolitan sensibilities and debates will have to find their ways back into national spaces of communication to be politically consequential. True, we have seen successful cases of global consumer campaigns that have been able to apply pressure on transnational corporations without resorting to political institutions, and those are likely to become even more influential in the future (cf. Bennett 2004). Similarly, religiously motivated charity work has helped motivate transnational campaigns and help the underprivileged around the world to receive basic education or medical support, often without much public funding. Yet these initiatives will not be enough for cosmopolitan citizens to achieve all their goals, since some political aims cannot be that easily adapted to the logic of branded communication and consumer preferences, or religious norms and values.

For the time being, nation-states, along with the international political bodies they are members of, remain the most powerful allies in wrestling cosmopolitan communicative exchanges out of the embrace of other institutional frameworks that can engender them – in particular, transnational corporations and transnational religious institutions – and thus ensure that such exchanges remain, at least in part, distanced from both religious and commercial imagery and the particular forms of exclusion they are likely to generate. It is the political infrastructure set up by the international order of nation-states that can also serve as an alternative anchor for many transnational civil society organizations. It is only by ensuring that cosmopolitan communication remains tied, through various feedback loops, to national public spheres and nation-state legislative and executive bodies, that we will be able to ensure that it continues to approach the ideal of limitless communication. It is only in this way that we will be able to pursue cosmopolitanism's full democratizing potential – akin to the one that saw nationalist ideologies mobilized for the pursuit of inclusion and extension of equal rights across gender, class, ethnic and religious divides.

All of this indicates that the route to cosmopolitan communication does not lead *past* the nation-state and national spaces of communication, but *through* them. We should also accept that, given the pace of technological and social change, the ideal of cosmopolitan communication and cosmopolitan media nations will remain elusive and one that we will never be able to fix in permanent policies and solutions.

Bibliography

Abu-Lughod, L. (2005) *Dramas of Nationhood: The Politics of Television in Egypt* (Chicago, IL: University of Chicago Press).

Adams, I. (2002) *Political Ideology Today* (Manchester: Manchester University Press).

Aksoy, A. and Robins, K. (2000) 'Thinking across Spaces: Transnational Television from Turkey', *European Journal of Cultural Studies* 3(3): 343–65.

Alasuutari, P. (2000) 'Review Essay: Globalization and the Nation-State: An Appraisal of the Discussion', *Acta Sociologica* 43(3): 259–69.

Albers-Miller, N. D. and Gelb, B. D. (1996) 'Business Advertising Appeals as a Mirror of Cultural Dimensions: A Study of Eleven Countries', *Journal of Advertising* 25(4): 57–70.

Allan, S. (1999) *News Culture* (Buckingham: Open University Press).

Altschull, H. J. (1984) *Agents of Power: The Role of the News Media in Human Affairs* (New York: Longman).

Anderson, B. (1991) *Imagined Communities: Reflections on the Origins and Spread of Nationalism*, 2nd edn (London: Verso).

Anderson, B. (1998) *The Spectre of Comparisons: Nationalism, South Asia and the World* (London: Verso).

Anderson, B. (2006) 'Travel and Traffic: On the Geo-biography of Imagined Communities', in B. Anderson, *Imagined Communities: Reflections on the Origins and Spread of Nationalism* (London: Verso).

Ansell, C. K. (2001) 'Political Legitimacy', in N. J. Smelser and P. Bates (eds) *International Encyclopedia of the Social and Behavioral Sciences* (Oxford: Pergamon Press).

Armbrust, W. (2006) 'Synchronizing Watches: The State, the Consumer, and Sacred Time in Ramadan Television', in B. Meyer and A. Moors (eds) *Religion, Media and the Public Sphere* (Bloomington, IN: Indiana University Press).

Armstrong, J. (1982) *Nations before Nationalism* (Chapel Hill, NC: University of North Carolina Press).

Arnason, J. P. (1993) *The Future That Failed: Origins and Destinies of the Soviet Model* (London: Routledge).

Arnason, J. P. (2000) 'Communism and Modernity', *Daedalus* 129(1): 61–90.

Arnason, J. P. (2006) 'Nations and Nationalism: Between General Theory and Comparative History', in G. Delanty and K. Kumar (eds) *The SAGE Handbook of Nations and Nationalism* (London: Sage).

Askew, K. (2002) *Performing the Nation: Swahili Music and Cultural Politics in Tanzania* (Chicago, IL: University of Chicago Press).

Aslama, M. and Pantti, M. (2007) 'Flagging Finnishness: Reproducing National Identity in Reality Television', *Television and New Media* 8(1): 49–67.

Bail, C. A. (2008) 'The Configuration of Symbolic Boundaries against Immigrants in Europe', *American Sociological Review* 73(1): 37–59.

Banerjee, S. (2003) 'Gender and Nationalism: The Masculinization of Hinduism and Female Political Participation in India', *Women's Studies International Forum* 26(2): 167–79.

Baranowski, S. (1995) *The Sanctity of Rural Life: Nobility, Protestantism, and Nazism in Weimar Prussia* (Oxford: Oxford University Press).

Barker, R. (2001) *Legitimating Identities: The Self-Presentations of Rulers and Subjects* (Cambridge: Cambridge University Press).

Barnett, C. (1999) 'Broadcasting the Rainbow Nation: Media, Democracy and Nation-Building in South Africa', *Antipode* 31(3): 274–303.

Bašić Hrvatin, S. (1997) 'The Role of the Media in the Transition', in D. Hafner-Fink, and J. R. Robbins (eds) *Making a New Nation: The Formation of Slovenia* (Aldershot: Ashgate).

Bašić-Hrvatin, S., Thompson, M. and Jusić, T. (eds.) (2008) *Divided They Fall: Public Service Broadcasting in Multiethnic Societies* (Sarajevo: Mediacentar).

Bauman, Z. (1989) *Modernity and the Holocaust* (Ithaca, NY: Cornell University Press).

Baycroft, T. and M. Hewitson (eds) (2006) *What is a Nation? Europe 1789–1914* (Oxford: Oxford University Press).

Beck, U. (1999) *World Risk Society* (Cambridge: Polity and Oxford: Blackwell).

Beck, U. (2002) 'The Cosmopolitan Society and Its Enemies', *Theory, Culture & Society* 19(1–2): 17–44.

Beissinger, M. R. (2002) *Nationalist Mobilization and the Collapse of the Soviet State* (Cambridge: Cambridge University Press).

Bell, D. (1976) *The Coming of Post-industrial Society: A Venture in Social Forecasting* (New York: Basic Books).

Bendix, R. (1964) *Nation-building and Citizenship: Studies of Our Changing Social Order* (New York: Wiley).

Ben-Ghiat, R. (2004) *Fascist Modernities: Italy, 1922–1945* (Berkeley, CA: University of California Press).

Bennett, L. W. (2004) 'Branded Political Communication: Lifestyle Politics, Logo Campaigns, and the Rise of Global Citizenship', in M. Micheletti, A. Follesdal and D. Stolle (eds) *The Politics behind Products* (New Brunswick, NJ: Transaction Books).

Benson, R. and Hallin, D. (2007) 'How States, Markets and Globalization Shape the News: The French and US National Press, 1965–97', *European Journal of Communication* 22(1): 27–48.

Berger, P. L. and Luckmann, T. (1967) *The Social Construction of Reality: A Treatise in the Sociology of Knowledge* (New York: Anchor Books).

Bergmann, W. (1992) 'The Problem of Time in Sociology: An Overview of the Literature on the State of Theory and Research on the "Sociology of Time", 1900–82'. *Time & Society* 1(1): 81–134.

Bergmeier, H. J. P. and Lotz, R. E. (1997) *Hitler's Airwaves: The Inside Story of Nazi Radio Broadcasting and Propaganda Swing* (New Haven, CT: Yale University Press).

Bertelsmann (2009) *Facts and Figures*, http://www.bertelsmann.com/, date accessed 14 November 2009.

Bielby, D. D. and Harrington, C. L. (2008) *Global TV: Exporting Television and Culture in the World Market* (New York: New York University Press).

Billig, M. (1992) *Talking of the Royal Family* (London: Routledge).

Billig, M. (1995) *Banal Nationalism* (London: Sage Publications).

Billig, M. (2005) 'Comic Racism and Violence', in M. Pickering and S. Lockyer (eds) *Beyond a Joke: The Limits of Humour* (Basingstoke: Palgrave Macmillan).

Bishop, H. and Jaworski, A. (2003) '"We Beat 'em": Nationalism and the Hegemony of Homogeneity in the British Press Reportage of Germany versus England during Euro 2000', *Discourse & Society* 14(3): 243–71.

Blanning, T. C. (2002) *The Culture of Power and the Power of Culture: Old Regime Europe 1660–1789* (Oxford: Oxford University Press).

Blouin, C. (2000) 'The WTO Agreement on Basic Telecommunications: A Reevaluation', *Telecommunications Policy* 24(2): 13–142.

Bonnell, V. E. (1997) *Iconography of Power: Soviet Political Posters under Lenin and Stalin* (Berkeley, CA: University of California Press).

Bourdieu, P. (1989) 'Social Space and Symbolic Power', *Sociological Theory* 7(1): 14–25.

Bourdon, J. (2003) 'La télévision est-elle un média global? Une perspective historique', in *Télévision, mémoire & identités nationales* (Paris: L'Harmattan).

Bourdon, J. (2007) 'Pan-European Television: Unhappy Engineers of the European Soul: The EBU and the Woes of Pan-European Television', *Gazette: The International Journal for Communication Studies* 69(3): 263–80.

Bowen, J. R. (2006) *Why the French Don't Like Headscarves: Islam, the State and Public Space* (Princeton, NJ: Princeton University Press).

Boxer, M. J. (2007) 'Rethinking the Socialist Construction and International Career of the Concept "Bourgeois Feminism"', *American Historical Review* 112(1): 131–58.

Boyd-Barrett, O. (ed.) (2006) *Communications Media, Globalization and Empire* (Eastleigh: John Libbey).

Boyd-Barrett, O. and Rantanen, T. (1999) *The Globalization of News* (London: Sage).

Brass, P. (1979) 'Elite Groups, Symbol Manipulation and Ethnic Identity among the Muslims of South Asia', in D. Taylor and M. Yapp (eds) *Political Identity in South Asia* (London: Curzon Press).

Bren, P. (2010) *The Greengrocer and His TV: The Culture of Communism after the 1968 Prague Spring* (Ithaca, NY: Cornell University Press).

Breuilly, J. (1993) *Nationalism and the State*, 2nd edn (Chicago, IL: Chicago University Press).

Breuilly, J. (1996) 'Approaches to Nationalism', in G. Balakrishnan (ed.) *Mapping the Nation* (London: Verso).

Brewer, J. (1990) *The Sinews of Power: War, Money, and the English State, 1688–1783* (Cambridge, MA: Harvard University Press).

British National Party (2004) *Constitution of the British National Party*, 8th edn (Weltham Cross: BNP).

Brook, V. (2009) 'Convergent Ethnicity and the Neo-platoon Show: Recombining Difference in the Postnetwork Era', *Television & New Media* 10(4): 331–53.

Brown, L. (2001) *Fables of Modernity: Literature and Culture in the English Eighteenth Century* (Ithaca, NY: Cornell University Press).

Brown, S. J. (2006) *Providence and Empire: Religion, Politics and Society in the United Kingdom, 1815–1914* (Harlow: Pearson Longman).

Brubaker, R. (1996) *Nationalism Reframed: Nationhood and the National Question in the New Europe* (Cambridge: Cambridge University Press).

Brubaker, R., Feischmidt, M., Fox, J. and Grancea, L. (2006) *Nationalist Politics and Everyday Ethnicity in a Transylvanian Town* (Princeton, NJ: Princeton University Press).

Bucur, M. (2008) 'An Archipelago of Stories: Gender History in Eastern Europe', *American Historical Review* 113(5): 1375–89.

Burbank, J. (1995) 'Lenin and the Law in Revolutionary Russia', *Slavic Review* 54(1): 23–44.

Burgess, J. and Green, J. (2009) *YouTube: Online Video and Participatory Culture* (Cambridge: Polity).

Burke, P. (2004) *Languages and Communities in Early Modern Europe* (Cambridge: Cambridge University Press).

Calabrese, A. and Burke, B. R. (1992) 'American Identities: Nationalism, the Media, and the Public Sphere', *Journal of Communication Inquiry* 16(2): 52–73.

Calhoun, C. (1997) *Nationalism* (Minneapolis, MN: University of Minnesota Press).

Calhoun, C. (2007) *Nations Matter: Culture, History, and the Cosmopolitan Dream* (London: Routledge).

Cammaerts, B. and Van Audenhove, L. (2005) 'Online Political Debate, Unbounded Citizenship, and the Problematic Nature of a Transnational Public Sphere', *Political Communication* 22(2): 179–96.

Carruthers, S. L. (2000) *The Media at War* (Basingstoke: Palgrave Macmillan).

Casanova, J. (1994) *Public Religions in the Modern World* (Chicago, IL: University of Chicago Press).

Castells, M. (2009) *The Rise of the Network Society*, 2nd edn (Cambridge, MA: Blackwell).

Castles, S. and Miller, M. J. (2009) *The Age of Migration*, 4th edn (Basingstoke: Palgrave Macmillan).

Chaffee, S. H. and E. M. Rogers (1997) 'The Establishment of Communication Study in America', in W. L. Schramm, S. H. Chaffee and E. M. Rogers, *The Beginnings of Communication Study in America: A Personal Memoir* (London: Sage).

Chan, B. (2005) 'Imagining the Homeland: The Internet and Diasporic Discourse of Nationalism', *Journal of Communication Inquiry* 29(4): 336–68.

Chan, J. M. and McIntyre, B. T. (2002) 'Transculturating Modernity: A Reinterpretation of Cultural Globalization', in J. M. Chan and B. T. McIntyre (eds) *In Search of Boundaries: Communication, Nation-States, and Cultural Identities* (Westport, CT: Ablex Publishing).

Chatterjee, P. (1986) *Nationalist Thought and the Postcolonial World: A Derivative Discourse?* (London: Zed Books).

Chatterjee, P. (1990) 'The Nationalist Resolution of the Women's Question', in K. Sangari and S. Vaid (eds) *Recasting Women: Essays in Indian Colonial History* (New Brunswick, NJ: Rutgers University Press), pp. 233–53.

Chatterji, P. C. (1991) *Broadcasting in India*, revised and updated edn (London: Sage).

Cheah, P. (2003) 'Grounds of Comparison', in P. Cheah and J. Culler (eds) *Grounds of Comparison: Around the Work of Benedict Anderson* (London: Routledge) pp. 1–20.

Chernilo, D. (2007) *A Social Theory of the Nation-State: The Political Forms of Modernity beyond Methodological Nationalism* (London: Routledge).

Christensen, W. M. and Ferree, M. Marx (2008) 'Cowboy of the World? Gender Discourse and the Iraq War Debate', *Qualitative Sociology* 31(3): 287–306.

Christians, C. G. (2004) 'Ubuntu and Communitarianism in Media Ethics', *Ecquid Novi* 25(2): 235–56.

Christians, C. G., Glasser, T., McQuail, D., Nordenstreng, K. and White, R. A. (2009) *Normative Theories of the Media: Journalism in Democratic Societies* (Urbana, IL: University of Illinois Press).

Clausen, L. (2004) 'Localizing the Global: "Domestication" Processes in International News Production', *Media, Culture & Society* 26(1): 25–44.

Coble, P. M. (2007) 'China's "New Remembering" of the Anti-Japanese War of Resistance, 1937–1945', *The China Quarterly* 190: 394–410.

Cohen, A. A. (2002) 'Globalization Ltd.: Domestication and the Boundaries of Foreign Television News', in J. M. Chan and B. T. McIntyre (eds) *In Search of Boundaries: Communication, Nation-States, and Cultural Identities*, (Westport, CT: Ablex Publishing).

Coleman, J. A. (1992) 'Catholic Integralism as a Fundamentalism', in L. Kaplan (ed.) *Fundamentalism in Comparative Perspective* (Amherst, MA: University of Massachusetts Press).

Collins, R. (1990) *Culture, Communication, and National Identity: The Case of Canadian Television* (Toronto: University of Toronto Press).

Connor, W. (1994) *Ethnonationalism: The Quest for Understanding* (Princeton, NJ: Princeton University Press).

Conway, J. and Singh, J. (2009) 'Is the World Social Forum a Transnational Public Sphere? Nancy Fraser, Critical Theory and the Containment of Radical Possibility', *Theory, Culture & Society* 26(5): 61–84.

Coover, G. E. (2001) 'Television and Social Identity: Race Representation as "White" Accommodation', *Journal of Broadcasting & Electronic Media* 45(3): 413–31.

Copsey, N. (2007) 'Changing Course or Changing Clothes? Reflections on the Ideological Evolution of the British National Party, 1999–2006', *Patterns of Prejudice* 41(1): 61–82.

Crotty, W. (2003) 'Presidential Policymaking in Crisis Situations: 9/11 and Its Aftermath', *The Policy Studies Journal* 31(3): 451–64.

Davis, H. B. (1978) *Towards a Marxist Theory of Nationalism* (New York and London: Monthly Review Press).

Dayan, D. (1998) 'Particularistic Media and Diasporic Communications', in T. Liebes and J. Curran (eds) *Media, Ritual and Identity* (London: Routledge).

Dayan, D. and Katz, E. (1992) *Media Events: The Live Broadcasting of History* (Cambridge, MA: Harvard University Press).

Deacon, D. (2008) *British News Media and the Spanish Civil War* (Edinburgh: Edinburgh University Press).

De Gouges, O. ([1791] 1980) 'The Declaration of the Rights of Woman', in D. G. Levy, H. B. Applewhite and M. D. Johnson (eds) *Women in Revolutionary Paris, 1789–1795* (Urbana, IL: University of Illinois Press).

De Grand, A. (1995) *Fascist Italy and Nazi Germany: The 'Fascist' Style of Rule* (London: Routledge).

Dembinska, M. (2008) 'Adapting to Changing Contexts of Choice: The Nation-Building Strategies of Unrecognized Silesians and Rusyns', *Canadian Journal of Political Science* 41(4): 915–34.

Denich, B. (1994) 'Dismembering Yugoslavia: Nationalist Ideologies and the Symbolic Revival of Genocide', *American Ethnologist* 21(2): 367–90.

Derné, S. (2000) 'Men's Sexuality and Women's Subordination in Indian Nationalisms', in T. Mayer (ed.) *Gender Ironies of Nationalism: Sexing the Nation* (London: Routledge).

De Sola Pool, I. (1977) 'The Changing Floor of Television', *Journal of Communication* 27(2): 139–49.

De Sola Pool, I. ([1975] 1998) 'Direct Broadcast Satellites and Cultural Integrity', *Society* 35(2): 140–51.

Deutsch, K. W. (1953) *Nationalism and Social Communication. An Inquiry into the Foundations of Nationality* (Cambridge, MA: MIT Press).

Deutsch, K. W. (1961) 'Social Mobilization and Political Development', *The American Political Science Review* 55(3): 493–514.

Deutschmann, P. J., Ellingsworth, H. and McNelly, J. T. (1968) *Communication and Social Change in Latin America: Introducing New Technology* (New York: Praeger).

Dirlik, A. (2003) 'Global Modernity? Modernity in an Age of Global Capitalism', *European Journal of Social Theory* 6(3): 275–92.

Djokić, D. (2002) 'The Second World War Two: Discourses of Reconciliation in Serbia and Croatia in the late 1980s and early 1990s', *Journal of Southern Europe and the Balkans* 4(2): 127–40.

Domke, D. (2004) *God Willing? Political Fundamentalism in the White House, the "War on Terror", and the Echoing Press* (London: Pluto Press).

Donner, J. (2008) 'Research Approaches to Mobile Use in the Developing World: A Review of the Literature', *The Information Society* 24(3): 140–59.

Douglas, S. J. (2004) *Listening In: Radio and the American Imagination* (Minneapolis, MN: University of Minnesota Press).

Dowler, L. (2002) 'Women on the Frontlines: Rethinking War Narratives Post 9/11', *GeoJournal* 58(2/3): 159–65.

Downey, J. and Koenig, T. (2006) 'Is There a European Public Sphere? The Berlusconi-Schulz Case', *European Journal of Communication* 21(3): 165–87.

Dragović-Soso, J. (2002) *'Saviours of the Nation': Serbia's Intellectual Opposition and the Revival of Nationalism* (London: Hurst and Montreal: McGill-Queen's University Press).

Duits, L. and Van Zoonen, L. (2006) 'Headscarves and Porno-Chic: Disciplining Girls' Bodies in the European Multicultural Society', *European Journal of Women's Studies* 13(2): 103–17.

Dunn, A. (2005) 'Television News as Narrative', in H. Fulton, with R. Huisman, J. Murphet and A. Dunn (eds) *Narrative and Media* (Cambridge: Cambridge University Press).

Dunn, K. (2009) 'Public Attitudes Towards Hijab-wearing in Australia', in T. Dreher, and C. Ho (eds) *Beyond the Hijab Debates: New Conversations on Gender, Race and Religion* (Newcastle: Cambridge Scholars Publishing).

Dupagne, M. and Waterman, D. (1998) 'Determinants of U.S. Television Fiction Imports in Western Europe', *Journal of Broadcasting & Electronic Media* 42(2): 208–20.

Durkheim, É. ([1893] 1984) *The Division of Labour in Society*, translated by W. D. Halls (Basingstoke: Palgrave).

Edy, J. A. (1999) 'Journalistic Uses of Collective Memory', *Journal of Communication* 49(2): 71–85.

Edy, J. A. and Daradanova, M. (2006) 'Reporting through the Lens of the Past: From Challenger to Columbia' *Journalism* 7(2): 131–51.

Eghigian, G. (2008) 'Homo Munitus: The East German Observed', in K. Pence and P. Betts (eds) *Socialist Modern: East German Everyday Culture and Politics* (Ann Arbor, MI: University of Michigan Press).

Eisenstadt, S. N. (1974) 'Studies of Modernization and Sociological Theory', *History and Theory* 13(13): 225–52.

Eisenstadt, S. N. (1999) *Fundamentalism, Sectarianism and Revolution* (Cambridge: Cambridge University Press).

Eisenstadt, S. N. (2000) 'Multiple Modernities', *Daedalus* 129(1): 1–29.

Eisenstadt, S. N. and Rokkan, S. (eds) (1973) *Building States and Nations: Models, Analyses, and Data across Three Worlds* (London: Sage).

Eisenstein, E. L. (1979) *The Printing Press as an Agent of Change* (Cambridge: Cambridge University Press).

Ellis, J. (1992) *Visible Fictions* (London: Routledge).

El-Nawawy, M. and Powers, S. (2010) 'Al-Jazeera English: A Conciliatory Medium in a Conflict-driven Environment?' *Global Media and Communication* 6(1): 61–84.

Emad, M. C. (2006) 'Reading Wonder Woman's Body: Mythologies of Gender and Nation', *The Journal of Popular Culture* 39(6): 954–84.

Entman, R. M. (2004) *Projections of Power: Framing News, Public Opinion, and the U.S. Foreign Policy* (Chicago: University of Chicago Press).

Eriksen, T. H. (2007) 'Nationalism and the Internet', *Nations and Nationalism* 13(1): 1–17.

Erk, J. (2003) 'Swiss Federalism and Congruence', *Nationalism and Ethnic Politics* 9(2): 50–74.

Ermert, M. and Hughes, C. R. (2003) 'What's in a Name? China and the Domain Name System', in C. R. Hugh and G. W. (eds) *China and the Internet: Politics and the Digital Leap Forward* (London: Routledge).

Esser, F. (1999) '"Tabloidization" of News: A Comparative Analysis of Anglo-American and German Press Journalism', *European Journal of Communication* 14(3): 291–324.

Esser, A. (2009) 'Trends in Television Programming: Commercialization, Transnationalization, Convergence', in A. Charles (ed.) *Media in the Enlarged Europe: Politics, Policy and Industry* (Bristol: Intellect Books).

Evans, H. (1999) '"Comrade Sisters": Gendered Bodies and Spaces', in H. Evans and S. Donald (eds) *Picturing Power in the People's Republic of China: Posters of the Cultural Revolution* (Lantham: Rowman & Littlefield).

Evas, T. (2007) 'Elitist with a Russian Twist: Mass Media Discourses on European Constitutional Ratification in Estonia and Latvia', *Perspectives on European Politics and Society* 8(3): 374–413.

Everard, J. (2000) *Virtual States: The Internet and the Boundaries of the Nation-state* (London: Routledge).

Favell, A. (1998) *Philosophies of Integration: Immigration and the Idea of Citizenship in France and Britain* (Basingstoke: Palgrave Macmillan).

Featherstone, M. and Lash, S. (1995) 'Globalization, Modernity, and the Spatialization of Social Theory: An Introduction', in M. Featherstone, S. Lash and R. Robertson (eds) *Global Modernities* (London: Sage).

Fehérváry, K. (2009) 'Goods and States: The Political Logic of State-Socialist Material Culture', *Comparative Studies in Society and History* 51(2): 426–59.

Figenschou, T. U. (2010) 'A Voice for the Voiceless? A Quantitative Content Analysis of Al-Jazeera English's Flagship News', *Global Media and Communication* 6(1): 85–107.

Fitzpatrick, S. (2008) *The Russian Revolution*, 3rd edn (Oxford: Oxford University Press).

Fodor, E. (2002) 'Smiling Women and Fighting Men: The Gender of the Communist Subject in State Socialist Hungary', *Gender & Society* 16(2): 240–63.

Foster, R. J. (2002) *Materializing the Nation: Commodities, Consumption, and Media in Papua New Guinea* (Bloomington, IN: Indiana University Press).

Fowler, B. (2007) *The Obituary as Collective Memory* (London: Routledge).

Fraser, N. (2007) 'Transnationalizing the Public Sphere: On the Legitimacy and Efficacy of Public Opinion in a Post-Westphalian World', *Theory, Culture & Society* 24(4): 7–30.

Frosh, P. and Wolfsfeld, G. (2007) 'ImagiNation: News Discourse, Nationhood and Civil Society', *Media Culture & Society* 29(1): 105–29.

Gallagher, M. (1995) *An Unfinished Story: Gender Patterns in Media Employment* (Paris: UNESCO).

Gallagher, T. (2000) 'The Media and the Search for Democracy in the Balkans', in G. Pridham and T. Gallagher (eds) *Experimenting with Democracy: Regime Change in the Balkans* (London: Routledge).

Gans, H. (1979) *Deciding What's News: A Study of CBS Evening News, NBC Nightly News, Newsweek, and Time* (New York: Random House).

Gellner, E. (1983) *Nations and Nationalism* (Ithaca, NY: Cornell University Press).

Georgiou, M. (2006) *Diaspora, Identity and the Media: Diasporic Transnationalism and Mediated Spatialities* (Cresskill, NJ: Hampton Press).

Gezduci, H. and D'Haenens, L. (2007) 'Culture-specific Features as Determinants of News Media Use', *Communications* 32(2): 193–222.

Giddens, A. (1991) *Modernity and Self-identity: Self and Society in the Late Modern Age* (Stanford, CA: Stanford University Press).

Gilman, N. (2007) *Mandarins of the Future: Modernization Theory in Cold War America* (Baltimore, MD: Johns Hopkins University Press).

Gillespie, M. (1995) *Television, Ethnicity and Cultural Change* (London: Routledge).

Gitlin, T. (1998) 'Public Sphere or Public Sphericules?', in T. Liebes and J. Curran (eds) *Media, Ritual and Identity* (London: Routledge).

Glennie, P. and Thrift, N. (2009) *Shaping the Day: A History of Timekeeping in England and Wales, 1300–1800* (Oxford: Oxford University Press).

Goldman, W. Z. (1993) *Women, the State, and Revolution: Soviet Family Policy and Social Life, 1917–1936* (Cambridge: Cambridge University Press).

Goodman, B. (2004) 'Networks of News: Power, Language and Transnational Dimensions of the Chinese Press, 1850–1949', *The China Review* 4(1): 1–10.

Gray, A. (1992) *Video Playtime: The Gendering of a Leisure Technology* (London: Routledge).

Grasso, J. M., Corrin, J. P. and Kort, M. (2004) *Modernization and Revolution in China: From the Opium Wars to World Power* (New York: M.E. Sharpe).

Greenfeld, L. (1992) *Nationalism: Five Roads to Modernity* (Cambridge, MA: Harvard University Press).

Greer, S. L. (2007) *Nationalism and Self-government: The Politics of Autonomy in Scotland and Catalonia* (Albany, NY: SUNY Press).

Gries, P. H. (2004) *China's New Nationalism: Pride, Politics and Diplomacy* (Berkeley, CA: University of California Press).

Griffin, D. (2005) *Patriotism and Poetry in Eighteenth-Century Britain* (Cambridge: Cambridge University Press).

Gronnvoll, M. (2007) 'Gender (In)Visibility at Abu Ghraib', *Rhetoric & Public Affairs* 10(3): 371–98.

Guild, E., Groenendijk, K. and Carrera, S. (eds) (2009) *Illiberal Liberal States: Immigration, Citizenship and Integration in the EU* (Aldershot: Ashgate).

Habermas, J. ([1962] 1989) *The Structural Transformation of the Public Sphere: An Inquiry into a Category of Bourgeois Society*, translated by Thomas Burger and Frederick Lawrence (Cambridge, MA: MIT Press).

Habermas, J. (1998) 'The European Nation-State: On the Past and Future of Sovereignty and Citizenship', *Public Culture* 10(2): 397–416.

Hafez, K. (2007) *The Myth of Media Globalization* (Oxford: Polity).

Ha-Ilan, N. (2001) 'Images of History in Israel Television News: The Territorial Dimension of Collective Memories, 1987–1990', in G. R. Edgerton and P. C. Rollins (eds) *Television histories: Shaping collective memory in the media age* (Lexington, KY: University Press of Kentucky).

Hall, D. (2002) 'Brand Development, Tourism, and National Identity: The Re-imaging of Former Yugoslavia', *Brand Management* 9(4–5): 323–34.

Hall, P. A. and Soskice, D. W. (2001) *Varieties of Capitalism: The Institutional Foundations of Comparative Advantage* (Oxford: Oxford University Press).

Hallin, D. (1986) *The 'Uncensored War': The Media and Vietnam* (Berkeley, CA: University of California Press).

Hallin, D. and Mancini, P. (1984) 'Speaking of the President: Political Structure and Representational Form in US and Italian Television News', *Theory and Society* 13(4): 829–50.

Hallin, D. and Mancini, P. (2004a) *Comparing Media Systems: Three Models of Media and Politics* (Cambridge: Cambridge University Press).

Hallin, D. and Mancini, P. (2004b) 'Americanization, Globalization, and Secularization: Understanding the Convergence of Media Systems and Political Communication', in F. Esser and B. Pfetsch (eds) *Comparative Political Communication: Theories, Cases, and Challenges* (Cambridge: Cambridge University Press).

Hallin, D. and Papathanassopoulos, S. (2002) 'Political Clientelism and the Media: Southern Europe and Latin America in Comparative Perspective', *Media, Culture & Society* 24 (2): 175–95.

Hansen, T. B. (1999) *The Saffron Wave: Democracy and Hindu Nationalism in Modern India* (Princeton, NJ: Princeton University Press).

Hardt, H. (1988) 'Comparative Media Research: The World According to America', *Critical Studies in Mass Communication* 5(2):129–46.

Harris, L. J. (2008) 'Modern Times: The Meaning of Dates and Calendars in Modern China, 1895–1935', *International Institute for Asian Studies Newsletter* 48: 20.

Harrison, H. (2000) *The Making of the Republican Citizen: Political Ceremonies and Symbols in China, 1911–1929* (Oxford: Oxford University Press).

Harvey, D. (1990) *The Condition of Postmodernity: An Inquiry into the Origins of Cultural Change* (Oxford: Blackwell Publishing).

Harvey, D. A. (2001) *Constructing Class and Nationality in Alsace, 1830–1945* (DeKalb, IL: Northern Illinois University Press).

Hasian, M. and Bialowas, A. (2009) 'Gendered Nationalism, the Colonial Narrative, and the Rhetorical Significance of the *Mother India* Controversy', *Communication Quarterly* 57(4): 469–86.

Hastings, A. (1997) *The Construction of Nationhood: Ethnicity, Religion and Nationalism* (Cambridge: Cambridge University Press).

Hayes, J. E. (2000) *Radio Nation: Communication, Popular Culture, and Nationalism in Mexico 1920–1950* (Tucson, AZ: University of Arizona Press).

He, Y. (2007) 'History, Chinese Nationalism and the Emerging Sino-Japanese Conflict', *Journal of Contemporary China* 16(50): 1–24.

Headrick, D. R. (1991) *The Invisible Weapon: Telecommunications and International Politics, 1851–1945* (Oxford: Oxford University Press).

Hearn, J. (2006) *Rethinking Nationalism: A Critical Introduction* (Basingstoke: Palgrave Macmillan).

Hechter, M. (1975) *Internal Colonialism: The Celtic Fringe in British National Development, 1536–1966* (Berkeley, CA: University of California Press).

Hedetoft, U. (1999) 'The Nation-state Meets the World: National Identities in the Context of Transnationality and Cultural Globalization', *European Journal of Social Theory* 2(1): 71–94.

Herbst, S. (1994) *Politics at the Margins: Historical Studies of Public Expression outside the Mainstream* (Cambridge: Cambridge University Press).

Herf, J. (1986) *Reactionary Modernisms: Technology, Culture and Politics in Weimar and the Third Reich* (Cambridge: Cambridge University Press).

Herzog, D. (2008) 'East Germany's Sexual Revolution', in K. Pence and P. Betts (eds) *Socialist Modern: East German Everyday Culture and Politics* (Ann Arbor, MI: University of Michigan Press).

Hewitson, M. (2006) 'Conclusion: Nationalism and the 19th Century', in T. Baycroft and M. Hewitson (eds) *What is a Nation? Europe 1789–1914* (Oxford: Oxford University Press).

Higgott, R. A., Underhill, G. R. D. and Bieler, A. (eds) (2000) *Non-state Actors and Authority in the Global System* (London: Routledge).

Hitchens, L. (2006) *Broadcasting Pluralism and Diversity: A Comparative Study of Policy and Regulation* (Portland, OR: Hart Publishing).

Hjerm, M. (1998) 'National Identities, National Pride and Xenophobia: A Comparison of Four Western Countries', *Acta Sociologica* 41(4): 335–47.

Hjort, M. and MacKenzie, S. (eds) (2000) *Cinema and Nation* (London: Routledge).

Hobsbawm, E. (1990) *Nations and Nationalism since 1780: Programme, Myth, Reality* (Cambridge: Cambridge University Press).

Hock, B. (2010) 'Sites of Undoing Gender Hierarchies: Women and/in Hungarian Cinema (Industry)', *Media Research/Medijska istraživanja* 16(1): 9–30.

Hofstede, G. (2001) *Culture's Consequences: Comparing Values, Behaviors, Institutions and Organizations across Nations*, 2nd edn (London: Sage).

Holton, R. J. (1998) *Globalization and the Nation-State* (Basingstoke: Macmillan Press).

Höpken, W. (1997) 'History Education and Yugoslav (Dis-)integration', in M. Bokovy, J. Irvine and C. Lilly (eds) *State–Society Relations in Yugoslavia, 1945–1992* (New York: St. Martin's Press).

Hopkins, M. (1970) *The Media in the Soviet Union* (New York: Pegasus).

Hopper, P. (2007) *Understanding Cultural Globalization* (Cambridge: Polity).

Horowitz, R. B. (2001) *Communication and Democratic Reform in South Africa* (Cambridge: Cambridge University Press).

Horsti, K. (2009) 'Antiracist and Multicultural Discourses in European Public Service Broadcasting: Celebrating Consumable Differences in the Prix Europa Iris Media Prize', *Communication, Culture & Critique* 2 (3): 339–60.

Hroch, M. (1985) *Social Preconditions of National Revival in Europe: A Comparative Analysis of the Social Composition of Patriotic Groups among the Smaller European Nations* (Cambridge: Cambridge University Press).

Hung, C. (2007) 'Mao's Parades: State Spectacles in China in the 1950s', *The China Quarterly* 190: 411–31.

Hutcheson, J., Domke, D., Billaeudeaux, A. and Garland, P (2004) 'U.S. National Identity, Political Elites, and a Patriotic Press Following September 11', *Political Communication* 21: 27–50.

Hutchinson, J. (2005) *Nations as Zones of Conflict* (London: Sage).

Ignatieff, M. (1993) *Blood and Belonging: Journeys into the New Nationalism* (London: Chatto and Windus).

Imre, A. (2009) *Identity Games: Globalization and the Transformation of Media Cultures in the New Europe* (Cambridge, MA: MIT Press).

Innis, H. (2007 [1951]) *Empire and Communications* (Toronto: Durndurn Press).

Ives, S. (2007) 'Mediating the Liberal Nation: Television in Post-Apartheid South Africa', *ACME: An International E-Journal for Critical Geographies* 6(1): 153–73.

Jaggar, A. M. (1999) 'Multicultural Democracy', *The Journal of Political Philosophy* 7(3): 308–29.

Janmaat, J. G. (2006) 'Popular Conceptions of Nationhood in Old and New European Member States: Partial Support for the Ethnic–Civic Framework', *Ethnic and Racial Studies* 29(1): 50–78.

Jayawardena, K. (1986) *Feminism and Nationalism in the Third World* (London: Zed Books).

Jarvie, I. C. (1992) *Hollywood's Overseas Campaign: The North Atlantic Movie Trade, 1920–1950* (Cambridge: Cambridge University Press).

Jones, F. L. and Smith, P. (2001) 'Diversity and Commonality in National Identities: An Exploratory Analysis of Cross-National Patterns', *Journal of Sociology* 37(1): 45–63.

Joppke, C. (2007) 'Beyond National Models: Civic Integration Policies for Immigrants in Western Europe', *West European Politics* 30(1): 1–22.

Joppke, C. (2008) 'Immigration and the Identity of Citizenship: The Paradox of Universalism', *Citizenship Studies* 12(6): 533–46.

Jordan, S. (2003) *The Anxieties of Idleness: Idleness in Eighteenth-Century British Literature* (Lewisburg, PA: Bucknell University Press).

Jović, D. (2003) 'Yugoslavism and Yugoslav Communism: From Tito to Kardelj', in D. Djokić (ed.) *Yugoslavism: Histories of a Failed Idea* (London: Hurst).

Juergensmeyer, M. (1993) *The New Cold War? Religious Nationalism Confronts the Secular State* (Berkeley, CA: University of California Press).

Kaldor, M. (2004) 'Nationalism and Globalisation', *Nations and Nationalism* 10(1/2): 161–77.

Katz, E. (1996) 'And Deliver Us from Segmentation', *Annals of the American Academy of Political and Social Science* 546: 22–33.

Katz, E. and Wedell, G. (1977) *Broadcasting in the Third World: Promise and Performance* (Cambridge, MA: Harvard University Press).

Kedourie, E. ([1960] 1996) *Nationalism* (London: Hutchinson).

Khiabany, G. (2007) 'Is There an Islamic Communication? The Persistence of "Tradition" and the Lure of Modernity', *Critical Arts* 21(1): 106–124.

Kitch, C. (2005) *Pages from the Past: History and Memory in American Magazines* (Chapel Hill, NC: University of North Carolina Press).

Kitch, C and Hume, J. (2008) *Journalism in a Culture of Grief* (London: Routledge).

Kluckhohn, F. R. and Strodtbeck, F. L. (1963) *Variations in Value Orientations.* (Westport, CT: Greenwood Press).

Koenig, T., Mihelj, S., Downey, J. and Gencel Bek, M. (2006) 'Media Framings of the Issue of Turkish Accession to the European Union: A European or National Process?', *Innovation: The European Journal of Social Science Research* 19 (2): 149–69.

Kogut, B. (2003) 'Introduction: The Internet has Borders', in Bruce Kogut (ed.) *The Global Internet Economy* (Cambridge, MA: MIT Press).

Kohn, H. (1944) *The Idea of Nationalism: A Study of Its Origins and Background* (London: Macmillan).

Kolar-Panov, D. (1997) 'Crowded Airwaves: Ethnic, National and Transnational Identities in Macedonian Television', in K. Robins (ed.) *Programming for People: From Cultural Rights to Cultural Responsibilities* (Rome: Radiotelevisione Italiana in association with the European Broadcasting Union).

Kolar-Panov, D. (2004) 'Troubled Multicultural Broadcasting in Macedonia', in N. Busch and H. Kelly-Holmes (eds) *Language, Discourse and Borders in the Yugoslav Successor States* (Clevedon: Multilingual Matters).

Koopmans, R., Statham, P., Giugni, M. and Passy, F. (2005) *Contested Citizenship: Immigration and Cultural Diversity* (Minneapolis, MN: University of Minnesota Press).

Krabill, R. (2001) 'Symbiosis: Mass Media and the Truth and Reconciliation Commission of South Africa', *Media Culture & Society* 23(5): 567–85.

Krzyżanowski, M. (2009) Europe in Crisis?, *Journalism Studies* 10(1):18–35.

Kuhn, R. (2008) 'The Public and the Private in Contemporary French Politics', *French Cultural Studies* 18(2): 185–200.

Kuipers, G. (2006) *Good Humor, Bad Taste: A Sociology of the Joke* (Berlin: Mouton de Gruyter).

Kuipers, G. and de Kloet, J. (2009) 'Banal Cosmopolitanism and *The Lord of the Rings*: The Limited Role of National Differences in Global Media Consumption', *Poetics* 37(2): 99–118.

Kumar, S. (2006) *Gandhi Meets Primetime: Globalization and Nationalism in Indian Television* (Urbana, IL: University of Illinois Press).

Kunovich, R. M. (2009) 'The Sources and Consequences of National Identification', *American Sociological Review* 74(4): 573–93.

Kymlicka, W. and Norman, W. (eds) (2000) *Citizenship in Diverse Societies* (Oxford: Oxford University Press).

Lambert, Y. (1999) 'Religion in Modernity as a New Axial Age: Secularization or New Religious Forms?', *Sociology of Religion* 30(3): 303–33.

Lampe, J. R. (2000) *Yugoslavia as History: Twice There Was a Country*, 2nd edn (Cambridge: Cambridge University Press).

Landy, M. (1986) *Fascism in Film: The Italian Commercial Cinema, 1931–1943* (Princeton, NJ: Princeton University Press).

Landy, M. (2000) *Italian Film* (Cambridge: Cambridge University Press).

Lane, C. (1981) *The Rites of Rulers: Ritual in Industrial Society: The Soviet Case* (Cambridge: Cambridge University Press).

Lash, S. and Lury, C. (2007) *Global Culture Industry: The Mediation of Things* (Cambridge: Polity).

Lee, J. W. and Maguire, J. (2009) 'Global Festivals through a National Prism: The Global–National Nexus in South Korean Media Coverage of the 2004 Athens Olympic Games', *International Review for the Sociology of Sport* 44(1): 5–24.

Legge, J. S. and Alford, J. R. (1986) 'Can Government Regulate Fertility? An Assessment of Pronatalist Policy in Eastern Europe', *Political Research Quarterly* 39(4): 709–28.

Lerner, D. (1958) *The Passing of Traditional Society: Modernizing the Middle East* (New York: Free Press).

Letham, M. E. (2000) *Modernization as Ideology: American Social Science and 'Nation Building' in the Kennedy Era* (Chapel Hill, NC: University of North Carolina Press).

Leurdijk, A. (2006) 'In Search of Common Ground: Strategies of Multicultural Television Producers in Europe', *European Journal of Cultural Studies* 9(1): 25–46.

Levitt, P. and Glick Schiller, N. (2004) 'Conceptualizing Simultaneity: A Transnational Social Field Perspective on Society', *International Migration Review* 38(3): 1002–39.

Lewis, M. W. and Wigen, K. E. (eds) (1997) *The Myth of Continents: A Critique of Metageography* (Berkeley, CA: University of California Press).

Li, Hongmei (2009) 'Marketing Japanese Products in the Context of Chinese Nationalism', *Critical Studies in Media Communication* 26(5): 435–56.

Liberal Democratic Party (2006) *The Constitution of the Liberal Democrats*, www.libdems.org.uk, date accessed 14 October 2009.

Liebes, T. (1998) 'Television's Disaster Marathons: A Danger for Democratic Processes?', in T. Liebes and J. Curran (eds) *Media, Ritual and Identity* (London: Routledge).

Liebes, T. and Katz, E. (1993) *The Export of Meaning: Cross-Cultural Readings of Dallas* (Cambridge: Polity).

Liebich, A. (2007) 'Introduction: Altneuländer of the Vicissitudes of Citizenship in the New EU States', in R. Bauböck, B. Perchinig and W. Sievers (eds) *Citizenship Policies in the New Europe* (Amsterdam: Amsterdam University Press).

Liew, L. H. and Wang, S. (eds) (2004) *Nationalism, Democracy and National Integration in China* (London: Routledge).

Liklanter, A. (1998) 'Cosmopolitan Citizenship', *Citizenship Studies* 2(1): 23–41.

Liklanter, A. (2007) 'Public Spheres and Civilizing Processes', *Theory, Culture & Society* 24(4): 31–37.

Lin, C. A. (2001) 'Cultural Values Reflected in Chinese and American Television Advertising', *Journal of Advertising* 30(4): 83–94.

Liu, J. H. and Hilton, D. J. (2005) 'How the Past Weighs on the Present: Social Representations of History and their Role in Identity Politics', *British Journal of Social Psychology* 44(4): 537–56.

Łobodzińska, B. (ed.) (1995) *Family, Women and Employment in Central-Eastern Europe* (Westport, CT: Greenwood Press).

Lockyer, S. and Pickering, M. (2008) 'You Must be Joking: The Sociological Critique of Humour and Comic Media', *Sociology Compass* 2(3): 808–20.

Lomnitz, C. (2001) *Deep Mexico, Silent Mexico: An Anthropology of Nationalism* (Minneapolis, MN: University of Minnesota Press).

Luke, T. W. (1995) 'New World Order or Neo-world Orders: Power, Politics and Ideology in Informationalizing Glocalities', in M. Featherstone, S. Lash and R. Robertson (eds) *Global Modernities* (London: Sage).

Lule, J. (2002) 'Myth and Terror on the Editorial Page: The *New York Times* Responds to September 11, 2001', *Journalism and Mass Communication Quarterly* 79(2): 275–93.

Lyon, D. (2001) *Surveillance Society: Monitoring Everyday Life* (Buckingham: Open University Press).

Machek, J. (2010) '"The Counter Lady" as a Female Prototype: Prime Time Popular Culture in 1970s and 1980s Czechoslovakia', *Media Research/Medijska istraživanja* 16(1): 31–52.

Madianou, M. (2005) *Mediating the Nation: News, Audiences and the Politics of Identity* (London: UCL Press).

Magó-Maghiar, A. (2010) 'Representations of Sexuality in Hungarian Popular Culture of the 1980s', *Media Research/Medijska istraživanja* 16(1): 73–96.

Malik, S. (2010) 'From Multicultural Programming to Diasporic Television: Situating the UK in a European Context', *Media History* 16(1): 123–28.

Mankekar, P. (1998) 'Entangled Spaces of Modernity: The Viewing Family, the Consuming Nation, and the Television in India', *Visual Anthropology Review* 14(2): 32–45.

Mankekar, P. (1999) *Screening Culture, Viewing Politics: An Ethnography of Television, Womanhood, and Nation in Postcolonial India* (Durham, NC: Duke University Press).

Mankekar, P. (2004) 'Dangerous Desires: Television and Erotics in Late Twentieth-Century India', *The Journal of Asian Studies* 63(2): 403–31.

Mann, M. (1992) 'The Emergence of Modern European Nationalism', in J. A. Hall and I. C. Jarvie (eds) *Transition to Modernity* (Cambridge: Cambridge University Press).

Mann, M. (1993) *The Sources of Social Power*, Volume II (Cambridge: Cambridge University Press).

Mann, M. (1997) 'Has Globalization Ended the Rise and Rise of the Nation-State?', *Review of International Political Economy* 4(3): 472–96.

Mansfield, E. D. and Snyder, J. (eds) (2005) *Electing to Fight: Why Emerging Democracies go to War* (Cambridge, MA: MIT Press).

Marko, M. (1998) 'An Evaluation of the Basic Telecommunications Service Agreement', *CIES – Policy Discussion Paper* 98/09, http://www.adelaide.edu.au/cies/papers/9809.pdf, date accessed 9 March 2009.

Marx, A. W. (1998) *Making Race and Nation: A Comparison of the United States, South Africa, and Brazil* (Cambridge: Cambridge University Press).

Marx, K. and Engels, F. ([1848] 2002) *The Communist Manifesto* (London: Penguin).

Maxwell, R. (1995) *The Spectacle of Democracy: Spanish Television, Nationalism, and Political Transition* (Minneapolis, MN: University of Minnesota Press).

Mayo, K. ([1927] 1969) *Mother India* (New York: Greenwood Press).

Mazower, M. (1998) *Dark Continent: Europe's Twentieth Century* (London: Penguin).

Mazzoleni, G., Stewart, J. and Horsfield, B. (eds) (2003) *The Media and Neo-Populism: A Contemporary Comparative Analysis* (Westport, CT: Praeger).

McGarry, J. and O'Leary, B. (1993) 'Introduction: The Macro-Political Regulation of Ethnic Conflict', in J. McGarry and B. O'Leary (eds) *The Politics of Ethnic Conflict Regulation: Case Studies of Protracted Ethnic Conflicts* (London: Routledge).

McGuire, J. and Reeves, G. (2003) 'The Bharatiya Janata Party, Ayodhya, and the Rise of Populist Politics in India', in G. Mazzoleni, J. Stewart and B. Horsfield (eds) (2003) *The Media and Neo-Populism: A Contemporary Comparative Analysis* (Westport, CT: Praeger).

McLelland, J. (2009) 'Visual Dangers and Delights: Nude Photography in East Germany', *Past & Present* 205(1): 143–74.

McLeod, H. (2000) *Secularisation in Western Europe, 1848–1914* (New York: St. Martin's Press).

McMillin, D. C. (2001) 'Localizing the Global: Television and Hybrid Programming in India', *International Journal of Cultural Studies* 4(1): 45–68.

Meyrowitz, J. (1985) *No Sense of Place: The Impact of Electronic Media on Social Behaviour* (Oxford: Oxford University Press).

Mežnarić, S. (1990) 'Bivanje nacijom danas', in B. Anderson, *Nacija: zamišljena zajednica*, translated by Nata Čengić and Nataša Pavlović (Beograd: Plato).

Michalowski, I. (2009) 'Citizenship Tests in Five Countries – An Expression of Political Liberalism?', *WZB Discussion Papers* SP IV 2009–702: 1–37.

Mickiewicz, E. (1988) *Split Signals: Television and Politics in the Soviet Union* (Oxford: Oxford University Press).

Mihelj, S. (2005) 'The Mass Media and Nationalizing States in the Post-Yugoslav Space', in Mojca Pajnik and Tonči Kuzmanić (eds) *Nation-States and Xenophobias: In the Ruins of Ex-Yugoslavia* (Ljubljana: Peace Institute).

Mihelj, S. (2007) 'The European and the National in Communication Research', *European Journal of Communication* 22(4): 443–59.

Mihelj, S. (2009) 'Between Segmentation and Integration: Media Systems and Ethno-cultural Diversity in Post-communist CEE', paper presented at the conference *Beyond East and West: Two decades of Media Transformation after the Fall of Communism,* 25–27 June 2009, Budapest.

Mihelj, S. (2010) 'Drawing the East–West Border: Narratives of Modernity and Identity in the Julian Region, 1947–1954', in T. Lindenberger, M. M. Payk, B. Stoever and A. Vowinckel (eds) *European Cold War Cultures: Perspectives on Societies in the East and West* (Oxford: Berghahn Books).

Mihelj, S., Bajt, V. and Pankov, M. (2009) 'Reorganising the Identification Matrix: Televisual Construction of Identity in the Early Phase of Yugoslav Disintegration', in P. Kølsto (ed.) *Media Discourse and the Yugoslav Conflicts: Representations of Self and Other* (Aldershot: Ashgate).

Misa, T. J. and Schot, J. (2005) 'Inventing Europe: Technology and the Hidden Integration of Europe', *History and Technology* 21(1): 1–19.

Moore, B. ([1966] 1993) *Social Origins of Dictatorship and Democracy: Lord and Peasant in the Making of the Modern World* (Boston, MA: Beacon Press).

Morley, D. (1986) *Family Television: Cultural Power and Domestic Leisure* (London: Routledge).

Morley, D. (2000) *Home Territories: Media, Mobility and Identity* (London: Routledge).

Mosse, G. L. (1964) *German Ideology: Intellectual Origins of the Third Reich* (New York: Grosset & Dunlap).

Mosse, G. L. (1975) *The Nationalization of the Masses: Political Symbolism and Mass Movements in Germany from the Napoleonic Wars through the Third Reich* (New York: H. Fertig).

Mowlana, H. (1997) 'Islamicizing the Media in a Global Era: The State-Community Perspective in Iranian Broadcasting', in K. Robins (ed.) *Programming for the People* (Rome: RAI).

Moyo, L. (2010) 'The Global Citizen and the International Media: A Comparative Analysis of CNN and Xinhua's Coverage of the Tibetan Crisis', *The International Communication Gazette* 72(2): 191–207.

Müller, F. (2009) 'Entertaining Anti-racism: Multicultural Television Drama, Identification and Perceptions of Ethnic Threat', *Communications* 34(3): 239–56.

Müller, J.-W. (2007) *Constitutional Patriotism* (Princeton, NJ: Princeton University Press).

Murdock, G. and Pickering, M. (2009) 'The Birth of Distance: Communications and Changing Conceptions of Elsewhere', in M. Bailey (ed.) *Narrating Media History* (London: Routledge).

Nairn, T. (1977) *The Break-up of Britain: Crisis and Neonationalism* (London: New Left Books).

Nattrass, N. and J. Seekings (2001) '"Two Nations?" Race and Economic Inequality in South Africa Today', *Daedalus* 130(1): 45–70.

Nerone, J. C. (ed.) (1995) *Last Rights: Revisiting Four Theories of the Press* (Urbana, IL: University of Illinois Press).

Newman, S. P. (1997) *Parades and the Politics of the Street: Festive Culture in the Early American Republic* (Philadelphia, PA: Philadelphia University Press).

Nokia (2009) *Nokia in Brief*, http://www.nokia.com/, date accessed 14 November 2009.

Nordenstreng, K. and Varis, T. (1974) *Television Traffic: A One-way Street?* (Paris: UNESCO).

Nowicka, M. and Rovisco, M. (eds) (2009) *Cosmopolitanism in Practice* (Aldershot: Ashgate).

Oettinger, A. G. and Zapol, N. (1974) 'Will Information Technologies Help Learning?' *Annals of the American Academy of Political and Social Science* 412(1): 116–26.

Ohmae, K. (1996) *The End of the Nation-State: The Rise of Regional Economies* (New York: The Free Press).

Oza, R. (2006) *The Making of Neoliberal India: Nationalism, Gender and the Paradoxes of Globalisation* (London: Routledge).

Özkırımlı, U. (2005) *Contemporary Debates on Nationalism: A Critical Engagement* (Basingstoke: Palgrave Macmillan).

Ozouf, M. (1988) *Festivals and the French Revolution*, translated by Alan Sheridan (Cambridge, MA: Harvard University Press).

Pashupati, K., Sun, H. L. and McDowell, S. D. (2003) 'Guardians of Culture, Development Communicators, or State Capitalists? A Comparative Analysis of Indian and Chinese Policy Responses to Broadcast, Cable and Satellite Television', *Gazette: The International Journal for Communication Studies* 65(3): 251–71.

Patterson, P. H. (2003) 'Truth Half Told: Finding the Perfect Pitch for Advertising and Marketing in Socialist Yugoslavia, 1950–1991', *Enterprise and Society* 4(2): 179–225.

Peri, Y. (1999) 'The Media and Collective Memory of Yitzhak Rabin's Remembrance', *Journal of Communication*, 49(3): 106–24.

Perica, V. (2002) *Balkan Idols: Religion and Nationalism in Yugoslav States* (Oxford: Oxford University Press).

Pehrson, S., Vignoles, V. L. and Brown, R. (2009) 'National Identification and Anti-Immigrant Prejudice: Individual and Contextual Effects of National Definitions', *Social Psychology Quarterly* 72(1): 24–38.

Pickering, M. (2001) *Stereotyping* (Basingstoke: Palgrave Macmillan).

Plamenatz, J. (1976) 'Two Types of Nationalism', in E. Kamenka (ed.) *Nationalism: The Nature of an Evolution of an Idea* (London: Edward Arnold).

Podkalicka, A. (2008) 'Public Service Broadcasting as an Infrastructure of Translation in the Age of Cultural Diversity: Lessons for Europe from SBS

Australia', *Convergence: The International Journal of Research into New Media Technologies* 14(3): 323–33.

Postill, J. (2006) *Media and Nation Building: How the Iban Became Malaysian* (Oxford: Berghahn).

Price, M. E. (1995) *Television, the Public Sphere, and National Identity* (Oxford: Clarendon Press).

Price, M. E. (2002) *Media and Sovereignty: The Global Information Revolution and Its Challenge to State Power* (Cambridge, MA: MIT Press).

Prividera, L. C. and Howard III, J. W. (2006) 'Masculinity, Whiteness, and the Warrior Hero: Perpetuating the Strategic Rhetoric of U.S. Nationalism and the Marginalization of Women', *Women and Language* 29(2): 29–37.

Prokhorova, E. (2006) 'The Post-Utopian Body Politic – Masculinity and the Crisis of National Identity in Brezhnev-Era TV Miniseries', in H. Goscilo and A. Lanoux (eds) *Gender and National Identity in Twentieth-Century Russian Culture* (DeKalb, IL: Northern Illinois University Press).

Puijk, R. (2000) 'A Global Media Event? Coverage of the 1994 Lillehammer Olympic Games', *International Review for the Sociology of Sport* 35: 309–30.

Pye, L. W. (ed.) (1963) *Communications and Political Development* (Princeton, NJ: Princeton University Press).

Queen Elizabeth II (1957) 'The Queen's Christmas Broadcast 1957', http://www.royal.gov.uk/ImagesandBroadcasts/TheQueensChristmasBroadc asts/ChristmasBroadcasts/ChristmasBroadcast1957.aspx, date accessed 15 November 2009.

Radhakrishnan, S. (2009) 'Professional Women, Good Families: Respectable Femininity and the Cultural Politics of a "New" India', *Qualitative Sociology* 32(2): 195–212.

Rajagopal, A. (1993) 'The Rise of National Programming', *Media, Culture & Society* 15(1): 91–111.

Rajagopal, A. (1998) 'Advertising, Politics, and the Sentimental Education of the Indian Consumer', *Visual Anthropology Review* 14(2): 14–31.

Rajagopal, A. (2001) *Politics after Television: Religious Nationalism and the Reshaping of the Indian Public* (Cambridge: Cambridge University Press).

Randiera, S. (2007) 'De-politicization of Democracy and Judicialization of Politics', *Theory Culture Society* 24(4): 38–44.

Rantanen, T. (2002) *The Global and the National: Media and Communications in Post-communist Russia* (London: Rowman and Littlefield).

Rantanen, T. (2005) *The Media and Globalization* (London: Sage).

Real, M. (1989) *Super Media: A Cultural Studies Approach* (London: Sage).

Reid, W. H. (1976) *America's Mass Media Merchants* (Baltimore, MD: Johns Hopkins University Press).

Renan, E. (2001 [1892]) 'What is a Nation?', in V. P. Pecora (ed.) *Nations and Identities* (Oxford: Blackwell).

Ricci, S. (2008) *Cinema and Fascism: Italian Film and Society, 1922–1943* (Berkeley, CA: University of California Press).

Richardson, J. E. (2006) *Analysing Newspapers: An Approach from Critical Discourse Analysis* (Basingstoke: Palgrave Macmillan).

Richardson, J. E. and Wodak, R. (2009) 'Recontextualising Fascist Ideologies of the Past: Rightwing Discourses on Employment and Nativism in Austria and the United Kingdom', *Critical Discourse Studies* 6(4): 251–67.

Robbins, B. (1998) 'Actually Existing Cosmopolitanism', in P. Cheah and B. Robbins (eds) *Cosmopolitics: Thinking and Feeling beyond the Nation* (Minneapolis, MN: University of Minnesota Press).

Robertson, R. (1992) *Globalization: Social Theory and Global Culture* (London: Sage).

Robinson, G. J. (1977) *Tito's Maverick Media: The Politics of Mass Communications in Yugoslavia* (Urbana. IL: University of Illinois Press).

Robinson, W. I. (1998) 'Beyond Nation-State Paradigms: Globalization, Sociology, and the Challenge of Transnational Studies', *Sociological Forum* 13(4): 561–94.

Roche, M. (2000) *Mega Events and Modernity: Olympics and Expos in the Growth of Global Culture* (London: Routledge).

Rodell, M. (2009) 'Mediating the Nation: Celebrating 6th June in Sweden', in D. McCrone and G. McPherson (eds) *National Days: Constructing and Mobilizing National Identity* (Basingstoke: Palgrave Macmillan).

Rogers, E. M. (1965) 'Mass Media Exposure and Modernization among Columbian Peasants', *Public Opinion Quarterly* 29: 614–25.

Rogers, E. M. (1974) 'Communication in Development', *Annals of the American Academy of Political and Social Science* 412(1): 44–54.

Rosie, M., Petersoo, P., MacInnes, J., Condor, S. and Kennedy, J. (2004) 'Nation Speaking unto Nation: Newspapers and National Identity in the Devolved UK', *The Sociological Review* 52(4): 437–58.

Roth-Ey, K. (2007) 'Finding a Home for Television in the USSR, 1950–1970', *Slavic Review* 66(2): 278–306.

Roushanzamir, Elli Lester (2004) 'Chimera Veil of "Iranian Woman" and Processes of U.S. Textual Commodification: How U.S. Print Media Represent Iran', *Journal of Communication Inquiry* 28(1): 9–28.

Rudra, N. (2002) 'Globalization and the Decline of the Welfare State in Less-Developed Countries', *International Organization* 56(2): 411–45.

Ryan, R. (2002) *Ireland and Scotland: Literature and Culture, State and Nation, 1966–2000* (Oxford: Oxford University Press).

Salovaara-Moring, I and T. Kallas (2007) *Mapping Communication and Media Research: Estonia* (Helsinki: University of Helsinki).

Scannell, P. (1996) *Radio, Television and Modern Life* (Oxford: Blackwell).

Scannell, P. and Cardiff, D. (1991) *A Social History of British Broadcasting: Volume One 1992–1939 – Serving the Nation* (London: Basil Blackwell).

Schierup, C.-U., Hansen, P. and Castles, S. (2006) *Migration, Citizenship, and the European Welfare State: A European Dilemma* (Oxford: Oxford University Press).

Schiller, H. ([1969] 1992) *Mass Communication and American Empire* (Boulder, CO: Westview Press).

Schlesinger, P. (1978) *Putting 'Reality' Together: BBC News* (London: Methuen).

Schlesinger, P. (1991) *Media, State and Nation* (London: Sage).

Schlesinger, P. (1999) 'Changing Spaces of Political Communication: The Case of the European Union', *Political Communication* 16(3): 263–79.

Schlesinger, P. (2000) 'The Nation and Communicative Space', in H. Tumber (ed.) *Media Power, Professionals and Politics* (London: Routledge).

Schramm, W. (1964) *Mass Media and National Development: The Role of Information in Developing Countries* (Stanford, CA: Stanford University Press and Paris: UNESCO).

Schudson, M. (1982) 'The Politics of Narrative Form: The Emergence of News Conventions in Print and Television', *Daedalus* 111(4): 97–112.

Schudson, M. (1986) 'When? Deadlines, Datelines, and History', in R. K. Manoff and M. Schudson (eds) *Reading the News* (New York: Pantheon).

Schudson, M. (2003) *The Sociology of News* (New York: Norton).

Scordato, M. R. and Monopoli, P. A. (2002) 'Free Speech Rationales after September 11th: The First Amendment in Post-World Trade Center America', *Stanford Law and Policy Review* 13(1): 185–203.

Scrase, T. J. (2002) 'Television, the Middle Classes and the Transformation of Cultural Identities in West Bengal, India', *Gazette: The International Journal for Communication Studies* 64(4): 323–42.

Senjković, R. (2008) *Izgubljeno u prijenosu: Pop iskustvo soc kulture* (Zagreb: Institute of Ethnology and Folklore Research).

Shirk, S. (2007) 'Changing Media, Changing Foreign Policy in China', *Japanese Journal of Political Science* 8(1): 43–70.

Shoup, P. (1968) *Communism and the Yugoslav National Question* (New York: Columbia University Press).

Shulman, S. (2002) 'Challenging the Civic/Ethnic and West/East Dichotomies in the Study of Nationalism', *Comparative Political Studies* 35(5): 554–85.

Siapera, E. (2010) *Cultural Diversity and Global Media: The Mediation of Difference* (Oxford: Wiley-Blackwell).

Siebert, F. S., Peterson, T. and Schramm, W. ([1956] 1969) *Four Theories of the Press: The Authoritarian, Libertarian, Social Responsibility and Soviet Communist Concepts of What the Press Should Be and Do* (Urbana, IL: University of Illinois Press).

Sinclair, J. and Harrison, M. (2004) 'Globalization, Nation, and Television in Asia: The Cases of India and China', *Television & New Media* 5(1): 41–54.

Sinclair, J., Jacka, E. and Cunningham, S. (eds) (1996) *New Patterns in Global Television: Peripheral Vision* (Oxford: Oxford University Press).

Singhal, A. and Rogers, E. M. (1988) 'Television Soap Operas for Development in India', *International Communication Gazette* 41(2): 109–24.

Sinha, M. (1995) *Colonial Masculinity: The 'Manly Englishmen' and the 'Effeminate Bengali' in the Late Nineteenth Century* (Manchester: Manchester University Press).

Skey, M. (2006) ' "Carnivals of Surplus Emotion?" Towards an Understanding of the Significance of Ecstatic Nationalism in a Globalising World', *Studies in Ethnicity and Nationalism* 6(2): 143–61.

Skrbis, Z., Kendall, G. and Woodward, I. (2004) 'Locating Cosmopolitanism Between Humanist Ideal and Grounded Social Category', *Theory, Culture & Society* 21(6): 115–36.

Skrbis, Z. and Woodward, I. (2007) 'The Ambivalence of Ordinary Cosmopolitanism: Investigating the Limits of Cosmopolitan Openness', *The Sociological Review* 55(4): 730–47.

Smith, A. ([1776] 1999) *The Wealth of Nations: Volume 2* (London: Penguin).

Smith, A. (1979) *The Newspaper: An International History* (London: Thames and Hudson).

Smith, A. D. (1986) *The Ethnic Origins of Nations* (Oxford: Basil Blackwell).

Smith, A. D. (1995) *Nations and Nationalism in a Global Era* (Cambridge: Polity).

Smith, A. D. (1998) *Nationalism and Modernism* (London: Routledge).

Smith, A. D. (2003) *Chosen Peoples: Sacred Sources of National Identity* (Oxford: Oxford University Press).

Smith, D. (1983) *Barrington Moore: Violence, Morality and Political Change* (Basingstoke: Macmillan).

Smith, M. M. (1998) 'Culture, Commerce, and Calendar Reform in Colonial America', *The William and Mary Quarterly* 55(4): 557–84.

Snyder, J. (2000) *From Voting to Violence: Democratization and Nationalist Conflict* (New York: WW Norton).

Snyder, J. and Ballentine, K. (1996) 'Nationalism and the Marketplace of Ideas', *International Security* 21(2): 5–41.

Sonwalkar, P. (2001) 'India: Makings of Little Cultural/Media Imperialism?', *Gazette: The International Journal for Communication Studies* 63(6): 505–19.

Sparks, C. (2007) 'What is Wrong with Globalization?', *Global Media and Communication* 3(2): 133–55.

Sparks, C. (2009) 'South African Media in Transition', *Journal of African Media Studies* 1(2): 195–220.

Spencer, P. and Wollman, H. (2002) *Nationalism: A Critical Introduction* (London: Sage).

Spigel, L. (2001) *Welcome to the Dreamhouse: Popular Media and Postwar Suburbs* (Durham, NC: Duke University Press).

Spigel, L. (2004) 'Entertainment Wars: Television Culture after 9/11', *American Quarterly* 56(2): 235–70.

Spitulnik, D. (1998) 'Mediated Modernities. Encounters with the Electronic in Zambia', *Visual Anthropology Review* 14(2): 63–84.

Stalin, I. ([1913] 1994) 'The Nation', in J. Hutchinson and A. D. Smith (eds) *Nationalism* (Oxford: Oxford University Press).

Stanyer, J. and Wring, D. (2004) 'Public Images, Private Lives: An Introduction', *Parliamentary Affairs* 57(1): 1–8.

Starr, P. (2004) *The Creation of the Media: Political Origins of Modern Communications* (New York: Basic Books).

Štětka, V. (2009) 'From Global to Local? Audiovisual Media Flows and Consumption Patterns in CEE Region' Paper presented at the conference

Beyond East and West: Two decades of Media Transformation after the Fall of Communism, 25–27 June 2009, Budapest.

Storsul, T. (2008) 'Telecom Liberalization. Distributive Challenges and National Differences', in P. Ludes (ed.) *Convergence and Fragmentation. Media Technology and the Information Society* (Bristol: Intellect).

Straubhaar, J. (1991) 'Beyond Media Imperialism: Asymmetrical Interdependence and Cultural Proximity', *Critical Studies in Mass Communication* 8(1): 39–59.

Swanson, D. L. and Mancini, P. (eds) (1996) *Politics, Media and Modern Democracy: An International Study of Innovations in Electoral Campaigning and Their Consequences* (Westport, CT: Praeger).

Sztompka, P. (1994) *The Sociology of Social Change* (Oxford: Blackwell).

Temin, P. (1991) 'Soviet and Nazi Economic Planning in the 1930s', *The Economic History Review* – New Series 44(4): 573–93.

Thapan, M. (2004) 'Embodiment and Identity in Contemporary Society: Femina and the 'New' Indian Woman', *Contributions to Indian Sociology* 38 (3): 411–44.

Therborn, G. (2003) 'Entangled Modernities', *European Journal of Social Theory* 6(3): 293–305.

Thomas, A. O. (2001) 'Global Media Corporations and the Nation-state: Balancing Politico-economic and Socio-cultural Globalization', *Global Business Review* 2(1): 71–82.

Thompson, J. (1995) *The Media and Modernity* (Cambridge: Polity).

Thompson, M. (1999) *Forging War: The Media in Serbia, Croatia and Bosnia-Herzegovina*, 2nd edn (Luton: University of Luton Press).

Tickner, J. A. (2002) 'Feminist Perspectives on 9/11', *International Studies Perspectives* 3(4): 333–50.

Tilly, C. (ed.) (1975) *The Formation of National States in Western Europe* (Princeton, NJ: Princeton University Press).

Tilly, C. (1990) *Coercion, Capital, and European States, AD 990–1990* (Oxford: Basil Blackwell).

Tipps, D. C. (1973) 'Modernization Theory and the Comparative Study of Societies: A Critical Perspective', *Comparative Studies in Society and History* 15(2): 199–226.

Tismaneanu, V. (1998) *Fantasies of Salvation: Democracy, Nationalism and Myth in Post-Communist Europe* (Princeton, NJ: Princeton University Press).

Todorova, M. (1997) *Imagining the Balkans* (Oxford: Oxford University Press).

Tomaselli, K. (1989) *The Cinema of Apartheid: Race and Class in South African Film* (London: Routledge).

Tomlinson, J. (1991) *Cultural Imperialism: A Critical Introduction* (London: Continuum).

Tønnesson, S. (2004) 'Globalising National States' *Nations and Nationalism* 10(1–2): 179–94.

Trebbe, J. (2007) 'Types of Integration, Acculturation Strategies and Media Use of Young Turks in Germany', *Communications* 32 (2): 171–91.

Trenz, H.-J. (2004) 'Media coverage on European Governance: Exploring the European Public Sphere in National Quality Newspapers', *European Journal of Communication* 19(3): 291–319.

Tunstall, J. (2008) *The Media Were American: U.S. Mass Media in Decline* (Oxford: Oxford University Press).

Turner, V. (1969) *The Ritual Process: Structure and Antistructure* (London: Routledge and Kegan Paul).

Underwood, D. (2002) *From Yahweh to Yahoo!: The Religious Roots of the Secular Press* (Urbana, IL: University of Illinois Press).

Urry, J. (2000) *Sociology beyond Societies* (London: Routledge).

Van den Bulck, H. and Sinardet, D. (2006) The Nation: Not Yet the Weakest Link? The Articulation of National Identity in a Globalized Popular Television Format', in L. Højbjerg and H. Søndergaard (eds) *European Film and Media Culture* (Copenhagen: Museum Tusculanums Press).

Van der Veer, P. (2001) *Imperial Encounters: Religion and Modernity in India and Britain* (Princeton, NJ: Princeton University Press).

Van de Steeg, M. (2002) 'Rethinking the Conditions for a Public Sphere in the European Union', *European Journal of Social Theory* 5(4): 499–519.

Van Gennep, A. ([1909] 1960) *The Rites of Passage*, translated by M. B. Vizedom and G. L. Caffee (Chicago, IL: University of Chicago Press).

Van Zoonen, L., Vis, F. and Mihelj, S. (2010) 'Performing Citizenship on YouTube: Activism, Satire and Online Debate around the Anti-Islam Video *Fitna*', *Critical Discourse Studies* 7(4): 249–61.

Veljanovski, R. (2002) 'Zaokret elektronskih medija', in N. Popov (ed.) *Srpska strana rata: Trauma i katarza u istorijskom pamćenju* – Part II, 2nd edn (Belgrade: Samizdat Free B92).

Verdery, K. (1996) 'Whither "Nation" and "Nationalism"?', in G. Balakrishnan (ed.) *Mapping the Nation* (London: Verso).

Vermeersch, P. (2009) 'National Minorities and International Change: Being Ukrainian in Contemporary Poland', *Europe–Asia Studies* 61(3): 435–56.

Vertovec, S. (2004) 'Cheap Calls: The Social Glue of Migrant Transnationalism', *Global Networks* 4(2): 219–24.

Vihalemm, T. (1999) 'Local and Global Orientations of Media Consumption in Estonia, 1993–1998', in *Estonian Human Development Report 1999* (Tallinn: UNDP).

Vincent, D. (1993) *Literacy and Popular Culture: England 1750–1914* (Cambridge: Cambridge University Press).

Vincent, D. (2000) *The Rise of Mass Literacy: Reading and Writing in Modern Europe* (Cambridge: Polity).

Vogrinc, J. (1996) 'Close Distance. Dilemmas in the Presentation of the War in Bosnia in the Daily News Bulletin of TV Slovenia', in J. Gow, R. Paterson and A. Preston (eds) *Bosnia by Television* (London: BFI).

Volčič, Z. (2007) 'Yugo-Nostalgia: Cultural Memory and the Media in the Former Yugoslavia', *Critical Studies in Media Communication* 24(1): 21–38.

Von Saldern, A. (2004) '*Volk* and *Heimat* Culture in Radio Broadcasting during the Period of Transition from Weimar to Nazi Germany', *Journal of Modern History* 76(2): 312–46.

Waisman, C. H. (2002) 'The Multiple Modernities Argument and Societies in the Americas', in L. Roniger and C. H. Waisman (eds) *Globality and Multiple Modernities: Comparative North American and Latin American Perspectives* (Brighton: Sussex Academic Press).

Walby, S. (2006) 'Gender Approaches to Nations and Nationalism', in G. Delanty and K. Kumar (eds) *The Sage Handbook of Nations and Nationalism* (London: Sage).

Wallerstein, I. M. (1984) *The Politics of the World Economy: The States, the Movements, and the Civilizations* (Cambridge: Cambridge University Press and Paris: MSH).

Walsh, M. (1996) 'National Cinema, National Imaginary', *Film History* 8(1): 5–17.

Wang, G. (2002) 'Restrictions on Foreign Ownership and National Sovereignty: Whose Issue Is It?', in J. M. Chan and B. T. McIntyre (eds) *In Search of Boundaries: Communication, Nation-States, and Cultural Identities* (London and Westport: Ablex Publishing).

Wang, J. (2006) 'The Politics of Goods: A Case Study of Consumer Nationalism and Media Discourse in Contemporary China', *Asian Journal of Communication* 16(2): 187–206.

Wang, Z. (2008) 'National Humiliation, History Education, and the Politics of Historical Memory: Patriotic Education Campaign in China', *International Studies Quarterly* 52(4): 783–806.

Wark, M. (1994) *Virtual Geography: Living with Global Media Events* (Bloomington, IN: Indiana University Press).

Weber, C. (2003) 'The Media, the "War on Terrorism" and the Circulation of Non-Knowledge', in D. K. Thussu and D. Freedman (eds) *War and the Media: Reporting Conflict 24/7* (London: Sage).

Weber, I. (2003) 'Localizing the Global: Successful Strategies for Selling Television Programmes to China', *Gazette: The International Journal for Communication Studies* 65(3): 273–90.

Weiss, L. (1998) *The Myth of the Powerless State* (Cambridge: Polity).

Welch, D. (1995) 'Nazi Film Policy. Control, Ideology, and Propaganda', in G. R. Cuomo (ed.) *National Socialist Cultural Policy* (Basingstoke: Palgrave Macmillan).

Welch, D. (2004) 'Nazi Propaganda and the *Volksgemeinschaft*: Constructing a People's Community', *Journal of Contemporary History* 39(2): 213–38.

West, L. A. (ed.) (1997) *Feminist Nationalism* (London: Routledge).

Wiener, J. M. (1975) 'The Barrington Moore Thesis and His Critics', *Theory & Society* 2(3): 301–30.

Wilmer, S. E. (2002) *Theatre, Society and the Nation: Staging American Identities* (Cambridge: Cambridge University Press).

Winfield, B. H., Friedman, B. and Trisnadi, V. (2002) 'History as the Metaphor through Which Current World is Viewed: British and American Newspapers' Uses of History Following September 2001 Terrorist Attacks', *Journalism Studies*, 3(2): 289–300.

Winseck, D. (2008) 'The State of Media Ownership and Media Markets: Competition or Concentration and Why Should We Care?', *Sociology Compass* 2(1): 34–47.

Wong, L. L. and Trumper, R. (2002) 'Global Celebrity Athletes and Nationalism: Fútbol, Hockey, and the Representation of Nation', *Journal of Sport and Social Issues* 26(2): 168–94.

Woodward, I., Skrbis, Z. and Bean, C. (2008) 'Attitudes towards Globalization and Cosmopolitanism: Cultural Diversity, Personal Consumption and the National Economy', *British Journal of Sociology* 59(2): 207–26.

World Bank (2007) *World Development Indicators* (Washington, DC: World Bank).

World Bank (2009) *World Development Indicators* (Washington, DC: World Bank).

Xinhua (2005) 'China to Revive Traditional Festivals to Boost Traditional Culture', *People's Daily Online*, 25 June 2005, http://english.peopledaily. com.cn/200506/25/eng20050625_192259.html, date accessed 28 January 2010.

Yanru, C. (2004) 'From National Day to National Way: The Story of October 1', in L. K. Fuller (ed.) *National Days/National Ways: Historical, Political, and Religious Celebrations around the World* (Westport, CT: Praeger).

Yeğenoğlu, M. (2005) 'Cosmopolitanism and Nationalism in a Globalized World', *Ethnic and Racial Studies* 28(1): 103–31.

York, Q. Y. and Zhang, H. Q. (2010) 'The Determinants of the 1999 and 2007 Chinese Golden Holiday System: A Content Analysis of Official Documentation' *Tourism Management* 31(6): 881–90.

Young, C. (1976) *The Politics of Cultural Pluralism* (Madison, WI: Wisconsin University Press).

Yuval-Davis, N. (1997) *Gender and Nation* (London: Sage).

Yuval-Davis, N. (2001) 'Nationalism, Feminism and Gender Relations', in M. Guibernau and J. Hutchinson (eds) *Understanding Nationalism* (Cambridge: Polity).

Zelizer, B. (1992) *Covering the Body: The Kennedy Assassination, the Media, and the Shaping of Collective Memory* (Chicago, IL: University of Chicago Press).

Zerubavel, E. (1982) 'The Standardization of Time: A Sociohistorical Perspective', *The American Journal of Sociology* 88(1): 1–23.

Zerubavel, E. (1985) *Hidden Rhythms: Schedules and Calendars in Social Life* (Berkeley, CA: University of California Press).

Zerubavel, E. (2003) 'Calendars and History: A Comparative Study of the Social Organization of National Memory', in J. K. Olick (ed.) *States of Memory: Continuities, Conflicts, and Transformations in National Retrospection* (Durham, NC: Duke University Press).

Zhang, B. (2001) 'Assessing the WTO Agreements on China's Telecommunications Regulatory Reform and Industrial Liberalization', *Telecommunications Policy* 25: 461–83.

Zhao, S. (1998) 'A State-Led Nationalism: The Patriotic Education Campaign in Post-Tiananmen China', *Communist and Post-Communist Studies* 31(3): 287–302.

Zhao, Y. (2003) '"Enter the World": Neoliberal Globalisation, the Dream for a Strong Nation, and Chinese Press Discourses on the WTO', in C.-C. Lee (ed.) *Chinese Media, Global Contexts* (London: Routledge).

Zheng, Y. (1999) *Discovering Chinese Nationalism in China: Modernization, Identity and International Relations* (Cambridge: Cambridge University Press).

Žikić, B. (2010) 'Dissidents Liked Pretty Girls: Nudity, Pornography and Quality Press in Socialism', *Media Research/Medijska istraživanja* 16(1): 53–72.

Zimmer, O. (2003) 'Boundary Mechanisms and Symbolic Resources: Towards a Process-Oriented Approach to National Identity', *Nations and Nationalism* 9(2): 173–93.

Index